kamera
BOOKS

THANDI LUBIMBI

RACE AND ENTERTAINMENT

REFLECTIONS ON RACISM IN FILM, TV AND THE MEDIA

kamera
BOOKS

First published in 2024 by Kamera Books,
an imprint of Oldcastle Books Ltd.,
Harpenden, Herts, UK

oldcastlebooks.com
@OldcastleBooks

978-0-85730-566-4 (Paperback)
978-0-85730-567-1 (eBook)

2 4 6 8 10 9 7 5 3 1

Typeset in Franklin Gothic

Printed and bound in Great Britain by
CPI Group (UK) Ltd, Croydon CR0 4YY

MIX
Paper | Supporting
responsible forestry
FSC® C171272

CONTENTS

ACKNOWLEDGEMENTS

Firstly, I give thanks to the Great Divine Creator for all the love and blessings that I have received in this life.

Thank you to my family and friends who have supported me and believed in me.

Thank you to my writing partner Richard Kurti, who suggested I write and speak on the topic of race and entertainment.

A big thank you to Desi Andrea Lyon who started the ball rolling when it came to writing this book. I would also like to thank Julian Friedmann of Blake Friedmann Agency.

Thank you to Hannah Patterson and Kamera Books for your patience and commitment to publishing this work.

Thank you to all the people who contributed to this work and who agreed to be interviewed about their experiences.

A very special thank you to Eugene "Rod" Rodenberry for taking the time to be interviewed.

And a big thank you to my manager Rowena Wallace of Peach House Management for believing in me and working tirelessly on my behalf.

With love and gratitude,
Thandi
XX

'I'm going to tell it like it is. I hope you can take it as it is.'

Malcolm X

CHAPTER 1

INTRODUCTION

My first experience of racism is etched in my mind. Every now and then I get a flashback to that event. Not to how I was feeling but to the look of humiliation and powerlessness on my mother's face.

I was about five years of age, and we were living in Morecambe, Lancashire and it was the late 1970s. My mother had taken me to a fete of some kind. I did notice that we seemed to be the only Black people there.

It started out as a nice day, but as I've come to learn over the years of living in Britain, rain and racism appear out of nowhere and happen frequently. Suddenly it began to pour with rain. People started to take cover in the many tents. As my mum took me to various tents, they all said the same thing: *'There's no room,'* even though there clearly was in some of them. Then some of the tents began to close their flaps.

The final tent we went to had one white male occupant. My mum asked for shelter. She was met with hostility, aggression and a clear refusal of entry. The tent flap closed. So we stepped out of the tent and there we were, stood in the middle of the fete getting soaking wet: all tents closed to us and some of the occupants staring at us in silence. As we stood alone getting soaked through, I looked at my mum's face. I'll never forget it. It was one of pain, humiliation and helplessness. I knew what had happened to us had happened because we were Black. That was my first experience of racism before I even knew the word and what it meant.

What I didn't know was that I would continue to experience it throughout my life, and what I realise now, at the age of fifty, is that even if I live another fifty years, I will probably die knowing it hasn't been eradicated.

Now for those of you who are white and have just read that story, I'm sure that some of you are thinking: *'Maybe all the tents were full,'* or *'maybe it was another reason'.* Perhaps some of you are even thinking: *'I'm sure it wasn't racism, maybe it was something else.'* Undoubtedly some of you simply don't believe the experience related to race at all and think I'm imagining it. Some of you may even be feeling a bit triggered by the story.

Your reaction – if that was what you were thinking – is not a surprise to me at all. Part of the problem of living and dealing with racism in this country, and perhaps in the Western world, is that our experiences as people of colour are very often not believed. It adds insult to injury and it also perpetuates the issue of racism, because if you don't believe it is happening, you won't address it.

Life continued after that day and so did the racism. Despite all of the racism I have faced and endured, I went on to become a barrister educated to master's level as well as a screenwriter. So, despite incidences of racism I went on to succeed, but it has been a marring experience.

At primary school I took the eleven plus and apparently passed with flying colours. The result of passing the eleven plus is that you are supposed to be offered a place at grammar school. I wasn't offered this. The education authorities acknowledged I had done well, passed even, but they refused to give me the grammar school option. My mum kept me out of secondary school because she wasn't going to give in, but the authorities then threatened her with prosecution for not sending me to school. That is the power of racism at play; you can engage in it and use the power of the state and its institutions to support you.

At most of the schools I attended there was racial abuse, harassment and racial jokes. I remember at a school in Blackpool when I was about fourteen years of age, the history teacher was absent for some reason. A number of students began making racist jokes. The whole class appeared to be entertained at my expense. The flurry of racist jokes kept coming until I was in tears. It was painful and humiliating and there was no escape.

Students in the education system were not the only problem. Certain teachers did not believe I was intelligent and one insinuated I had cheated (I hadn't) without any evidence, because they couldn't accept that I had scored that highly in an exam.

Initially I didn't do very well at school as I'd given up on making an effort and preferred to party, so I spent my teenage years and early twenties doing low-paid jobs such as waitressing, shop work, bar work and cleaning. The casual and overt racism from staff, managers and customers was – in certain employs – frequent.

While working as a waitress at a hotel in Blackpool, one manager said to a hotel guest in my presence: *'If you go on any more holidays, you'll come back looking like a bloody ni**er.'* At which they both laughed. At the same hotel, a chef shouted at me, *'The best ni**er I ever saw was a dead one.'* At twenty years old, this was the climate I worked in. Thankfully I was able to take them to a tribunal and win. It was evident that I was also held to a different standard. At the employment tribunal my former manager complained that I was *'unreliable'*, lamenting my absences. This appeared to stump the tribunal because I'd only been absent two days in two years.

'Why are you telling me this?' I hear you ask. Well, I understand you want to write scripts. The chances are you may even have a Black character. Are you aware of the Black experience? I mean really aware? I'm telling you this because it is my experience as a Black woman in the not so United Kingdom and because, undoubtedly in one form or another, my experience has been replicated across the country. I say from the outset that it is obvious that I cannot speak for every Black person. We have had different experiences and we will obviously have different views as to how to deal with our experiences of racism. I'm putting forward my experiences as a Black woman in Britain and to some extent in the United States. I'm also going to be referring to data and asking you, the reader, questions.

I'm telling you this because it is the background as to how this book came about and I'm telling you this so you can get a flavour of the Black experience so what you write will hopefully have some authenticity.

So, having done low-paid, thankless jobs for a few years I became sick and tired of it and decided to change my life. I decided to join Her Majesty's Armed Forces, as you do! In order to determine your corps you have to take the military entrance test. The higher you score, the more corps options you have. I scored fairly highly which seemed surprising to some. This meant that I had a decent pick of the corps I wanted to join. However, my height excluded me from some and not being third generation British, I was excluded from Army Intelligence.

In any event I ended up as a gunner in the Royal Artillery. I won't relive my whole time in the army, but needless to say there was plenty of racism. A substantial amount of the racism was blatant. There were also death threats and threats of physical violence. There was name-calling while on parade, which was not challenged by the senior ranks. In one barracks where I stayed overnight, there were swastikas on the lockers, along with daubs and scrawls of: *'There ain't no Black in the Union Jack'*. That was my reality of life in the army. I'm grateful that it wasn't an everyday experience and I was not subjected to racial violence, but I know that for other Black soldiers their experience was much worse.

I will say that there were some very decent men and women in the army who would not tolerate that behaviour, but in my experience they were in the minority. I'm not saying that every soldier I came across was a racist; what I am saying is that there were a significant number who were. There were also those who would react with hostility when the issue of racism was raised.

That leads me to my script and how this book came about. I wrote a television pilot about a Black woman in the army. There is a scene where the protagonist suffers racist abuse on a number of occasions. On one occasion everyone stands around either ignoring it or laughing. Later on she is seriously assaulted. I'd sent the script to a script editor, and he wrote the following note:

'Everyone sees what Morgan does to her prior to the attack yet no one really bats an eyelid beyond the bombardier.'

I sat with that script note for days. It irked me and it perturbed me and I decided I couldn't let the comment slide because it seemed to me that he was disbelieving my lived experience, and, in a nutshell, he was saying *don't make white people feel uncomfortable. If you do, the entertainment gates will be closed to you.* And herein lies the problem: many of the guardians of the entertainment gates are not willing to honestly and accurately reflect the minority experience.

I discussed this issue with my co-writer Richard Kurti and he suggested I write an open letter to the entertainment industry expressing my thoughts and feelings on the situation. This is what I wrote:

Dear Entertainment Industry, Why I'm Asking White People to Get Uncomfortable

I wrote a script containing racist abuse in public. An experience I have had to endure a number of times. In the scene, all the white people stand by and do nothing. Also, a situation I have experienced on a number of occasions.

The white script editor gave a note to me on this scene. In effect he said it wasn't credible that people would stand by and do nothing. This note sat with me for days. It niggled me and it disappointed me, but it didn't surprise me. As a Black person I know our experiences are often not believed.

I wrote back to the editor. An excerpt from what I said was:

'Case in point Derek Chauvin. He felt comfortable and happy to murder a Black man in broad daylight in public view. That wasn't in a bubble. That happened because the structure of racism led him to believe that the social structure would protect him. A structure that allows him to behave in that way. George Floyd was not the first Black person to be murdered with impunity because of the colour of his skin. He certainly won't be the last.'

I received a lengthy response from the editor. The salient part of it being:

'If you want to make a point about racism, you need to thread a very fine needle... Otherwise you risk a situation where the people reading it decide you're painting everyone who isn't Black with the same negative brush. They'll feel like it's a personal attack on them. Does this make sense?'

Yes it does. In effect he is saying that white people are not comfortable dealing with racism and it can have an adverse effect on the person of colour raising the issue.

Herein lies the problem. The realities of racism are not portrayed because it makes most white people – in this case the guardians of the entertainment gates – uncomfortable. Racism is an evil structure that has seen non-whites murdered, assaulted and abused with impunity, discriminated against and disenfranchised; yet it can't be discussed openly or portrayed honestly because it makes most white people uncomfortable. That is the epitome of white privilege. We suffer from the aforementioned, but it can't be discussed or portrayed because of your discomfort.

Despite being a staunch pacifist, Martin Luther King Junior was hated by many whites at the time because of the injustice he was trying to dismantle. Taking the knee has been vociferously criticised as have peaceful protests. Our experiences throughout are often denied. There is all too often a palpable rejection by white people to acknowledge what is happening to Black people in their society.

So, I ask the following questions. Are you willing to get uncomfortable with yourself? Are you willing to truly listen to our experience and not censor it because it makes you uncomfortable? Are you willing to not censor what we say because it doesn't fit in with your world view? Are you willing to acknowledge the existence of white privilege that you benefit from in almost every way in society?

> Racism is an evil structure. Like any structure it can be deconstructed. It requires you to get uncomfortable. In the meantime, we Black people will be getting our necks leaned on until we can't breathe, spat at, abused, assaulted and discriminated against on a daily basis and the structure will continue to deny that our experiences are really happening.
>
> Thandi Lubimbi

As a result of that letter I was asked to deliver a lecture on the topic. The lecture was entitled: Race and Entertainment – Can White Write Black? I then delivered the lecture to the London Screenwriters' Festival and thanks to Desi Lyon and Julian Friedmann of Blake Friedmann Literary Agency I was commissioned to write this book.

The book will look at how Black people are portrayed within the entertainment industry and examine whether Black characters are still being portrayed in stereotypical roles. There will be a comparative look at race and discrimination within British institutions and sectors and at whether or not the portrayal of Black people in film and television is a realistic portrayal of the Black experience within those institutions and sectors. The three sectors and institutions I will be looking at are the criminal justice system (CJS), healthcare and entertainment itself.

Within entertainment, the book will look at issues of race and will consider why Black actors and crew are not given the same opportunities within the industry as their white counterparts, and why there is still a lack of representation on and off the camera.

This book may be uncomfortable reading at times if you are white, but I ask you to get uncomfortable for a while and understand just how intrinsic and pernicious racism is within British and other Western societies, and understand that the true extent of it is often not portrayed in drama. If you are able to get past the discomfort hopefully you will have an understanding of the Black or minority experience and not revert to tired tropes or negative stereotyping.

Throughout this book there will be questions and exercises for you to consider and complete, which will hopefully get you thinking about race, racism and how that fits into the characters you are looking to write and the stories you wish to tell. The power of storytelling should not be underestimated. Films and television dramas have the ability to become mainstream and part of the public consciousness on a national or international level. People across the globe know the saying: *'Use the force Luke,'* or *'May the odds be ever in your favour'*. Films and television dramas have been used to educate and change public perceptions and opinions and formed part of the zeitgeist.

I will also be looking at historical events and attitudes that have shaped society and society's views of Black people, as well as possible solutions in respect of anti-racism, representation and racial portrayals in the entertainment industry.

'Tolerance, intercultural dialogue and respect for diversity are more essential than ever in a world where peoples are becoming more and more closely interconnected.'

Kofi Annan

CHAPTER 2

SO YOU WANT TO WRITE A BLACK CHARACTER!

You have an idea for a script and I'm assuming you are going to plot it out and establish your characters. If you live in a multicultural society, especially in a city, I'd say that at least one of your characters is going to be Black or some other ethnic minority.

I would like you to answer the following questions:

....

EXERCISE 1

1. Can you write a Black character?
2. Do you know what it is like to be Black in the Western world?
3. Do you understand the issues that Black people face on a regular basis?
4. Is what you write going to be authentic?
5. Is what you are going to write stereotypical?

....

I want to ask you some further questions and I'd like you to take the time to answer each one carefully and thoughtfully. I'd also like you to answer the question purely based on your current understanding without looking up the meanings and definitions or asking anyone else before answering.

....

EXERCISE 2

In your own words write down your answers to the following:

1. What is racism?
2. How does it manifest?
3. How does it play out in the world and society?
4. What is systemic racism?
5. What is institutional racism?
6. How do institutions and people react to racism when it is highlighted?
7. How do Black people working in institutions fare when it comes to treatment, opportunities and advancement?
8. What are common stereotypes in society and entertainment about Black people?
9. What is critical race theory?
10. What is intersectionality?

....

I hope the questions have given you pause for thought and focused your mind on the issues that Black people face in everyday situations. I would also like you to consider your answers and contemplate whether or not you are well informed on the topic because the depth and strength of your character is going to depend on how well informed you are.

I'm going to pose another set of questions below. Again, I would like you to take your time and consider each question carefully and thoughtfully, based on your current knowledge.

....

EXERCISE 3

In your own words write down your answers to the following:

1. Have you ever been a victim of racism?
2. What was your experience?
3. How was it resolved, if at all?
4. If you complained about being subjected to racism, what was the response?
5. Have you ever challenged a person being racist towards you; if so, what was the response?
6. If you have a child and they experienced racism, how did you deal with it?
7. Have you been a victim of racism in front of your child?
8. What impact did it have on you and your child?
9. Have you spoken to any Black people about their experiences of racism?
10. Do you have any empirical data on the subject of racism?

....

If you have not experienced any of the aforementioned, then ask yourself: how can I write about it? Similarly, if you do not understand the basic terms and structures then ask yourself: how can I portray it competently and appropriately?

My initial lecture was entitled 'Race and Entertainment – Can White Write Black?' It questioned whether or not white people can write a Black character or write the Black experience.

The initial answer must of course be no! Not unless you are informed and do your research. You need to understand what it means to be Black in the country you reside in and globally. You need to understand what the Black experience is on a regular basis, because it affects the decisions that are made and the attitudes that can be taken in certain situations.

Without understanding the issues of race and racism, then, as per a substantial amount of television and film, you will highly likely end up with inauthentic and stereotypical tropes. I say inauthentic because if you have a Black character in a television series which is lucky enough to get one hundred episodes, and they never experience racism, then that is going to be wholly inauthentic and the issue of race is completely ignored, which is unrealistic.

I'm not saying that each and every week your character needs to be subjected to racism, or that each and every week the story is about racism. I am mindful that as screenwriters we are first and foremost entertainers. We need to write great scripts that are entertaining and engaging. If your script is based on reality, then you need to write your characters realistically. It simply wouldn't be credible to have a long-running television series and write a Black character in modern times who never experiences racism.

If you are not aware of the Black experience and write your Black character based on what you have seen in the media, on television and in films, there is a good chance that what you write will be stereotypical in a negative way. That is because those mediums, particularly the media, often write in a racist, stereotypical and divisive way. Television and film can also write stereotypical content, so what you would be writing would not only be a copy of a perception, it could also potentially be perpetuating racist stereotypes.

Perhaps you want to engage in race blind casting in order to have a diverse cast. That is an admirable goal and in many ways will open doors and break down barriers, but I would say that you still need to make your characters authentic according to their race and the period. A prime example of successful race blind, or diversified casting is *Grey's Anatomy*, created by the formidable Shonda Rhimes, which is now in its twentieth season. There is also the Shondaland production *Station 19* which is one of ABC's top rated shows. If the work is a fantasy story then race is irrelevant but if it is set in a real period, then that is another story. It would not be authentic or credible to write about the genocide of one race by people of another race and then mix up the races in the casting. It would not be authentic, credible or believable if Martin Luther King was played by someone white or Lyndon B Johnson was played by someone

Black. Diversify yes, but I would say that there are going to be times and places and stories where it just isn't feasible.

As a result of the creation of racism, racial stereotyping became a main feature of western society that is still prevalent today. Stereotyping occurs in all walks of life and is often perpetuated by the media and the entertainment industry. The portrayal of Black characters and characters of colour has often resulted in stereotypical and offensive roles that became mainstream remaining in the consciousness of society.

I will end this chapter by asking you three questions.

....

EXERCISE 4

1. Is your only Black character a criminal, a sportsperson, or a musician?
2. If so, why?
   If it is a genuine story with something to say, then fair enough. However, if it is simply your imagination and how you perceive the character and by extension Black people, then what you have imagined and created is playing to a stereotype.
3. At this stage, do you still think you can write a Black character?

....

'Racism is a system of oppression of African Americans and other people of color by White Europeans and Americans'.

Joe R. Feagin – White Racism: The Basics

CHAPTER 3

RACISM AND **DISCRIMINATION**

Before we dive further into the subject of race and entertainment, it is helpful to understand a number of relevant definitions in relation to race, racism and its construction. In order to keep things simple, I will be using the terms Black and white from hereon in, but racism happens to all ethnic minorities in one form or another.

racism
Definition 1
a A belief in the supremacy of a particular race; prejudice based on this. *b* Antagonism towards other races, especially as a result of this.
Oxford English Dictionary

Definition 2
When a racial group's collective prejudice is backed by the power of legal authority and institutional control.
Robin DiAngelo – White Fragility

WHITE RACISM

Trigger warning! Only white people can be racist. But, but, but, I hear you say as you cite examples of people of colour who have said hateful or bigoted things about other races. Those people would be bigots, or hateful or prejudiced but they are not racist. Racism isn't just about disliking another person based on their skin colour. Racism is prejudice backed by the state, institutions and cultural norms and as such, only white people can be racist and yes that applies globally. Racism is a situation and power dynamic unique to white people. Like it or not, be triggered by it or not, it is a fact of life.

In his book *White Racism: The Basics*[1] Joe R. Feagin eloquently and forcefully sets out what racism is and why it can only be committed by white people. He explains that: *'In the United States, white racism is a centuries old system intentionally designed to exclude people of colour from full participation in the economy, polity and society.'* He explains that academic writing between the seventeenth and twentieth centuries was designed to support and perpetuate racism. Centuries later the system of racism is fully entrenched into Western societies and African countries where white people were the colonisers. Feagin explains how it manifests in the modern world and states: *'AntiBlack feelings, ideas and actions are widely developed, disseminated by parents, peers, the media and the educational system. They have been passed along from generation to generation now for more than three centuries.'*

IN THE BEGINNING

Racism is not a biological fact of life; it is an evil social construct created by white Western society to justify and rationalise slavery.

Prior to the Atlantic slave trade, Africa was – and still is – one of the most biologically diverse continents on the planet. Throughout the land there was enough food and resources to feed its people. Nick Hazlewood[2] refers to the traveller Leo Africanus who ventured in Africa during the sixteenth century and observed that: *'The West Africans were intelligent resourceful people.'* Regarding the people of Mali he noted: *'They excelled at wit, civility and industry, with no shortage of merchandise to be bartered. Furthermore they had a complex social structure[3].'* Clearly the European travellers in the fifteenth and sixteenth centuries had seen prosperous nations with structured societies and plenty of natural resources.

Eric Williams[4] suggests that slavery created racism and not the other way around and both were a product of mercantilism. Williams explains that after America was discovered and the Europeans began to settle there (having subjected the Native Americans to genocide and stolen their land), the British mercantile industry exploded.

As the Europeans gained a foothold and had an abundance of land, slavery commenced. The first slaves were Indian, but were not deemed suitable due to the high mortality rates as a result of brutal conditions, disease and suicide. Next came the indentured servants. These consisted of poor whites and criminals from Britain. Williams explains that once the profitability of indentured servants became apparent mass kidnappings on the streets of London and Bristol ensued and were positively encouraged, causing it to become rampant. Husbands, wives, drunks and children were drugged, kidnapped and sent abroad and forced into indenture.

Criminals in England who were facing harsh penalties or a death sentence were advised to beg for indenture says Williams. Here then it seems that the mercantile trade system which was the precursor to capitalism was exploiting and brutalising the poor, criminals and those without power.

Those caught up in the mercantile system would be shipped to America or the Caribbean to serve their period of indenture. The mercantilists realised that the issue with indentured poor whites was that after a period of time they would be free. As Williams points out, Africans were seen as the solution and slave laws were developed accordingly. Racism was born and thus, through the system of slavery, solidified. As Williams quotes in his book:

> 'Tho' to traffic in human creatures, may at first sight appear barbarous, inhuman and unnatural, yet the traders herein have as much to plead in their own excuse as can be said of some other branches of trade, namely the advantage of it. In a word from this trade proceed benefits, far outweighing all, either real or pretended mischiefs and inconveniences[5].'

Slavery was hugely profitable for European nations, particularly Britain. In order to justify it, it meant the systematic dehumanisation and brutalisation of Black people in order to make that profit. With that malevolent intent and purpose, racism was constructed. Let me be clear, racism is an evil social construct. It was created by white society in order to brutalise and slaughter people of colour, steal their land and enslave Black people and amass an obscene amount of wealth through unjust enrichment. Because racism is a social construct it can be deconstructed, but capitalism in its current form and white privilege have no interest in doing so.

WHITE SUPREMACY AND THE CONSTRUCTION OF RACISM

white supremacy
The belief that the white race is inherently superior to other races and that white people should have control over people of other races. *Merriam-Webster Dictionary*

Every area of Western life helped to construct the lie of racism and born of racism was the false concept and myth of white supremacy, and Black or non-white inferiority. Having constructed this social lie, it underpinned and enabled the Atlantic slave trade that lasted four hundred and thirty years.

That's four hundred and thirty years of stealing millions of Black people from their land. Slavery stole lives, futures, men, women and children. It also stole their humanity and dignity. According to Williams[6] the British Empire's annual income from the West Indies plantations was £4 million in 1798. In today's money that's £547,680,000.

Hugh Thomas[7] estimates that between ten and thirteen million Africans were transported out of Africa within the Atlantic slave trade period which was 1440 to 1870. During this time Britain, Europe, America and South America made countless billions, developed their nations and amassed fortunes and power that are still seen today.

Law, education, science and religion all helped to create and maintain the myth of white supremacy. White supremacy had to take root in the hearts and minds of white society and the state in order for slavery and racism to occur and be sustained.

In Britain slavery was permissible under common law and then legalised when the Royal African Company was chartered (originally called the Company of Royal Adventurers Trading into Africa). Subsequent legislation and case law in Britain regarded Black people as property. Slavery, segregation, apartheid – all white social constructs – were enabled by lawful authority. Remember that law is not an abstract. It is made up of lawyers, judges and officials, presidents and prime ministers, many of whom could be regarded as the educated intelligentsia.

This educated intelligentsia created, implemented and applied laws based on the false notion of white supremacy, not just through the Atlantic slave trade period but also in the colonial years which saw the brutal repression of non-white nations.

Religion also played its part in maintaining the structure of racism and adhering to this false concept. Both Catholic and Christian churches partook in the slave trade, and upheld or supported slavery as well as segregation and apartheid throughout their existence.

Last, but by no means least, is the education system which was used to indoctrinate people in this false ideology. The education system determined who it would educate and how. To this day issues surrounding the allocation of resources to schools exist, particularly in the United States with ethnic minority schools being woefully underfunded. Although they have moved on from enforced segregation and busing, access to good-quality education remains an issue. While studying in America in 1999, I came across Jonathan Kozol's work on racial inequality in the American education system. For anyone wanting to write a drama on education, I would highly recommend his work which is a shocking indictment of the American education system and how it plays out. Kozol was writing two decades ago but I am sure that there is a plethora of books and academic articles on racism within the British education system.

In *Biased*, Jennifer Eberhardt, a professor of psychology, recalls the horrors she faced when writing the chapter 'The Science of the

Scary Monsters'. She is referring to British surgeon Charles White who in 1799 studied skulls and assessed the features of the races and claimed that whites were the furthest from the brute creation and Blacks were on the lowest rung. By the same token, Samuel George Morton, an internationally renowned scientist, doctor and Harvard professor, decreed that Caucasians were distinguished by the highest intellectual endowments and his work became internationally prominent[8].

Others were to follow. In their 1854 book, *Types of Mankind*, Josiah Nott and George Gliddon instigated the false science of racial inferiority. Paul Broca discovered the area of the brain responsible for the ability to produce speech and falsely hypothesised *'frontal lobes responsible for higher reasoning were grossly underdeveloped in Blacks, while occipital lobes that handle sensory processing were overdeveloped[9]'*. In effect, Broca was asserting that Black people were intellectually inferior, unable to reason and emotionally volatile. This undoubtedly created the stereotypes relating to Black people in respect of anger, rage, immaturity and dangerousness. It is a stereotype that is still being perpetuated today, particularly when it comes to associations with crime. How many crime dramas have you seen featuring the stereotypical Black man who is either in a gang or is carrying a knife? Are there too many to mention? How many dramas and films portray the Black man as mentally slow who needs to be taken care of by white people or the system? How many dramas have you watched that portrayed the *Angry Black Woman*?

There were a whole slew of scientists from the period of slavery to the 1980s who achieved world renown for expounding the false ideology of white supremacy and Black inferiority.

So what relevance does that have in today's world, you may ask. White supremacy is the basis on which racism continues to exist in Western society and across the globe. You might think that is melodramatic or over the top, but if you are white, consider your world view at this very moment.

THE WHITENING OF SCIENCE

When you think of world-renowned scientists, you are probably thinking of white scientists: Einstein, Tesla, Pasteur, Bell, Edison and so forth. Even the films about scientists are (except for *Hidden Figures*) about white scientists. I'm not saying these were not great. I'm saying that these were probably the only scientists that you were taught about, these are the scientists that films are made about.

Now think of a Black scientist! Think of an Asian scientist! An Arab scientist? Stumped? Coming up empty? You may well think, *'Well all the great scientists happened to be white!'* If you are, then think about what you just thought. I mean *really* think about it. Are you honestly saying that in humanity's existence there has never been a great African, South Asian, East Asian or Middle Eastern scientist? Of course there has. They are just systematically erased from history and are never in the mainstream. That is the construct of white supremacy being maintained. That's why, if you are white, you probably equate science with whiteness. If you think back to all the television and films you have watched, I'd wager that the scientist was almost always portrayed as white. Breaking the mould was the excellent *Loki* series and one of my favourites, *The Flash* TV series. Here are 12 Black scientists who changed the world that you never hear about:

1.	**Charles Drew**	(1904–1950)
	Invented the blood bank	
2.	**Dr Daniel Hale Williams**	(1856–1931)
	Performed the first successful open-heart surgery	
3.	**Percy Julian**	(1899–1975)
	Created a drug to treat glaucoma	
	Created aero-foam to put out fires	
	Synthesised cortisone to treat rheumatoid arthritis	

4.	**Patricia Bath** Developed laser technology to treat cataracts	(1942–2019)
5.	**Alice Ball** Chemist who developed the first effective treatment of leprosy	(1892–1916)
6.	**Garrett Morgan** Invented the first three-way traffic signal First patented the gas mask	(1877–1963)
7.	**Lewis Latimer** Invented the carbon filament	(1848–1928)
8.	**Maria Van Brittan Brown** Home security system and CCTV	(1922–1999)
9.	**Benjamin Banneker** Invented America's first functioning clock	(1731–1806)
10.	**George Washington Carver** Botanist and innovator of agricultural science	(1864–1943)
11.	**James West** Invented the microphone	(1931–)
12.	**Thomas Jennings** Invented dry-cleaning	(1791–1856)

If the above scientists had been white, they would have been world-renowned and in the consciousness of the world. They created life-changing inventions that are used today and yet there is no knowledge or recognition of them, who they are and what they did. There are no films celebrating their work and their life stories and the obstacles they faced.

DO PEOPLE OF COLOUR WRITE?

Next, take literature. When you think of the global classical works you're probably thinking: Shakespeare, Hemingway, Shelley, Austen, Dickens and so forth. Now think of a Black classical writer. Again, can you really believe that in the centuries that passed the only great writers were white? There is no mention of Terence, the African Roman playwright whose plays went on to influence the Middle Ages and Renaissance period as well as Shakespeare. His plays were taught throughout Europe. No mention of great Black literary talents throughout the centuries such as William Wells Brown, Phillis Wheatley, Gwendolyn Brooks or Zora Neale Hurston. What about other writers of colour from the ages? Don't you think it is strange that the only world-renowned playwrights from history are white? Is it really credible to believe that across the continents hundreds of millions of people simply weren't writing? Or that people in other continents just couldn't tell stories like white people could?

AND THE LIST GOES ON

Inventors, academics, economists to name but a few. If you are white, your world view may well be that all the greats have been white. That is how white supremacy operates today, systematically and intrinsically. That is what you have been taught. That is the mainstay of education and culture. White supremacy is a socialisation process and it means erasing people of colour from the mainstream consciousness in areas such as science and literature. In a nutshell it is the normalisation of whiteness at the expense and exclusion of any other race.

GOVERNANCE

Think of governance and white supremacy. The portrayal of Africa is as depressing as it is racist. Most European nations regard Africa and Africans as people who cannot govern themselves – who do not have the intellectual, moral or technical ability to govern themselves. If you look at the adverts, there's usually a celebrity with a white saviour complex begging the seemingly benevolent European citizens of their nation for money because Africans can't feed themselves or don't have access to clean water. There is never any calling out of the Western politicians, corporations, NGOs, institutions and systems that have created this situation and are perpetuating it.

Seemingly well-meaning adverts show Africa as a dark and desperate place. Take the Band Aid song: *'Where nothing ever grows, no rain nor rivers flow...'* Really! I mean really? Africa, one of the most biologically diverse continents on the planet and yet in the minds of people listening to that song, they believe such nonsense. The tropes are the same as they are tired. *'If only Africans could govern themselves.'* Strangely enough, eons ago they built pyramids that can't be replicated today with all the available technology. Pyramids that are calculated to Pi before Pythagoras. There were great baths in Egypt and they understood hygiene (as did many non-white nations) before the Europeans did.

Western culture claims the Greeks were the founders of civilisation but according to Martin Bernal[10] it was the Egyptians who civilised the Greeks. The Greeks were known to attend the great libraries in Egypt. Libraries that were later sacked by the Catholic Church, in effect they stole knowledge and education from an African nation.

Moving through time, Africa had established societies, language and trade. Starvation was a situation created by Europe. First by stealing Africans, then by stealing African land and its resources. The slave trade did not care if the person they stole was a scientist, a healer, an engineer, a writer, a poet or a sage. Stealing all of those people often decimated that community of its knowledge, its progress and its ability to prosper.

In her 2015 Tedx Talk, 'Change Your Channel', the amazing and graceful Mallence Bart-Williams talks about the richness of Sierra Leone and the African continent. She explains that they have an abundance of natural resources including gold, platinum, diamonds and other materials which are all used by the West. Bart-Williams explains: *'The West needs Africa's resources most desperately.'* She asks two questions. The first is why five thousand units of Sierra Leone's currency is worth one unit of western currency. The second question is how does the West ensure that free aid keeps coming.

In effect, she makes clear that the West is giving publicly with one hand and taking in the shadows with the other. She makes it abundantly clear that the resources are not coming from the West to Africa but the other way around and questions why Africa is in the predicament it is in. Her answer to the above question is: *'By systematically destabilising the wealthiest African nations and their systems and backed by a PR campaign leaving the entire world under the impression that Africa is poor and dying and merely surviving on the mercy of the West.'*

African debt is a Western creation. African conflicts are for the most part a Western creation caused by partition and installing murderous tyrants. The British strategy of divide and rule has been working well for centuries.

Africa was not given self-determination. It was subjected to slavery, colonisation, genocide, apartheid, poverty and economic and social democide. Don't get me wrong, Africa now has serious problems, but most of them were caused by Europe and continue to be caused by Europe, the United States of America and international organisations who are engaging in profiteering. Unfortunately, they are the ones who also control the narrative and how its citizens see those African nations.

Some of the myths you may have bought into:

Africa needs to learn how to deal with its money responsibly.
IN TRUTH: The West created the debt problem. African nations have more than paid back their debt but the West is going to keep Africa impoverished.

Africa is a continent made up of many countries, so it's a nonsense to make the assertion anyway.

Africa has a problem with tyrants.
<u>IN TRUTH:</u> A number of dictators in Africa have been installed and/or supported by European nations or America.

Revolutionaries and socialists who have tried to implement social justice measures and undo Western harms have frequently met brutal ends, often as a result of Western input.

Thomas Sankara the prime minister of Burkino Faso or what was then known as Upper Volta, from 1983–87 is a prime example of Western intervention preventing self-determination. The leader's Pan-African policies and anti-imperialist stance resulted in the loss of 'allies' such as France and the Ivory Coast, and led to his subsequent assassination on 15 October 1987.

Africa needs our aid.
<u>IN TRUTH:</u> Africa needs the West to stop stealing its resources and land. It is one of the most biologically diverse continents on the planet containing: food, gold, other precious metals, diamonds and other gems which are in mostly white hands. The West needs to stop robbing Africa blind, stop subsidies and trade fairly.

As you can see the construction of white supremacy maintained through the socialisation process clearly benefits white people at the expense of other races and nations.

EVEN THE HEROES ARE WHITE

In the consciousness of the West, especially up to the first decade of the twenty-first century, the heroes have almost always been white. This is portrayed in history, in film and television which is an extension of that narrative. Think about World War Two, particularly if you are white and you live in Europe.

The reality is that more than a million African soldiers fought on behalf of the Allies in the Second World War[11] of which more than 600,000 fought on behalf of the British[12] yet most films about the war contain an all-white cast and there is no portrayal of Black people or other people of colour. In respect of African Americans, more than one million African American men and women fought in the Second World War[13], despite being subject to segregation at home. So two million Black people fought in the war and yet they are not recognised, remembered or portrayed. Two and a half million Africans fought in World War One[14].

After World War Two, African soldiers returned to their homes only to be subjected to brutal colonisation by the very people they had fought for. Their efforts in the war were disregarded. Furthermore, their efforts and participation were erased from history and many died and are in unmarked graves and the British refused to commemorate them. In America Black soldiers returned home to a still segregated society. To many African Americans who had fought in the war and returned home they could see no difference between the Nazis and the Americans. Of course, there wouldn't be because they both believed in the concept of white supremacy. The same can be said of the Europeans. The British still maintained a system of white supremacy and this was clearly apparent in Kenya. As Caroline Elkins[15] points out, the British were engaging in systematic internment, torture, murder and sexual abuse of Kenyans. They had decided that the Universal Declaration of Human Rights did not apply to Black people. Now, if you're white, you see the Allies as heroes. If you're Black, maybe not so much.

In the documentary *The Unremembered*[16] David Lammy MP visits Kenya and Tanzania. In Voi, Kenya, following World War One, the graves for the British soldiers were given individual headstones and kept in a pristine condition. The Black soldiers were buried in a mass unmarked grave. The Commonwealth War Graves Commission was supposed to have a policy of *'what was done for one should be done for all'*. There was supposed to be equality in death regardless of rank, but that equality only applied to white people.

In Tanzania, which was German held, the British provided marked graves to honour the enemy soldiers but the Black soldiers in Tanzania were also left in unmarked graves. In the documentary it is established that this wasn't down to random acts of racism but policy, and an excerpt from the decision reads: '...most of the natives who have died are of a semi-savage nature and do not attach any sentiment to marking the graves of their dead'. Further, '...the erection of individual headstones would constitute a waste of public money'. That meant no recognition then and no remembrance by current and future generations, whether they be family members, or the British for whom they died. It is not in the consciousness of most Europeans that World War One was also fought in Africa.

THE WHITE RACIAL FRAME

This erasing of people of colour – the creation of white dominance in all aspects of society and across the globe – is deliberate and systematic. In his book *The White Racial Frame* and in his lectures, Joe R. Feagin explains that *'the white racial frame greatly helps to preserve the dominance of racial inequality'*. He observes that the white racial frame has a number of methodologies to *'legitimise and rationalise a racist society'*. Feagin explains that the WRF utilises racist stereotypes and prejudices, expounds racist narratives that are steeped in myths and untruths, portrays racist images and racialised emotions. He then goes on to explain that there are subsets within the WRF that ensure white dominance by portraying white culture, white people as virtuous, white people as civilised and white people as scholars or people of science. It is, he asserts, a culture of *'anti-others'*. The effect is a white global view which in turn leads to large-scale discrimination.

OMG

Bloody hell, Thandi, that's a bit heavy, you may be thinking, I just want to write scripts. Well write a great script I say. Understand the true impact of racism and the role race plays. If you are white you may have a positive view of the country you reside in and the systems and institutions within it, but if you are Black your view of them could be completely different due to adverse experiences and history.

You should understand that if you are white you have the benefit of this structure of white supremacy. If you are Black you are often adversely affected by the same structure. With two completely different experiences in the same world, the characters cannot have the same viewpoint or thought processes. A relatively well-off white person can go through life not having to ever think about their race. A Black person in the same economic situation still has to navigate life in this social construct; as such the characters are simply not going to be the same.

If you understand this structure and racism, you can build worlds, you can understand the views of a person of colour you can have realistic characters. Writing the Black Jane Austen character is not authentic. Writing the stereotypical Black or other person of colour is just lazy and uninformed and it will show.

I hope you will write a great script with great characters. So bear in mind when you write a Black character, they may reside in the same country as you but it is highly likely they will live in a completely different world to yours if you are white. We have to navigate and negotiate because sometimes our lives really do depend on it and so do our livelihoods, both of which can be so easily taken away.

The socialisation process starts young as Eberhardt pointed out[17] when she referred to a University of Washington study relating to Seattle preschool children. In the study a woman is hostile to one person in front of the children. She is then friendly to another person and gives them a toy. The children expressed hostility or prejudice to the person on the receiving end of the hostility, not the person engaging in the hostility. Therefore it follows, when children see white people being hostile to people of a different race, that behaviour is replicated.

The 1981 Scarman Report[18] and the 1999 Macpherson Report[19] both recognised the problem of racism and racial prejudice in children as young as five. They had both implored the governments of the day to address this issue. Unsurprisingly, successive governments have failed to tackle the issue and the most recent Conservative government have chosen to dilute institutional racism and its existence, as evidenced by the 2021 Commission on Race and Ethnic Disparities[20]. The published report has disappointed many who have been addressing the issues of institutional and systemic racism within the United Kingdom.

There is a plethora of material on race, racism and prejudice. Racism manifests in all areas of our lives whether you benefit from it or are on the receiving end of it. If you are going to write a character who is Black or another person of colour, then you should be informed as to what racism is, how it manifests, who benefits from it and who is disadvantaged by it.

As a writer of science fiction and fantasy and an avid fan of television and film in that genre, the thought crossed my mind that utopian creations are free of racism in those worlds. In respect of those creations that are set on earth but in the future, I pose the question: how was racism eliminated? Now, as a writer in the present day, if your character or characters were going to eliminate racism/white supremacy, how would they do it? That is a story and a character arc. If your protagonist is going to find the solution, they need to know what the problem is.

racial stereotyping
Racial stereotype or cultural stereotype involves part of a system of beliefs about typical characteristics of members of a given ethnic group, their status, societal and cultural norms.
https://en.wikipedia.org/wiki/Ethnic_stereotype

One of the biggest problems Black people face is stereotyping, which is making assumptions about a person or a group of people based on their race. A UN General Assembly Report[21] clearly set out that stereotyping began as a way to commodify Black bodies and justify enslavement. It continues to this day and results in racial discrimination. The report is twenty-two pages long and worth reading for an introduction to racism and stereotyping. In her book, *Biased*, Jennifer Eberhardt points out that one of the most problematic stereotypes is linking Black people, particularly Black men, with criminality.

I don't seek to write at length about stereotyping, suffice to say the most common stereotypes relating to Black people are in respect of crime, drugs, gangs, sports, music, violence, poverty. In respect of Middle Eastern people, it's usually terrorism, extremism and/or misogyny. In respect of Asian people, again it's terrorism, owning a corner shop, working in IT. You get the picture. How many characters have you seen in television and film that portray those stereotypes? Stereotypes that remain in human consciousness.

At this point it might be worth examining your character of colour. Have you stereotyped them? If you have created a character based on your belief about their race, then that is a stereotype. If you haven't given them a name but only given them a designation such as 'prisoner', 'gang member', or 'prostitute' and it is based on your perception of a race of people, or specified a racial designation, then guess what? You've stereotyped them. If you have, you should go back to the drawing board and research where your character was born, what their heritage is and what the issues they are facing today are… and I would strongly urge you to read the UN report on stereotyping.

systemic racism

Systemic racism includes the complex array of antiBlack practices, the unjustly gained political-economic powers of whites, the continuing economic and other resource inequalities along racial lines, and the white racist ideologies and attitudes created to maintain and rationalise white privilege and power.
Joe R. Feagin – *Racist America: Roots, Current Realities and Future Reparations* (Routledge, 2000)

Another definition is:

'Systemic racism' can be defined as an infrastructure of rulings, ordinances or statutes promulgated by a sovereign government or authoritative entity, whereas such ordinances and statutes entitled one ethnic group in a society certain rights and privileges, while denying other groups in that society these same rights and privileges because of long-established cultural prejudices, religious prejudices, fears, myths, and Xenophobia's [sic] held by the entitled group.

MD Shahid – Office of the United Nations High Commissioner for Human Rights – taken from the Out of Africa Monologue Series.

institutional racism

The collective failure of an organisation to provide an appropriate and professional service to people because of their colour, culture, or ethnic origin. It can be seen or detected in processes, attitudes and behaviour which amount to discrimination through unwitting prejudice, ignorance, thoughtlessness and racist stereotyping which disadvantage minority ethnic people.

The Macpherson Report, 1999 para 6.34

racial discrimination

A person discriminates against another in any circumstances… if… on racial grounds he treats that other less favourably than he treats or would treat other persons; or he applies to that other a requirement or condition which he applies or would apply equally to persons not of the same racial group as that other…

Section 1(1) Race Relations Act 1976

The result of racism and white supremacy is racial discrimination. As per the Race Relations Act 1976, it is treating a person less favourably on the grounds of race. In Britain racial discrimination cuts across all areas of life and society, and is active in most, if not all British institutions.

As will be discussed later, in healthcare Black nurses are subjected to harsher discipline than their white counterparts and less likely to be promoted. In certain circumstances Black women are five times more likely to die during pregnancy and childbirth than their white counterparts.

In the British criminal justice system Black people are between four and twenty-four times more likely to be stopped and searched compared to their white counterparts. In the United States and Britain, Black people have been victims of homicide either by shooting, restraint or neglect at the hands of the police and often those deaths have occurred with impunity.

In the education system Black children are more likely to receive harsher sanctions in school such as suspension or exclusion than their white counterparts. In employment Black people are further discriminated against in respect of being offered employment and their access to training and promotion.

The above are not an exhaustive list of where and how racism operates, but they are an example of how racism operates. They are also examples of how prevalent and entrenched racism is.

critical race theory

Critical race theory (CRT) is a cross-disciplinary intellectual and social movement of civil rights scholars and activists who seek to examine the impact of racism across all aspects of society.
https://en.wikipedia.org/wiki/Critical_race_theory

intersectionality

Kimberlé Crenshaw is credited with coining the term intersectionality. Intersectionality posits that concentrating on one aspect of discrimination focuses on the dominant group, e.g. race or gender, but can erase others from the group and not have regard to the additional discrimination that they face. For example, addressing sex discrimination tends to focus on white women but it will not take into account Black women and the fact that race is an additional factor when they are discriminated against.

white fragility

A white person becoming angry, defensive or fragile at any attempt to connect them to the system of racism or challenging their racial comfort.
Robin DiAngelo – *White Fragility*

Robin DiAngelo is a white woman who pulls no punches when it comes to recognising the state of society in racial terms. Indeed she starts with:

'White people in North America live in a society that is deeply separate and unequal by race, and white people are the beneficiaries of that separation and inequality[22].'

DiAngelo asserts that white supremacy is a socialisation process and, throughout time, white people have been able to benefit from the process to the point that in today's world they no longer need to explicitly talk about race, racism and privilege. She further suggests that any suggestion to a white person that they are complicit in or engaging in racism causes a shock to the system and henceforth triggers white fragility leading to behaviours of anger, denial or silence from the said white person.

The issue, she contends, is that racism in their eyes is seen as a good/bad binary and that any connotations with racism are regarded as bad. Not wanting to be seen as bad, white people will shut down any discussion of racism or deny that it is happening.

DiAngelo concludes that as a result many white people are misinformed about the state of affairs when it comes to racism and inequality. She suggests that rather than be defensive about the label and adhere strictly to the good/bad binary, white people should understand they have been raised in the socialisation process and seek to confront racism from that place.

I've had my fair share of fragile white responses which included silence, denial, anger and sulking. These are also some common responses:

i. I didn't mean anything by it.
ii. I'm sure they didn't mean it.
iii. You can't say anything these days.
iv. If Black people can say it, why can't I?

white privilege

White privilege, or 'historically accumulated white privilege' as we have come to call it, refers to whites' historical and contemporary advantages in access to quality education, decent jobs and liveable wages, homeownership, retirement benefits, wealth and so on.

The following quotation from a publication by Peggy McIntosh can be helpful in understanding what is meant by white privilege: *'As a white person I had been taught about racism that puts others at a disadvantage, but had been taught not to see one of its corollary aspects, white privilege, which puts me at an advantage... White privilege is an invisible package of unearned assets which I can count on cashing in every day, but about which I was meant to remain oblivious'.*
Peggy McIntosh, 'White Privilege: Unpacking the Invisible Knapsack', *Peace and Freedom Magazine,* **July 1989**

I could write at length about white privilege but, in a nutshell, it is about benefit. It is benefiting from the socialisation process of white supremacy that white people can call on and use to their advantage. Now, I'm not saying white people don't have problems; there are still issues about poverty and class and gender that affect certain sections of white society. What I am saying is that your race isn't going to be a factor that will adversely affect you.

In respect of white privilege, it can be the difference between liberty and incarceration. It can be the difference between a polite and brief interaction with law enforcement or a fatal one. It can mean receiving appropriate medical treatment or dying. And crucially it can mean the difference between being believed or not believed.

In respect of being believed, you may recall the incident between Amy Cooper, a white woman and Christian Cooper, a Black man. Amy Cooper is in the park with her dog off the leash. Christian Cooper requested that she put her dog on the leash. Christian then beckoned the dog towards him with a treat. Despite Christian Cooper remaining calm, civil and at a distance, Amy Cooper weaponised her whiteness. She started with the threat of calling the police and telling Christian Cooper: *'I'm going to tell them there's an African American man threatening my life.'* He was doing no such thing and thankfully he was recording the incident. She then goes on to call the police and in a raised and hysterical voice she says: *'There's an African American man recording me and threatening me.'* She was relying on her whiteness as a weapon against a Black man.

Undoubtedly, she knew the potential for a fatal or life-changing outcome for Christian Cooper and it was all because she didn't get her way that she decided to play the race card. Unfortunately, it is a card that many white people have played throughout time which has led to incarceration or a brutal and fatal outcome for Black people.

My final example of white privilege and being believed is Brexit. For decades, politicians, the media and even British citizens have lauded Britain as multicultural and racism as a thing of the past, despite ethnic minorities and certain organisations saying that racism is still a problem in this country. Brexit happened and suddenly a lot of white people are saying: *'I can't believe how racist this country is.'* Now they are saying it, it must be true! That is a classic example of white privilege.

FROM BIRTH TO DEATH

If we look at society as a whole from birth until death, racism is often a factor as to whether or not you live or die, succeed or fail, prosper or perish. If you are white you are probably not going to engage in daily negotiations that have arisen out of being on the receiving end of racism. I'm going to take a short look at the stages of life and how they affect Black people. In the upcoming chapters I have expanded upon these issues further, not just because they are important topics but because they are often the subject of drama. At this stage, I would ask that you think about the age and stage of life that your Black character is in and what they are facing.

PREGNANCY AND CHILDBIRTH

In America the Population Reference Bureau studied death certificates between 2016 and 2017 and found that during that period, *'the maternal mortality rate among non-Hispanic Black women was 3.5 times that of non-Hispanic white women'*. Furthermore, that *'Postpartum cardiomyopathy and the blood pressure disorders pre-eclampsia and eclampsia were leading causes of maternal death for Black women with mortality rates five times those of white women'.* PRB went on to say *'The elevated risk of maternal mortality for Black women from multiple causes, reflects the impact of structural racism on health and health care in the United States[23].'* In the United Kingdom Black women are four times more likely to die during pregnancy and childbirth than their white counterparts[24]. This is not down to physiological differences, this is a result of systemic and institutional racism. A key finding was that Black women were not listened to, or ignored when they tried to highlight something was wrong. There was also stereotyping and erroneous assumptions relating to pain thresholds, aggression and drug use.

EARLY YEARS

According to Greenwood et al[25] in America Black newborn babies die at three times the rate of white newborns when treated by a white physician. When Black newborns are treated by Black doctors the mortality penalty is halved. They also found that there is no difference in mortality for white newborns when treated by a Black or white doctor.

EDUCATION

Education and race could be the subject of another book. Suffice to say that research shows that in the United States Black schools are more likely to be chronically underfunded and have fewer resources. In the United Kingdom Black Caribbean children are up to six times more likely to be expelled from school than their white counterparts[26], Gypsy and Roma children are nine times and mixed-race children four times more likely to be excluded than their white counterparts in some areas.

When it comes to educational attainment, class appears to be the biggest factor according to the government as white, mixed-race and Black boys have lower educational attainment if they are from a lower socio-economic background. Black boys from higher socio-economic status situations tend to fare worse than their white counterparts. The report does, however, suggest that the overwhelming picture is an advantage to ethnic minority students in relation to educational achievement at age 16[27].

EMPLOYMENT

Access to employment, training and promotion has long been at the centre of discrimination. Studies show that in the United Kingdom, Europe, America and Canada racial discrimination adversely affects Black people when it comes to employment and progression.

A Kings College University study[28] found *'Everyday experiences of bullying, harassment and discrimination mean that in London there is a culture of high diversity but low inclusion for racial and ethnic minority healthcare staff.'*

Healthcare is not the only institution to be singled out for racial discrimination in employment and it is not exclusive to government institutions. In all sectors public and private racial discrimination occurs. That is not to say that every employer is racist, I am saying that it is prevalent.

Eberhardt[29] refers to the Bertrand and Mullainathan 2003 study whereby they created 5000 fictitious resumes. The resumes were identical but given Black or white sounding names and sent out to 1300 job adverts in Chicago and Boston. An analysis of the results showed that applicants with white-sounding names received 50 per cent more call backs than their Black counterparts. Eberhardt points out that even though the study was in 2003, it still holds true in 2019 and had similar outcomes in Canada, America, the United Kingdom and Europe.

HEALTHCARE

Black people have suffered gravely at the hands of medical professionals and as the later chapter explains they have been subject to brutal experiments, are discriminated against when it comes to treatment, have more adverse health outcomes and Black staff are abused and bullied on the basis of race by staff and patients.

MEDIA

Covered in a later chapter, we find the media is often hostile to Black people who are successful: the adverse reporting in relation to Black footballers with wealth compared to their white counterparts; the treatment of Meghan Markle compared to Kate Middleton for the exact same behaviour. In a later chapter I will look at racism within the media and how state violence would appear to be supported and racial justice vilified.

POLITICS

Politicians have shamefully, dangerously and hatefully used racism to appeal to the worst character traits of their citizens. Whether it be the prime minister using racially offensive language in relation to Black people, immigrants and Muslims; or the Home Secretary creating hostile environments, denying the people of Windrush the right to remain in the United Kingdom, or sending immigrants on a plane to Rwanda.

Racism and xenophobia are used to appeal to the lowest common denominator, to garner votes and at the same time distract from what the real problems are. If a group of identifiable people can be blamed for the nation's troubles, they make a great scapegoat for corruption, incompetence, nepotism, lax taxation policies and a failure to govern properly.

Unfortunately for the people on the receiving end it makes them subject to verbal and physical abuse, violence and harassment.

CONCLUSION

At every stage of a Black person's life, there is racism. The statistics speak for themselves, yet individuals, institutions and very often the media deny it is happening. The same tired lip service of 'it's just a few individuals' is lazy and inaccurate.

I hope this chapter has given you an understanding of what racism is, how it manifests and how intrinsic it is in society. I also hope you are aware of the terms and what they mean and the implications they have for white people and people of colour, as well as society as a whole.

I finish this chapter by stating that a Black character would undoubtedly have had a fundamentally different experience to your white character in the same role. Their outlook and motivations may be completely different and so it must follow that their decisions and actions will be completely different. A great example of portraying the Black experience was the painfully funny 2017 film *Get Out* written, produced and directed by the amazing Jordan Peele. In *Get Out* Daniel Kaluuya's character Chris Washington is going out with a white woman and is going to meet her family for the first time. His experience as a Black man is intricately woven into the everyday whilst creating some excruciating but hilarious moments in respect of the Black experience.

It is clear that racism pervades society and that life experiences often differ according to race, as such it should be reflected in film and television. By the same token, stereotyping is still a problem in society and in the entertainment industry. In light of the above, I hope that when you write your script, your Black or ethnic minority characters and the world they inhabit are accurately portrayed and that you do not revert to stereotyping.

'We might not see confederate flags flying in parks or signs relegating colored people to separate facilities, but we do see minorities cast as criminals and leeches to "white upper-class" America.'

Horton, Price and Brown[30]

CHAPTER 4

RACE AND ENTERTAINMENT FROM A HISTORICAL PERSPECTIVE – PART 1

Film, television and media have played a role in perpetuating racism and stereotypes since their inception. Overtly racist programmes, stereotyping and cultural appropriation have all featured in the entertainment industry.

The first cinema was broadcast on 28 December 1895 in Paris. Its inventors were Louis and Auguste Lumière. America's first cinema theatre opened in 1896 at Vitascope Hall in New Orleans. Theatre became the way to not only reach the masses but also influence them.

It is worth bearing in mind that at the time of cinema theatres' inception, America – and in particular the southern states of America – was a deeply racist country. The Emancipation Proclamation which freed the American slaves had occurred in 1863. Although slaves were technically free, many were not and were forced to work on plantations that had enslaved them as a result of dire economic circumstances and/or exploitation.

While the southern states had engaged in the slave trade, it is worth pointing out some of the northern states were tied economically to the trade and the majority of the population held racist views. America was – and still is – a deeply racist country and that was

49

reflected *inter alia* in film. Britain was – and still is – a deeply racist country. Britain had engaged in the slave trade and indeed, slavery is largely responsible for Britain's wealth today. As Williams points out, Britain did not dismantle slavery due to some moral outrage, it did so for economic purposes. After slavery came colonisation and European countries made a scramble for Africa. Their impact had more deadly and devastating consequences for Africans.

One of the earliest and most notoriously racist films to be released in American theatres was *The Birth of a Nation*[31] originally entitled *The Clansman*. Writing in the *Washington Post* in 2015, Ed Rampell[32] called it *'The most reprehensibly racist film in Hollywood history.'* The film, which was three hours long, followed two families across the north-south divide of America during and after the time of Abraham Lincoln.

The film depicted Black people as subhuman and Black men were portrayed as aggressive sexual predators. It also suggested that if no action was taken white people would be living under Black rule. In the film the Ku Klux Klan are portrayed as the heroes. Most of the Black characters were played by white actors in Blackface but some Black actors were cast in the film.

According to Wikipedia: *'In spite of its divisiveness,* The Birth of a Nation *was a huge commercial success across the nation – grossing more than any previous motion picture – and it profoundly influenced both the film industry and American culture.'* The National Association for the Advancement of Colored People and local Black leaders tried to get the film banned before it was released in local theatres but were unsuccessful.

The Birth of a Nation's influence spread throughout America and it is clear that the film was not just meant for entertainment purposes. It perpetuated, if not increased racism. It was clearly designed to maintain the false notion of white supremacy and some regard it as being responsible for bringing the KKK back to life. The audiences across America who watched the film consisted of ordinary men and women. People who were doctors, lawyers, educators and politicians. Indeed, the film was given a special screening at the White House to Woodrow Wilson, a purported racist himself, who never denounced the film.

The people who watched the film made up society and they were being socialised into white supremacy. Many would have agreed with and adopted those views and have those views confirmed by their peers and, more concerningly, pass those views on to their children. The professionals influenced by the film would have been people who would have made decisions in the course of their employment regarding Black people. Consider then, as the film influenced white consciousness, the decisions those white people would have made in respect of Black people in their capacity as medical professionals, law enforcers, legal professionals. Undoubtedly and evidently the decisions made were discriminatory and adverse towards Black people.

AMERICAN FILMS

The Birth of a Nation was not the only reprehensibly racist film to be released in American theatres in the twentieth century that received critical acclaim. The most notorious examples are set out below.

---

1. **The Jazz Singer** (1927)
   Al Jolson singing in Blackface trying to make it as a jazz singer.

---

2. **Judge Priest** (1934)
   Set in a Kentucky town in 1890, the judge has a Black friend, but the friend is stereotypically slow-witted and Black women are mammies, happily singing while being a servant. Black men are referred to as 'boy'. The court is run by white people who are seen as fair-minded gentlemen.

---

3. **The Littlest Rebel** (1935)
   Benevolent slave owners are fighting against the bad Unionists, while stereotyping Black people as stupid and docile, who apparently don't want to be free. The Black people are always ready with a dumb smile and a dance. Cringeworthy, dishonest and racist.

---

4. Gone with the Wind (1939)

Sympathising with slave owners and the confederacy. Racist stereotyping.

5. Dumbo (1941)

Racist stereotyping. The crows are in Black voice and the lead crow is called Jim Crow. Jim Crow being a vile racist and segregationist.

6. Breakfast at Tiffany's (1961)

Mickey Rooney playing a Japanese man, false teeth inserted and stereotyping aplenty.

7. Mandingo (1975)

Obscenely racist and disturbing on so many levels. The male slave owner is known to rape the female slaves. He rapes his female slave but then they are regarded as *'being in a relationship'*. Female slave owner tells Black male slave to sleep with her or she will cry rape.

BRITISH FILMS

Although the British film industry of the early twentieth century was not the leviathan that Hollywood was, it still had significant output and released a number of films for the cinema and television.

While some British films were overtly racist, or stereotypical, some films took an anti-racist stance. Undoubtedly, some may seek to defend the films of the past but I would suggest that is engaging in more white fragility. To use the phrase *'it was a different time'* is to suggest that everyone was a racist and morally bankrupt throughout the periods. While racism was rife, there were still those who did not engage in it and those who actively fought against it and so to excuse the films is to tar everyone with the same brush. It's also fragility to not accept that in that period there was significant wrongdoing.

The British films below are a sample of racist portrayal.

1. The Dam Busters   (1955)

Following the story of the bouncing bomb. The Wing Commander's dog was called Ni**er.

---

2. Othello   (various)

The title character is Black but he has been played by various white actors who Blacked up.

---

3. Lawrence of Arabia   (1962)

Lawrence is a British army officer with a white saviour complex who is sent to find Prince Faisal and help in a war against the Turks. Alec Guinness is in brownface, playing an Arab. Casual racism and stereotyping aplenty in this very, very long film.

---

4. Zulu   (1964)

This film was subversive and clearly anti-war and made thought-provoking comments in respect of racism and stereotyping. The premise in issue is that the British are the defenders. Clearly the British were the invaders and the imperialists so to portray them as defenders is absurd. One may say it is ethnocentric; I'd say the premise is racist. It is suggested that a small number of British soldiers defeated thousands of Zulus at Rorke's Drift. History has often been written from a white perspective so who knows!

BRITISH TELEVISION

The year 1927 saw the beginning of the television, the impact of which was the ability to eventually reach and influence the masses in millions of households. In Britain the first television drama to be aired was *The Man with the Flower in His Mouth* in the 1930s. In the same decade, the BBC had become responsible for making and broadcasting programmes.

Television in Britain was suspended during the war years but in 1946 it made a return. Filmmakers and entertainers would have been aware of the impact of drama on the audience.

British television produced some of the most racist shows aired throughout the twentieth century that made their way into millions of households in Britain. Below are some of the programmes that I have had the misfortune of watching.

1. **The Black and White Minstrel Show – BBC**   (1958–1978)
    This was a Saturday evening primetime show consisting of white men made up in Blackface who would sing songs and engage in racism, racist stereotyping and mocking of Black people.

    Despite its racist tones and being warned about its racist content, the BBC refused to remove the show saying that *'coloured people should shut up'.*

2. **Curry and Chips – LWT for ITV**   (1969)
    This was a comedy show starring Spike Milligan in Blackface as an Irishman with Pakistani heritage called Kevin O'Grady. The show was set in a factory called Lillicrap and purported to mock racism but in reality it was just racist.

    In the pilot highly offensive racial slurs are used with no challenge. Black and Asian characters are subjected to constant racism and they also engage in bigotry.

3. **Till Death Us Do Part – BBC**   (1965–1975)
    Alf Garnett is the grumpy racist lamenting that the racist Enoch Powell is not in charge. This was a show that engaged in highly offensive racism without challenge. There would be a constant use of racial epithets.

    In 2000 Till Death Us Do Part was rated 86 out of 100 of the greatest British TV shows.

4. **Mind Your Language – LWT for ITV**   (1977–1986)
    This was a comedy series with a diverse cast about foreign students attending evening classes to learn English. It made use of every stereotypical and racist joke under the sun.

These were some of the most notoriously racist programmes throughout the twentieth century in film and television. There is a plethora of them out there. It would be worth trawling through archives and researching old television programmes and films that were overtly racist. Some of the above are available on YouTube or Amazon. Be warned if you are Black, a person of colour or an anti-racist as they are a depressing watch.

One may say, 'Well it was a different time back then,' but throughout time people have always known the difference between right and wrong. People have always known the difference between kindness and cruelty. If they didn't, life would have been a lot darker and there would not have been any social progress.

Not everyone in the Dark Ages engaged in murder or rape. Not everyone engaged in the slave trade or supported slavery. The same can be said of segregation and apartheid. While those regimes may have had the support of the white majority, there were those who opposed it and actively sought to dismantle it. Why? Because they knew it was wrong and they wanted no part of it. So for people to say it was a different time is just a lazy, thoughtless cop-out and a desperate attempt to defend racism and its horrific legacy.

The Western entertainment industry and audiences were clearly part of the socialisation process known as white supremacy and these films were told in a white racial frame. Think of the portrayals of Black people as stupid or slow-witted and Black men as aggressive and sexual predators.

Now recall the scientific findings discussed in Chapter 3: Charles White in 1799 asserting that whites are furthest from the brute creation and Blacks are on the lowest rung; Samuel Morton claiming during the 1830s to 1840s that whites were superior and Blacks were inferior morally and intellectually. Last but by no means least, Gliddon and Knott in their 1854 book *Types of Mankind* asserting Blacks were inferior. Considering the films mentioned it is clear that those scientists influenced society as a whole and those views were accepted by most whites at the time and continue to lurk in the consciousness of Western society. Clearly among those films there was a rank dishonesty that perpetuated racist myths. Some of them being:

i. White supremacy – that whites are the superior race and Blacks are the most inferior.

ii. White endangerment – that the so-called superior race is advanced and civilised and that they are in danger of being overrun or destroyed. As such, they must do all they can to protect their race, their racial purity and their way of life.

iii. White benevolence – that slavery wasn't so bad. Slave owners were wise and benevolent and if it wasn't for white slave owners or white dominance, people of colour would revert to ignorance and savagery and be lost without white people.

From a psychological and spiritual point of view, one may wonder if certain white people who made these films were engaging in projection or cognitive dissonance. There appears to be an obsession with portraying Black men as dangerous sexual predators, yet it was white men who were committing genocide, brutalising, raping, killing and enslaving people of colour across the continents. This appears to be textbook projection. The depravity of white enslavement and colonisation for more than four centuries knew no bounds and it was as sickening as it was brutal.

The following excerpts are a small snapshot of what was done over the centuries in Africa, the Americas, Asia and Australia.

The Spanish in the Caribbean

'They kicked their way into Indian villages, slaughtering everyone that they found there, including small children, old men, women who had just given birth. ... They grabbed suckling infants by the feet and ripping them from their mothers' breasts dashed them headlong against the rocks. Others laughing and joking.'

Slavery
Murdering, raping, trafficking, burning, beating, brandishing and general brutalising.

Segregation/Apartheid
White rule enforced through law as well as murder, lynching and brutalising.

The Kenya Emergency
'The white officers had no shame. They would rape women in full view of everyone. They would take whomever they wanted at one corner and just do it right there.'

It is worth reiterating that this is a small snapshot of the brutality perpetrated by white people across the globe for centuries. In Africa, America, South America, Asia and Canada, genocide and terror was brought to these nations. They were forced off their land, had their children taken away and even into the twentieth century indigenous people were being forcefully sterilised. However, if you watched American and British films in the first half of the twentieth century, white people were depicted as intelligent, benevolent, civilised, heroes and endangered. In comparison people of colour who had been the victims of extreme barbarity from whites were depicted as savages, stupid, lost and helpless.

Everyone participating in the production of racist films and television had a choice. Some had more choices than others. The more powerful their position, the more choice they had to either walk away or challenge the status quo. Television in particular is more egregious because the racism was long running. Actors, directors, producers and writers all chose whether or not to create and perpetuate racism and to transmit that racism into people's houses and say that racism is okay.

It was a choice to demean and dehumanise Black people and people of colour and make their lives harder. It should also be borne in mind that while those programmes were made to entertain the white audience, it was done at the expense of people of colour who would have been on the receiving end of the overt and casual racism. Throughout this chapter have you considered how these shows would impact and affect the Black or Asian audience? Imagine a Black or Asian parent having to sit down with their children as slurs such as 'coon, sambo, coolie and wog' are regularly used casually and without challenge. The shame and humiliation that national television was inflicting upon you. That hurt and humiliation being dismissed as 'just banter', or 'not being able to take a joke'. Now think about what your children are going to face at work because this racism is popular and spread into family homes across the country. You know your kids are going to face racial abuse and jokes as a result of those television shows. You know it, because when you go to work, you're going to face it too.

Those words were used so casually towards ethnic minorities in the 1970s and 1980s and I have no doubt the casualness of racism and racial abuse was accepted as a result of the part television and film played in broadcasting those portrayals. Indeed Horton, Price and Brown state: *'The media sets the tone for the morals, values, and images of our culture. Many people in this country, some of whom have never encountered Black people, believe that the degrading stereotypes of Blacks are based on reality and not fiction. Everything they believe about Blacks is determined by what they see on television. After over a century of movie making, these horrible stereotypes continue to plague us today, and until negative images of Blacks are extinguished from the media, Blacks will be regarded as second-class citizens*[33]*.'*

No doubt there will be some triggered white people reading this chapter who will undoubtedly start engaging in a bit of white fragility right now. I did say this would be an uncomfortable read for some. Ask yourself if you are engaging in white fragility at the moment. Some fragile responses might be:

i. It was a different time back then.
ii. You can't say anything these days.
iii. Snowflakes.
iv. People of Colour are just as racist as whites.
v. What about...
vi. This PC shit has gone mad.
vii. They didn't mean anything by it.

And on and on it can go: the whataboutery, the fragility and the hostility to what is being shown. Bear in mind the people working on those programmes trained and handed over the reins to the next generation, who handed the reins down to the next and so on. It wasn't just knowledge and skills that were handed down, but attitudes and behaviours. So, while we are unlikely to see programmes like *Curry and Chips* today, racist portrayals and stereotypes still make their way into film and television.

There was a lot of political and social upheaval in the twentieth century and the tone of film appears to change. By the 1980s it is doubtful that something like *The Birth of a Nation* would have been greenlit, but the racism and stereotyping portrayed still persist today in one form or another.

Below are some of the initial racist and stereotypical tropes about Black people that were on display in the nineteenth and twentieth centuries.

The Savage
The uncivilised Black person who can barely speak and can't understand basic conversations or etiquette. In Africa they will barely be clothed, will engage in cannibalism and brutality.

The Dangerous
Particularly relates to Black men. They are portrayed as dangerous, violent and lacking any impulse control. Often portrayed as a danger to white women.

The Criminal
The drug dealer, the robber, the gangster.

The Sexually Aggressive

Usually men but sometimes women. Again with no impulse control and white women are in danger.

The Mammy

She's usually non-sexual, has a heart of gold but lacks intelligence. She only wants to look after white people's children and puts them above the needs of her own.

The Harlot

A beautiful Black woman but oversexed and either lacks intellect or is dangerous and manipulative.

The Docile/Lost Soul

They may have a special talent (usually a sport) but they are too soft/docile/stupid to harness it, so they need a white saviour. They usually don't want to be freed from their white master.

The Stupid

Sometimes bug-eyed. They usually speak painfully slowly and can't string a comprehensible sentence together. Usually the loyal slave, servant or friend.

Like the Mammy, the male version has a heart of gold but no brains and struggles to understand anything complex.

The Angry

Last but by no means least, angry. Angry Black woman or angry Black man. They are always angry about absolutely everything and communicate via shouting or violence.

STEREOTYPING TRANSFORMED

Racist portrayals become a bit more subtle over time and are an offshoot of the stereotypes listed above. Below are some of the racist and stereotypical portrayals that were common from the 1970s onwards and continue to exist in film and television today.

Angry
Still exists today – the angry Black woman or the angry Black man.

Impoverished
In America the Black person is from the ghetto and in the UK they are from an estate.
   They are often broke and the situation is usually inevitable and hopeless.

Ghetto
As above but Black neighbourhoods are usually portrayed as impoverished, crime ridden and dangerous.

Criminal
In jail, on death row. A drug dealer or a gangster.

Drug Addicted
Needs no explanation.

Stupid/Slow
The Black person who can barely string a sentence together. They barely or never managed to see school through to the end.

I should say at this point that I am not saying that there is no such thing as a Black person who is impoverished and that there are no Black people who have issues with drugs or crime. What I'm saying is that the continual stereotyping of Black people into these roles is problematic. It begins with the writing and continues into the casting process and subsequent portrayal on screen.
   Films and television in the latter part of the twentieth century and into the twenty-first century often heavily relied on these stereotypes. The new programmes only seemed to portray Black neighbourhoods as ghettos. They were dangerous places – if a white person ventured there, they would need to be rescued or they'd end up dead. The only people venturing into such neighbourhoods were the police or some other white saviour.

The number of white saviour films also increased. You know the type, the one where the Black person is either in trouble or has a gift and only the white saviour can save them and turn their life around and take them to safety, fortune, fame or glory. Again, I'm not saying that a white person never helped a Black person; the problem is, it is a go-to story, and it is another tired trope.

EXERCISE 5

1. Think about the films you have watched so far, and ask yourself if any of them were stereotypical.
2. Think about the television you have watched lately, was any of it racist or stereotypical?
3. Thinking back to Chapter 3 and the scientists who expounded racist stereotypes about:
    i.   race and intellect,
    ii.   race and civilisation,
    iii. race and impulse control.

    What impact do you think those scientists had on film and television programme makers?
4. What impact do you think those false scientific theories had on society?
5. What influence do you think film and television had in respect of race and racism in the nineteenth and twentieth centuries.

Before I leave this chapter here's another exercise.

EXERCISE 6

1. Think of some of the stereotypes about race such as: inferiority, gangs, drugs, absent fathers, danger, crime, poverty and ghettos; do you have any ingrained beliefs about race and the above?

2. If so, were any of those views formed as a result of television, film or media?
3. If so, in what way?
4. Thinking of the films and television programmes that you grew up watching, do _you_ regard any of those programmes as racist or stereotypical?
5. If so, consider listing them and explaining why they were racist or stereotypical.
6. In terms of ground-breaking television in racial terms, what do you consider as ground-breaking?

....

This chapter has focused on the early portrayals of Black people in film and television, but it goes without saying that people of colour have also had to deal with racist and/or stereotypical portrayals. Looking back through films and television, there have been racist portrayals of Native Americans, Indians, Asians and people from the Middle East. The fact that every other race, except the white race, has been portrayed in negative racist and stereotypical ways confirms that racism is unique to white people. The portrayals of other races by the white majority in the entertainment industry lend credence to the fact that the construct of white supremacy is a socialisation process, and it is created in the context and purpose of maintaining the white racial frame that favours one race at the expense of all others. And it is clearly a process that is rife in the entertainment industry.

'One child, one teacher, one pen and one book can change the world.'

Malala Yousafzai

CHAPTER 5

RACE AND ENTERTAINMENT FROM A HISTORICAL PERSPECTIVE – PART 2

At a time when racism was rife within the film and television industry in Britain and America, there were white people in front of and behind the camera in both countries who refused to accept the status quo and remain silent. They took a stand and made films with a conscience. They made programmes that were thought-provoking and entertaining.

BRITISH FILM

Two films worth watching are *Sapphire* and *Flame in the Streets*.

Sapphire (1959)
An interesting film set in London. A young woman called Sapphire is found dead on Hampstead Heath. As the murder investigation takes place, it transpires she was mixed-race, passing as white.

As well as being a well-thought-out crime thriller, *Sapphire* examined racial attitudes in London, in the police and in society. It did, however, use the word coloured but they are to be applauded for having a Black man as a doctor and another Black man as a barrister in 1959.

Some profound insights:

'Given the right atmosphere you can organise riots against anyone: Jews, Catholics, Negroes, Irish, even policemen with big feet.'
'We didn't solve anything, Phil. We just picked up the pieces.'

Flame in the Streets (1961)

An interesting film about a union worker who stands up for the right of his Black co-worker to be treated equally and given a promotion based on merit. Pro-union and anti-racist, it tells a number of stories about racism, interracial relationships, community and violence. Sometimes a bit on the nose but still ahead of its time.

BRITISH TELEVISION

There were also some ground-breaking British television programmes that broke down barriers and did not revert to racist stereotyping but showed Black people in a different light or told a story from a Black perspective. Worthy of note are:

Desmond's (1989–1994)

A comedy set in a hairdresser's in Peckham portraying a Black family navigating life in London in the 1980s. Each week the titular character, his family and friends provided love, laughs and sometimes sought to address racism and stereotypes and break down barriers.

Chef! (1993–1996)

Lenny Henry was the perfectionist irritable chef. Ground-breaking in that it showed a hard-working Black man striving for excellence, as opposed to the usual stereotypical and racist roles. I used to love this show, not just because of the aforementioned, but also because it was funny.

Luther (2010 – 2019)

Idris Elba as the titular character playing a high-ranking detective. Ground-breaking in that it had a lead Black officer and in its gritty portrayal of the police. However, criticism was levelled at the show because Luther did not have any Black friends and was not really having a Black experience.

What these shows demonstrate is that there were people willing to stand up and buck the trend. People who made thoughtful and thought-provoking television that was non-racist, was entertaining and of good quality. There is a plethora of television programmes and films that have bucked the system and have been entertaining as well as diverse and authentic and it is worth taking a look at them.

AMERICAN FILM

While there was a plethora of films that were openly racist and stereotypical during the twentieth century there were ground-breaking films that sought to counter the narrative and either highlight the issues of racism or portray Black people in a different light.

Guess Who's Coming to Dinner (1967)
Sidney Poitier plays the boyfriend of a white woman who takes him home to meet her parents, who believe they are liberal and progressive until they meet their daughter's Black boyfriend. A great and thoughtful film that is dramatic while addressing the issue of race and racism.

In the Heat of the Night (1967)
Sidney Poitier plays a detective from Philadelphia who becomes embroiled in a murder in Mississippi. Throughout the investigation he faces racism and violence but remains defiant and dignified throughout.

AMERICAN TELEVISION

Two American television series worthy of note are *Star Trek* and *Julia*.

Star Trek Original series (1966)

The most famous avant-garde breakthrough television of the twentieth century was *Star Trek* created by the legendary Gene Roddenberry. Gene Roddenberry envisaged a world where society had gone beyond race and as such the crew of the *Enterprise* were multiracial. A bold move considering that America was racially segregated at the time.

Julia (1968–1971)

Julia, starring Diahann Carroll, was the first television series to cast a Black woman as its lead. Julia played a widowed nurse raising her young son who had lost his father during the Vietnam War. It was one of the first roles that did not portray a Black lead in a stereotypical fashion.

BEHIND THE SCENES

In the past, what was happening on set and behind the camera in the entertainment industry was just as important. In Britain there were rarely any Black people on screen or behind the camera and in America the situation was even worse. Hollywood pandered to segregationist or exclusionary practices on set and few took a stand to rectify this evil.

It is worthy of note that despite starring in *Gone with the Wind*, Clark Gable did try to take a stand against racism. He threatened to walk away from the film if the set was not desegregated. He was also willing to not appear at the awards ceremony because his Black co-stars were not permitted to attend the walkabout nor remain in the theatre.

Gene Roddenberry took a stand in respect of Riverboat, a series which was to be set in 1860s Mississippi. According to Wikipedia[34] he was asked to write the series but *'when he learned that the producers did not want any Black people on the show, Gene argued so much with them that he lost the job'*.

There were also Black trailblazers in Hollywood including Eric Monte, Sidney Poitier and Oscar Micheaux, whose films set out to challenge the mainstream racist status quo. I have thought long and hard about whether or not to include *The Cosby Show* in historical shows that made a difference to breaking down barriers, going against the grain and portraying a Black family in a non-stereotypical light, because, while all those things are true, one of its creators caused a significant amount of pain to a number of women. To not do so, however, would be to omit a show that made a substantial difference to anti-racism.

The point I make about the filmmakers, writers, directors and producers in the past is that they took a stand. Some went on to make great television and film and did not revert to stereotyping and racism but actively took a stand against it. They also paved the way for more diverse storytelling.

Consider the profound message in *Sapphire* about being able to turn the crowd, and then think about the hateful and racist rhetoric that politicians, the media and television utilise today. As storytellers and entertainers, our words and actions have power. We can stir up hatred through all the media at our disposal, or we can reveal, educate and dissipate hatred. We can also inspire people to be better and to bring about change in themselves or in their lives. The heroes of the past did the latter, all while entertaining and providing powerful drama or comedy.

EXERCISE 7

1. Consider the films and the television programmes of the past that can be considered racist – what legacy did they leave?
2. Consider the films and the television of the past that tried to address racism and break down barriers – what legacy did they leave?
3. Consider your own work and ask yourself
   i.   What legacy will it leave?
   ii. What legacy do you want to leave?

STAR TREK

To me *Star Trek* was and still is one of the most inspirational and hopeful television franchises of the times. I am most grateful to Eugene 'Rod' Roddenberry, Gene's son, who took the time to answer questions about his father, his vision and the *Star Trek* world. Below is a portion of the Q&A that Rod very kindly agreed to participate in and I yield the rest of this chapter to it.

*

What was your father's most endearing quality?
One of the qualities I loved about him and learned about after he passed was his ability to transport his intellect into the future and contemplate certain social and political issues. He was a man living ahead of his time and I think that's a perspective we should all consider most often.

What was his flaw?
My father's only flaw was that he was human and like all of us, gave in to many of his temptations. And sometimes his actions even contradicted his views. But I feel that this is all part of the human condition. We are not machines. We make plenty of mistakes. Some of us more often than others. And it's those mistakes that we grow and evolve from.

Gene Roddenberry took a principled stance in respect of race and racism on projects such as **Riverboat** *and* **The Lieutenant** *at great cost to himself. What made him stand his ground?*
My father had an incredible life. He was a bomber pilot in WWII flying somewhere around 80 missions over the South Pacific. He saw his friends killed and as a pilot contributed to the ugliness of war. He became a transcontinental pilot after the war and flew the longest legs of an airline from NY to Johannesburg and was deadheading on a flight that crashed in the Syrian desert. Out of something like

22 people, he was one of approximately 11 survivors. He became a police officer in the LAPD and rose to the rank of sergeant where he would often debate the then Chief of Police William Parker who is known for his prejudiced and bigoted tactics. My father saw the worst that humanity had to offer and saw us at our best. From these experiences I think he knew that the only way for us to survive and continue on as a species was to not just tolerate, but love the uniqueness between us both in form and in idea.

He was famous for creating Star Trek *which portrayed a multiracial world where racism was a thing of the past. What inspired him to create such a world?*

My father passed away when I was 17. I was in my teenage adolescence and rebellious years, so I never really had adult conversations with him. Certainly nothing on this level so sadly the only thing I can do is speculate. In terms of racism I can only assume that as a WWII pilot he travelled the world, and in doing so was introduced to the various people, perspectives and unique aspects of our planet. I think meeting different people and experiencing various cultures gave him a broader perspective of our existence. He also did a lot of reading. If I have one standout memory it's him on a Sunday morning reading a book. It was usually a book about a person of significance good or bad such as Gandhi, Kennedy, even Hitler and Stalin. He seemed to really want to understand the human condition, and mind. He could look at something like relationships and say to himself, *'In the future – whether it's 50, 100 or 500 years from now – this need to be connected with a single person in matrimony will not be something that we do because we will learn to differentiate between love, lust, sex and friendship. We will also be able to better communicate our feelings and better able to receive such communications from each other. Jealousy and insecurity will be a thing of the past because we will learn to love unconditionally.'* While I can't say for certain this was his exact way of thinking, I've heard enough interviews and read enough of his writing to know he looked at everything this way. He was definitely a humanist which is essentially an atheist saying that God didn't create the wonders of our world such as the pyramids, humans did. I think my father was able to look into the future and recognise the absurdities of who we are and what we do today.

What happened when he took the idea of Star Trek to the Networks?
My understanding of what happened when my father took *Star Trek* to the networks is that he was turned down by all of them but Desilu. This may not be fact, and there are probably better sources out there, but the story is that Desilu was one of the last ones and it was Lucille Ball who said let's give this guy a shot. To be honest, at the time my understanding is that *Star Trek* was a failure. When the season's ratings came in low, Lucille or the studio execs would call up Gene and say, *'You have to do something.'* He was always working his ass off to make the studio happy and increase the ratings, but sadly it wasn't enough. It was cancelled at the end of its third season. It wasn't until *Star Trek* went into syndication in the 70s that it became really popular.

What made your father persist?
He had been in the entertainment industry for a while prior to *Star Trek* and he knew a thing or two about how things worked. He knew that determination was essential. After being a WWII pilot and officer of the LAPD, I think there's a certain amount of life experience, which gives you perspective, confidence and even some authority on our existence here on earth. Perhaps mixed in with some arrogance.

Given the power dynamics between studios/networks and writers, how did your father convince the network to cast actors of colour in officer roles?
DC Fontana – who may have passed away before you started on this – shared a great story during an interview I did with her in the *Trek Nation* documentary. She said that when 'Plato's Stepchildren' first aired – that's the ST episode where Kirk kisses Uhura – there were TV stations in the south that said they weren't going to play the

episode if they kept the scene in the story and apparently my father's response was, *'Fuck em. They don't have to play it.'* So it definitely was a legitimate part of my father's views and personality. He was adamant about equality and had no tolerance for discrimination and probably didn't have the patience to deal with those kinds of backwards mindsets.

What do you think is the most inspiring thing about your father?
His ability to intellectually live in the future or intellectually weigh his forward-thinking views and perspectives against current day social constructs. I will say my father would on occasion sit down with other people of the era, usually stodgy old white men who probably had more conservative, narrow and short-sighted views, and would often take an extreme point of view. He wouldn't do this just to shock them or raise eyebrows, but more so he could get them to consider different points of view. For example, if it were a conversation about drugs and his peers would suggest locking up anyone caught doing them, he might say *'Why not legalise all drugs?'* and then he would proceed with many well-thought-out arguments and reasons to support such an extreme point of view. Again, he didn't do this because he necessarily felt that way, but because he wanted to kick people out of their comfort zones and consider drastically different points of view. He was an incredible debater and an incredible speaker. I would have loved to be in one of those rooms where he was taking such extreme (and well-thought-out) points of view and I wouldn't be surprised if he succeeded in getting a few people to at least reconsider their views.

What do you believe your father's legacy is?
That's a very good question. I would like to believe that in the future he will be remembered as a thinker and visionary of our time. Truthfully, in terms of writing and being a writer, I don't think he stands out. It's really more about his ideas, philosophies and vision. Hopefully he will be looked back on and held in regard as one of the visionaries who intellectually mapped out a better future for

humanity. Not that everyone needs to hang on his every word nor the exact ideology of *Star Trek* but the fact that coming together as a species and realising that it's the differences and uniqueness between us that make us special. And it is only with that uniqueness and those differences that we can grow and evolve intellectually. And from that intellectual growth we will be able to prosper in every way. I think he will be in a long line of great thinkers who stood on the shoulders of other great thinkers before them and showed us a vision through *Star Trek* of what we could someday become.

What do you think Star Trek's impact was when it first aired?
In the late 60s, I think the older or post-college working stiffs were just trying to get through life and probably didn't give it too much thought and dismissed it as just another sci-fi nonsense show. What I heard was that it was the younger kids and college kids who saw the messaging, ideas and philosophy. It was also during the era of Vietnam and many social injustices... and they were incredibly inspired by it. I think *Star Trek* spoke to the younger, open-minded people. College kids are typically searching for identities and searching for what it is 'to be human', and 'who they are' and 'how they fit in'. And what the world is about. Not to say it was solely them – there were still plenty people of all ages and backgrounds that had that forward-facing mindset and it probably spoke to them too.

What inspired you to become an executive producer?
I was inspired by my father. Not to become an executive or producer, but in the sense of seeing the potential for what can be done with television, movies, music and entertainment. I love *Star Trek* because throughout my entire life people have come up to me and told me that it inspired them to become better than they thought they could be. That it gave them more hope for humanity. *Star Trek* has messaging and gets people to think, so I love that part of Hollywood. So many people – my father included – are pouring their heart, soul and passion into an idea. It can affect your family life and consume you. It tore my father's previous marriage apart as he was always working.

Sometimes there can be a battle between the creative and the business side when the executive doesn't see the creative vision. I feel the return on investment can be substantial in the rare instance that everything aligns: your stories or ideas are top notch, and the right audience sees it at the right time. *Star Trek* is a great example of that. My father spent his life killing himself to make that and its success happened pretty much after his death. He died on the fifth season of *Next Generation*, so I am glad that he got to see some of *Star Trek*'s success, but of course he's not around to see what it has become today.

Passion is the most important thing. I'm not passionate about being a producer, I'm passionate about the philosophies and ideologies in the show. And in my own way, I try to carry that on through the Roddenberry Foundation by working on the shows in the way that I do, going to conventions, interacting with the fans and promoting the ideology.

What impact, if any, did Star Trek have on you personally?
It took me a while to see and recognise the values in *Star Trek*, and let them sink in. And actually become a fan of those ideas and ideologies myself. Of course when I did, it was very eye-opening that a television show could really make you think and reflect on your own views. To question and even expand them. I see the values in episodes I watch like fans do. They make me think and consider, and look at myself. *Star Trek* inspires me to try to be more open minded. To try and hear views that I strongly oppose. It certainly has shaped me because *Star Trek* is my family and I have spent the last 29, 30 years thinking about it multiple times a day. Also talking to people and doing a documentary and running a company that makes entertainment that should fit within the Roddenberry values. So it does impact me.

What message or theme do you think Star Trek conveys today?
My hope is it that it conveys the idea that we should be more willing to accept – not agree with, but accept – valid, rational, well-thought-out opposing or different ideas and or ideologies.

In terms of race and racism, what impact did your parents and* Star Trek *have on you?

My father was certainly open minded and progressive. I do think he lived ahead of his time and his intellect was ahead of his time. He was also a fallible human male. Just normal like the rest of us. And there were things he did that were not considered acceptable in today's society, to be more specific cheating on his wife and philandering. I'm not necessarily trying to justify it, but he obviously didn't look at relationships in the same way. My mother and father were members of the Bel Air Country Club; we're going back 38 or 40 years or so. They used to take me there as a young kid. Obviously I didn't really pay too much attention but I did remember that there was the men's grill on Thursdays. There was a men's section that didn't allow any women. And I don't really remember other ethnicities except some members who were of Asian and Latino descent. What I do remember is that there were a lot of old white men and I'm guessing they were conservative. I never really liked the place – it just felt stuffy and old-fashioned – but also I don't know why my parents were members considering who they were and my father's views. But perhaps it plays into what I've been saying all along – although my father may have had more of a progressive mindset on a lot of social topics and issues, he didn't necessarily let that stop him interacting with people with other points of view and beliefs. Maybe that's my takeaway from this – just because he may not have shared those more conservative points of view, he saw it as an opportunity to go there and converse. To grow and learn.

What themes in* Star Trek *inspire you the most and why?

Kirk. Going back to the original series, Kirk has his favourite famous risk speech. It's talking about their mission on the Enterprise and why they do it and he says risk is who we are. That it's up to humanity – to individuals – to take certain risks to grow and evolve and learn about the other. Not only is it a beautiful speech, it rings true for me. It feels important. Like something I should probably wake up and embrace every morning. Speaking about social and political issues and interacting with other humans. Talking to people who have contrary thoughts to mine so I can grow. The other episode that rings true to me in the original series is 'Devil in the Dark' with the rock monster. To this day that was when *Star Trek* clicked. When Spock says let's communicate with this creature instead of trying to kill it. Let's communicate. Let's stop seeing it as just a monster and recognise that it's intelligent and makes decisions based on its surroundings and information. That it is a being that is capable of having knowledge. We should realise that. We should try to communicate. And if we can communicate and understand one another, perhaps things can be resolved peacefully. I think that is probably the most important thing that humanity could learn and act on, and do on a daily basis. So those philosophies really resonate deeply with me.

The Star Trek *franchise appears to be egalitarian in race, gender and sexual orientation. What would you say is the best way to achieve equality in front of and behind the camera in respect of characters that are diverse and reflect that egalitarianism?*
To listen and truly hear rational, well thought-out, contradictory points of view without becoming emotional and reactive is very, very important. To let go of the ego, and your own points of view and ideas to really see the world and the people in it as more of a unified family as opposed to 'us and them'. I think it's huge – and it's so corny to say – but unconditional love of your fellow human beings, so when you meet someone from an entirely different part of the world with a contrary point of view, to have a conversation with them and not prejudge or assume they're wrong. Or to assume you're right, straight off, but to be curious and willing to hear what they have to say and then allow for a dialogue back and forth. Because when they see something that you maybe don't agree with or don't understand, then you can say *'I don't really agree with that but I'd like to hear more,'* and be able to have that dialogue. We're so divided today and reactive and we just think, *'That person's an idiot, they're wrong and stupid.'* And I do that constantly. So, if we can look at people with

unconditional love and be willing to hear them and try to understand them, you can educate yourself and expand your own sort of wisdom. The issue is how to get there and I think there's a missing part of education. Learning and critical thinking. Learning how to learn. I believe that many of us in society today don't question and we don't necessarily wonder. We take things as fact. But as young people it's important that we have life experience. That we travel everywhere as much as we can. And experience new cultures and new things around the world. I think from that experience we can have a greater perspective on the world and be more accepting of viewpoints that are counter to our own. So we should focus our efforts on teaching our young how to be critical thinkers. How to question and have more open minds. I think that's an important part of the *Star Trek* philosophy.

Does the Star Trek *franchise make positive efforts to ensure equality of opportunity?*

I have to give so much credit to Alex Kurtzman and Akiva Goldsman. They really don't discriminate. I mean there's five shows out there and no one is hired based on anything other than the quality of work they do and the calibre of person. If you went through everyone who's employed there, there's tons of women, tons of people of ethnicity, people of different social economic backgrounds and sexual orientations. I haven't heard of any discrimination. Now I am not going to say it's perfect – there never has been anything perfect – but from my understanding it really is an incredibly open minded and diverse group who just really want the most talented people for the job.

What do you believe is the best way to deal with racism when it arises?

Great question. I wish I could say I've been successful at it. When someone is racist I go back to my analogy of the dog that's been kept in the backyard its whole life and the fact that they have a lack of life experience. They were taught something from a young age and it's a learned response – no child is ever born being racist. So how to deal with it? Ideally in a *Star Trek* world, I'd say being empathetic. That you understand this is something they were taught. I mean people have to take responsibility and be held responsible for their actions, but you can also look at them with a little bit of understanding, realising that they simply don't know better. That might sound elitist of me to say, as if my point of view is the right point of view, but I can comfortably say being racist or bigoted in any way is the wrong point of view. I don't know of a scenario where it could be considered okay. I'm definitely not a Trump fan and of course I can sit here and rail about how much of an idiot he is – and forgive me if you have opposing point of views – but every now and then, when I have a quiet moment to myself, I'm able to think, *'This man was brought up a certain way.'* Of course I don't know what that is, but he was taught – probably by his parents and his surroundings – how to behave and conduct himself, and how to react to situations. And the ways that he does, I think are often atrocious and narrow minded, and not looking out for anyone's best interests but his own. But I can understand that he has been brought up a different way and he's somewhat of a victim of his own upbringing. But if you're really patient, have the conversation and let them say whatever they're saying and just gently, with love, say, *'Okay and why does it make you feel that way? Can you explain more? How did you learn?'* And maybe without being combative, because obviously the minute you're combative in any discussion, real discussions don't really happen. So with compassion, ask questions and try to get them to analyse their own thinking and come to their own conclusions. And if you're really good at it maybe you can get them to come the conclusion that it would be absurd to judge someone by the way they look, or their skin colour.

Today Western societies are deeply divided in terms of political ideology and race. Star Trek, which is set in the future, appears to be unified in all the above aspects. In light of that, if you could imagine the journey from our present conflicted society to the fairly utopian Star Trek *future, what one step might make a difference in eradicating racism?*

I would answer this with the education thing that I was talking about before. People need to be let out of their backyards and to have more life experiences with other people and cultures so they have a broader perspective and understanding of the vast uniqueness in the world in which they live. I definitely think that would have a huge impact on racism.

What event could change the course of the future and eradicate racism?

My mind immediately goes to contact by alien life which I do believe is out there, I just don't know in what form or how intelligent it is. I want to think it's more evolved, advanced and better off than we are. As if the *Star Trek* universe did exist, and there were countless life forms out there for us to learn from. Life forms that are incredibly different in form, skin colour, how they breathe, what sensory organs they have, the ways they communicate and how they think about the universe. Being a scuba diver, you see how just a different environment of water can allow for the evolution of such different, strange-looking life forms, from octopuses and jellyfish to sharks and whales. I would hope that when we learn of those various life forms that we would see just how similar we are here as humans on earth. How the differences between us are actually very minor and that the universe is filled with things that are far more unique and different. My only fear is that based on our current human mentality we would react with fear. And of course fear is the basis of all negativity. Fear is where hatred, anger and war comes from. And that we might somehow misinterpret their actions or their appearance and be hostile towards them, because as a species we are not intelligent enough to do what Spock said in the episode 'Devil in the Dark' and say, *'Hey let's communicate with these things.'*

*

There were some honest, beautiful and profound answers that I believe not only inspire writers, but people from all walks of life in the industry. It also demonstrates that when we love and accept people and fight to do the right thing beautiful art can be made. The *Star Trek* franchise is a great testament to that fact. *Star Trek: Strange New Worlds* (STSNW) which was created by Akiva Goldsman, Alex Kurtzman and Jenny Lumet has a Rotten Tomatoes approval rating of 98% and according to Parrot Analytics, the audience demand for STSNW has been 30 times and 21.2 times the demand for the average television series. *Star Trek: Discovery* created by Bryan Fuller and Alex Kurtzman had – according to Wikipedia – *'led to record subscriptions for CBS all Access and became the most viewed original series on both All Access and Paramount+*[35]*'*. Parrot Analytics indicated that audience demand for *Star Trek: Discovery* was 19.2 times the demand for the average television series.

'Race and racism is [sic] a reality that so many of us grow up learning to just deal with. But if we ever hope to move past it, it can't just be on people of color to deal with it. It's up to all of us – Black, white, everyone – no matter how well-meaning we think we might be, to do the honest, uncomfortable work of rooting it out.'

Michelle Obama

CHAPTER 6

RACE AND ENTERTAINMENT **TODAY**

Today's film and television have still not achieved true equality and diversity. Don't get me wrong, progress has been achieved and some great strides have been made but there is still a problem with access to employment, progression and portrayal when it comes to Black people and people of colour. There have been a number of seminal reports in respect of race and the entertainment industry providing ample evidence that racism is still a feature in the industry.

BRITISH FILM

The salient parts of the executive summary of the 2016 BFI London Film Festival Black Star Report[36] found as follows:

i. 13% of UK films have a Black actor in a leading role and 59% have no Black actors in any role.
ii. Decade sees little change in the number of roles for Black actors. Only four Black actors feature in the list of the 100 most prolific actors.

iii. Horror, drama and comedy films are the LEAST likely to cast Black actors.
iv. Crime, sci-fi and fantasy films are the MOST likely to cast Black actors.

The Black Star Report researched race and representation in the film industry from January 2006 to August 2016. It found that:

'Of the 1,172 UK films made and released in that period, 59% (691 films) did not feature any Black actors in either lead or named roles.' Page 1

The BFI's creative director suggested that roles for Black people had not really changed over the last decade and those roles made available were indicative of stereotyping. On page 4 it is explained that:

'the subjects that recur most frequently where a film has a cast with more Black actors are slavery, racism, colonialism, crime and gangs... limiting the range and depth of possible representation'.

It seems – unsurprisingly – that despite the report highlighting the inequalities, four years on nothing had really changed. On 23 June 2020 an open letter to the UK film and television industry was signed by 5000 people of colour, people who were prominent actors, writers and producers.

The actors included Michaela Coel, Chiwetel Ejiofor, Idris Elba, Lennie James, Sophie Okonedo and David Oyelowo. The letter was from Black and Asian people within the community calling on the industry to actively engage in tackling systemic and structural racism within the industry in the UK and around the world. It is a powerful letter setting out the inequality, racism and discrimination that is used to silence and ignore the voices of Black and brown people. It highlights that language is used in a pernicious way to enable a white person to repeatedly fail but never take a gamble on a Black or brown person. Furthermore, it asserted that the industry was not willing to listen to or portray the Black experience.

The letter is worth reading. It is powerful, on point and demonstrates that occurrences of racism and discrimination are happening to most people of colour and that it is widespread and systemic. At this stage if you are still trying to defend the industry and don't believe that racism is occurring, I would ask why you are not willing to believe the voices of 5000 people who are all having the same experience.

In the Racial Diversity Initiatives in UK Film & TV report (RDI) by Dr Clive Nwonka and Professor Sarita Malik[37] presented to the UK Film and TV Charity, the authors state: *'UK film and television has also been a space in which deep social inequalities have been produced and sustained.'* The RDI studied twenty years of diversity policies and practices within the UK film and TV industry.

At the outset they noted the distinction between diversity practices and anti-racism. The former seeks to address under-representation, but it does not mean that anti-racist policies are being adopted. The RDI suggests that there is a lack of accountability and evaluation in respect of diversity schemes and they do not adequately address structural racism. They found that schemes tend to be applied to younger BAME people who are entering the industry, as opposed to the older and/or more senior members who are not being given equality of opportunity. One aspect of this finding relates to the fact that there are very few Black, Asian or other ethnic minorities in senior or stakeholder roles.

In any event, the Black and person of colour experience within the industry suggests that diversity alone is not a solution. As the RDI points out (page 11): *'Black and minority ethnic creatives are often denied autonomy, editorial control, and must exist within an unaltered institutional climate where they remain subjected to various and habitual forms of racism.'*

Looking at film initiatives 2002–2020, there was the UK Film Council initiative from 2000–2008 although ethnic minorities only received 8% of the funding. The New Cinema Fund awarded 4%

to ethnic minority applicants and 70% to white able-bodied men (Bhavnani, 2007). Further they highlight that Film London 2012–2018 had loose criteria which meant that tokenism in casting or crew could qualify a white project for diversity funding.

The RDI concluded at page 21 '...across the last twenty years we can identify one outstanding common feature: an unwillingness to address the structural elements of the exclusions faced by Black and ethnic minorities in the sector'. They also conclude: 'From the above analysis... there remains no initiative, scheme or policy that has successfully responded to specific questions of racial inequality and in the UK Film Industry'.

BRITISH TELEVISION

Equally problematic is television. Looking at the 2018 Equity Report entitled: Diversity in Broadcast Peak Scripted Television 2018 by Equity's Race Equality Committee, the executive summary stated:

i. East Asians are severely under-represented on broadcast television.
ii. 8% of lead roles were played by African-Caribbean, South Asian, East Asian or Middle Eastern heritage.
iii. The depiction of Middle Eastern and/or South Asian characters continues to reinforce stereotypes by portraying narratives about terrorism.
iv. Stereotypes of African-Caribbeans as criminals persist in scripted narratives.
v. There is a high level of segregation within peak scripted programming.

The Equity Report studied peak hours prime time scripted drama and comedy between 6.30 pm and 11.00 pm for the calendar year on channels BBC1, BBC2, ITV and Channel 4. It consisted of 53 weeks from 06/01/2018 to 04/01/2019. Across 53 weeks they monitored 388 individual appearances in scripted comedy and drama. The majority of weeks there were 400 plus actors. Their findings were as follows:

i. Broadcast television remains predominantly white with 82% of performers being predominantly white across 992 episodes.
ii. 18% was spread across remaining non-white groups:
 – 9% were African-Caribbean.
 – 7% were South Asian.
 – 1% East Asian.
 – 1% Middle Eastern but virtually excluded.

Comedy had the lowest rate of inclusion which was 87% white and 34% of 156 episodes had all-white casts. Continuing drama was 85% white. Contemporary drama had 50 programmes totalling 197 episodes being monitored. It had a greater level of inclusion i.e., 70% white, but it was in a segregated context due to being set in Africa or Asia or in a British Pakistani context such as *Ackley Bridge*.

The report points out (page 5): *'Even in narratives that revolve around minority ethnic characters, white actors dominate the leading roles with scripted television.'* It also found that with the exception of *Death in Paradise*, mystery series were less inclusive than stand-alone episodes/dramas. Eighty-nine per cent (16 out of 18) programmes had a white leading actor. Period drama was the least inclusive – 95% white and no lead roles for ethnic minorities.

PORTRAYAL

In British film it is apparent that there is an issue with the portrayal of Black and ethnic minorities. As the studies show, in film there is a dearth of Black people in lead or named roles and the roles provided tend to be stereotypical. There appears to be a reluctance to portray Black and ethnic minorities that aren't a stereotype or a trope.

In television there are issues with the linking of Black people with criminality and Middle Eastern or South Asian people with terrorism that still persists. As stated earlier, television and film influence millions of people and they do so every day. If television and film continue to portray racist stereotypes on a regular basis into the homes of millions of people, then the industry and the people with the power must bear some responsibility for perpetuating racism, not just in the industry but in society as a whole.

REPRESENTATION AND OPPORTUNITY

One reason why racism is not being addressed is because diversity programmes are mistaken for anti-racism. Racism does not appear to be addressed on set and there is also a lack of equality and opportunity. Diversity programmes and diversity itself therefore are not the answer to eradicating racism. As Dr Nwonka and Professor Malik point out in their report, diversity seeks to address under-representation. It is not a tool of anti-racism.

I would suggest that what is required are anti-racist policies, practices and environments. It requires the white industry members to educate themselves on what racism is, how it manifests, how to deal with it when it arises, and how to ensure it does not affect decision-making processes.

Now, I'm imagining the triggered responses to the above information and suggestions, but take a moment to think about the last fifty years. Racism has been consistent and prevalent in society and the entertainment industry. There have been a multitude of reports, reviews, schemes, programmes, scholarships and mentorships with a view to improving diversity and *giving ethnic minorities a chance*. Honestly, they have been an abject failure. How do we know? Because racism is alive and well, and still an issue in the industry today.

In the industry there is still racism behind and in front of the camera. There is still a lack of inclusion of people of colour and it is clear that there is deliberate exclusion of the same people. Black people, people of colour and anti-racists are still fighting racism. They are still seeking equality and have yet to achieve that aim. The situation is exacerbated as, despite the numerous reviews, reports and findings, there is still denial that racism and discrimination are taking place and there is still a refusal to take any real action.

Do you recall DiAngelo's opening in *White Fragility*?

> *'White people in North America live in a society that is deeply separate and unequal by race, and white people are the beneficiaries of that separation and inequality.'*

Although she is talking about North America, I would say that the same can be said about the United Kingdom. The studies American sociologists have conducted have been in the United States, Britain, and Canada. British sociologists and researchers have also conducted extensive studies on race in this country. In the next few chapters I will briefly address the issues of race in healthcare, law and order, and the media and give an overview of the problems of racism within those sectors. I will then consider how those sectors are portrayed in the entertainment industry and ask if the portrayals – in terms of race – are an accurate representation. Having considered those sectors and their portrayal in film and television, it is quite clear that the realities of everyday racism are not always truly reflected.

There is an inequality in portrayal and representation and white people are the beneficiaries of that inequality. Perhaps it is time for the privileged in the film and television industry to recognise that benefit and the advantages they have, which are at the expense of other races.

Now consider DiAngelo's assertion about what white fragility is and how it manifests.

- Resistance to acknowledging racism or any complicity in it.
- Denial.
- Hostility/anger.
- Withdrawing or leaving when the issue is raised.
- Arguing.
- Crying (particularly white women).

There are a whole list of behaviours and feelings that DiAngelo asserts that white people revert to when engaging in white fragility.

Racism is happening in the film and television industry. Those with the power and all white people in the industry need to understand white supremacy as a social construct and a socialisation process. They also need to understand the privilege that pertains to their race and how racism manifests and how to combat it.

As an educated and fairly intelligent Black woman, I don't need a scheme, special treatment or positive discrimination in order to succeed in life. I, like most people, simply need equality. That is, being treated as an equal and being given equality of opportunity. I need my work and performance to be judged on their own merits. By the same token, I do not want additional barriers attached to opportunities, I do not want to be regarded as less, simply because my skin colour is different and I certainly do not want to be bullied, harassed and adversely discriminated against because of the colour of my skin. That requires the white members of the industry, particularly those with power, to examine their own attitudes and behaviours. Not just in relation to their views on race and racism but how they have behaved towards people of colour or reacted when issues of racism have arisen.

Below are a series of questions that I ask you to consider carefully and answer honestly. It is not for my benefit, but I hope it will give you some insight as to how ingrained racism and privilege is in our society.

....

EXERCISE 8

1. Have you ever heard anyone being racially offensive or abusive to a person of colour?
2. If yes, what action did you take?
3. If you supported or sided with the person making the remark,
    i.   Why did you support them?
    ii. What impact did it have on the person of colour?
4. If you ignored the remark, why did you do that?

5. Has a person of colour ever pointed out to you that what you have said was racially offensive?
6. If so,
    i. What was your reaction?
    ii. Why did you react in that way?
    iii. Was your response conducive to making that person feel safe and comfortable in the working environment?
    iv. In light of what you have read, what, if anything, would you do differently?
7. On the sets you have worked on, have you been aware of any anti-racist policies?
8. If you are a producer/director/senior manager,
    i. Has anyone ever complained to you about racism?
    ii. If so, what was your response?
    iii. Having read the preceding chapters, how do you regard your response now?
    iv. Have you ever responded with disbelief or hostility to a complaint about racism?
    v. If so, why.

....

Now, we are at that stage where some white people might be feeling uncomfortable or triggered; and may be tempted to stop reading, throw this book away and just give up. You may feel that you are being attacked personally – you are not. At this stage I would ask you to be mindful of the Black experience, and the experiences of people of colour, because once you put this book down, if you are white you can go on with your day, your life and not have to consider or worry about racism and its adverse effects if you don't wish to.

You won't be subjected to harassment, discrimination or bullying as a result of your skin colour. You won't be blacklisted if you try to complain about being subjected to racism and therefore susceptible to mental health problems that such a situation puts you in. You won't be denied roles and opportunities because of your race, so yes you may feel uncomfortable and triggered but perhaps that is because I am pointing out the advantages of white privilege that pertain to you at the expense of people of colour who are adversely affected. Race will not be a factor adversely affecting your treatment, career, opportunities and advancement. You can put this book down and return to the relative comfort of your working life.

If you are a white person reading this book, this is not an attack on you because of your race. It is an attack on the socialisation process of white supremacy which perpetuates racism and in which – if you are a white person – you are in many ways a beneficiary of that socialisation process. One of the benefits of that socialisation process is that a white person can engage in racism and discrimination in the industry with relative impunity, or they can ignore it when it happens. It does not, or it need not, affect you if you do not want it to and the numerous reviews, reports and findings support my assertion.

Consider that perhaps one reason why you may be feeling triggered is because you know that what I am saying is fundamentally true, that is:

1. White supremacy is a socialisation process.
2. White people are the beneficiaries of that process.
3. That benefit is at the expense of Black people and people of colour.

Therefore, if you are white, you are the beneficiary of the system of racism. I can imagine that's quite triggering, probably upsetting when you read it in black and white – but it is true. You and I were both born into this world. You and I did not have a choice what skin colour we would have. You and I were both socialised into this process. The difference is I, like many other people of colour, have had to fight it to survive. We've had to fight the false notions and labels of inferiority, we have had to fight mistreatment, we have had to fight discrimination. We have had to fight for a seat at the table and to remain at the table. If you are white, you may not have even noticed there was a struggle going on.

But, you are not helpless and neither am I. You are not powerless and neither am I. You can accept and acknowledge the truth and take the time to begin to understand it. You can educate yourself about it and be the person who decides to help dismantle it. You can be anti-racist. You can honestly examine your beliefs and attitudes, as can I, as can we all. You can question our socialisation and beliefs and above all you can let go of the white fragility.

It doesn't matter if you are the actor, writer, make-up artist, editor, producer or director; as individuals we all have a responsibility. As individuals we make up the collective. In his book *People of the Lie*, M. Scott Peck considered the notion of evil and wrongdoing in corporations. He found that a major factor enabling evil is that organisations were compartmentalised and that there was little or no regard for individual responsibility. As individuals, we have an impact on every person around us. That impact can be positive or negative.

I say all of this because there is a wealth of evidence to suggest that Black people and people of colour have been subjected to racism, harassment and denied opportunities in the UK film and television industry. The next set of reports shows that every Black person they interviewed had an experience of or were subjected to racist treatment. There is a suggestion that the treatment is prevalent. That means not only are individuals engaging in racism, but racism is being tolerated or ignored, or at worst, adversely affecting the complainant.

There are two further reports worthy of note. The first is, Race Between the Lines: Actors' Experience of Race and Racism in Britain's Audition and Casting Process and On Set[38] (RBL 2021). The report by Dr Jami Rogers for Birmingham City University and commissioned by the Sir Lenny Henry Centre for Media Diversity conducted a survey between March and April 2021 of 1300 British actors of colour. It found the following:

i. 79% felt roles continued to stereotype their ethnicities.
ii. 64% have experienced racist stereotyping in an audition.
iii. 55% have experienced racist behaviour in the workplace.
iv. 71% have had experience with hair and make-up departments unable to cater to their heritage, hair or skin tone.

v. 61% feel 'largely' unable to turn down an audition for a stereotypical character.

vi. 66% feel 'generally' unable to discuss issues openly with a director.

The report asserts (page 3): *'the quantitative results of the survey, combined with the qualitative nature of the range of comments by actors... demonstrate that the problems are not "isolated incidents", or a "few bad apples", but are systemic and far reaching'*. The report stresses that *'Stereotyping begins with the writing of characters for which performers of colour are considered.'* It is clear that people of colour are asked to play a stereotype and not a person. Furthermore, the report finds that the roles tend to be written as smaller parts that conform to racial, religious or cultural stereotypes.

In considering casting, RBL 2021 said (page 4): *'The survey would support the idea for some groups that the audition is one of the most pernicious sites of institutional racism in the industry, where decisions about casting are made before any performer is even invited into the room.'*

RBL 2021 indicates that auditions can be places where overt and casual racism occur frequently. The report also found that there was a litany of racially inappropriate language or requests during the audition process, examples of which were:

- Be more urban/street
- Be more sassy
- Could you do 'the Black thing'?
- Black it up a bit more
- Be fierce
- Have more attitude.

I'm curious: *'Can you do the Black thing?'* What exactly is 'the Black thing'? I mean there are 1.3 billion Black people in the world. I never knew there was a 'thing' that all 1.3 billion of us do and it was uniquely Black. It would be interesting to know what these people meant when they were asking Black auditionees to do *'the Black thing'*. If there is a 'Black thing', I wonder why I've never heard of it. Was it something bestowed upon us at birth? Is there a secret ritual or initiation I missed? Was there a global memo about it that I wasn't aware of?

RBL 2021 found that 64% of auditionees had been asked to exaggerate an accent or play to a stereotype. There were issues around Middle Eastern and North African (MENA) backgrounds too, such as being asked to play the terrorist. Stereotypes about Asian women where they were usually being asked to play the geisha or the Indian mother panicking because her son is gay. Despite the prevalent and pernicious stereotyping only 39% of people of colour felt that they could turn down an audition for a stereotypical role. This was in part due to a lack of power, lack of roles and the feeling that it was best to take the opportunities provided. Another issue RBL highlighted was the casting breakdown. It found that the majority of lead or supporting roles were listed as white or Caucasian.

I hope that you can now get the picture with stereotyping. Obviously it starts with the writing. As a writer you create the character and it would appear that what is being created is perpetuating racial stereotypes. Those stereotypes are often embraced and make their way from option to being greenlit without challenge. Back to individual responsibility. Every person in the chain has a voice, every person in the chain can challenge what is being said and done – to date – that is not being done anywhere near often enough. Remember the socialisation process I was talking about?

It is mostly actors of colour who get stereotyped. Playing a stereotype is dehumanising and quite humiliating and disempowering. Writing stereotypes is racist, lazy and unimaginative; so please, please, please refrain from doing so.

RBL 2021 is well worth a read. It clearly sets out the experiences of people of colour when they are auditioning. It's also a great resource to help you learn what not to say to people of colour. A point made by one of the auditionees surveyed in RBL 2021 is worthy of note:

'A panel comprised only of white people cannot and should not offer their opinion on how a non-white role should be played in regards to race and racial stereotyping.'

The report went on to look at the workplace, i.e., once the actor got the role. According to RBL 2021 71% of respondents said the biggest issue was hair and make-up; they had experienced hair and make-up artists who lacked the knowledge to work with them on an equal basis to their white colleagues. RBL highlighted that white make-up artists tend to get defensive when people of colour try to work collaboratively and can be dismissive when they try and explain what works best for their skin and hair. There have been occasions when the make-up artists have damaged the hair of a person of colour. The problem is particularly acute for Black people and people of colour find themselves having to do their own hair and make-up as a result of make-up artists getting it wrong[39].

One actor commented: *'The few Black hairstylists I worked with knew not only how to tend to Afro-centric hair texture, but also Caucasian and thick Asian or Hispanic. But I'm still yet to work with a white hair stylist who knows how to treat Afro-centric hair.'* It is yet again indicative of white privilege and the white racial frame, that a person working in hair and make-up in twenty-first century Britain only needs to be able to know and understand white hair to get the job. It may also be indicative of a different hiring standard if Black or ethnic minority make-up artists have to understand all hair in order to be hired.

One would have hoped that a set which has actors of differing races would at least make it a criterion for the make-up artist to hold the relevant qualifications and have the relevant experience.

RBL 2021 also reported that 55% of respondents had encountered culturally insensitive language in the workplace. Some of the issues also outlined in the report were:

- Micro aggressions.
- Mistaken identity.

- Being regarded as oversensitive if you don't laugh the racism off as a joke.
- Statements such as 'I don't see colour'.
- Being asked, 'Where are you from?' usually followed by 'Where are you really from?'

The majority of people of colour would not feel comfortable raising issues in the workplace and the percentages are as follows:

- 73% would feel uncomfortable or very uncomfortable or would not discuss the issues raised with the casting director.
- 76% say the same above but in respect of the producer.
- 66% say the same above but in respect of the director.

The next report worth reading is: Think Piece on Anti-Racism in the UK Film & TV Industry[40] by Sasha Salmon for the Film and TV Charity. This 2021 report pulls no punches. It is based on the accounts of 55 people. 48 were people of colour and 7 of those interviewed were white people working on an anti-racism or diversity agenda within institutions. 40 were personally interviewed by the author and 15 provided written submissions; all worked in off-screen roles such as producing, directing or writing.

The participants spoke on the basis of anonymity. There was a feeling that (page 5) *'There is not a safe space to talk about racism in the industry without being branded as a "troublemaker" or "blacklisted".'* There was a consensus among all those interviewed that racism was rife within the industry and that the structural racism based on relationships maintained the status quo and systematically excludes people of colour.

All 55 people had experienced racism in the industry and at page 10 it states: *'They had experienced feelings of being disrespected and othered because of their race.'* The Think Piece Report highlights (page 11) the *'close network of decision-makers, commissioners and heads of production companies... who were nearly exclusively white and from privileged backgrounds'.*

These relationships are maintained and the people who tend to be recruited, interned or mentored are usually from the same ethnicity and background. Clearly this is leading to an exclusion of under-represented groups, particularly people of colour but I would say that it is a class issue too.

One interviewee in the report commented that, *'While 90% of institutions have committed to anti-racism publicly, internally many have no idea what that meant.'* There appears to be a belief that diversity schemes and hiring a few more Black people is anti-racist, but it looks like there is little understanding of what racism is and how it manifests in all its forms.

The interviewees are of the view that the industry say they want more voices but the opposite appears to be true. One aspect corroborating that assertion is the hiring process. There appears to be little or no feedback for rejections of people of colour. The suggestion – and I would say it is an accurate one – is that feedback is lacking because there is no objective rationale for the rejection. In a nutshell, rejections were highly likely to have been based on race.

The report revealed that the interviewees had tried to get their stories about people of colour developed. Stories that had often been their experience; however, they found that a greenlight was not forthcoming. In comparison, production companies with an all-white team were seeking to tell stories about people of colour; stories that they had not lived or experienced. Additionally, many people of colour had then been approached and asked to work on those projects for advice. There was often an all-white team even when the lead character was a person of colour.

The report asserted that this all leads to stereotyping and racist stereotyping. The interviewees felt that the common excuse for a lack of people of colour in writing rooms was *'there was no qualified Black, Asian or other minority who could fill the role'*. Now clearly this excuse tends to lack any and all credibility. Those who are rejecting people of colour on that basis think it is believable that there is no qualified person of colour in the United Kingdom who can write a script based on their lived experience. It would also suggest that new writers of colour, who may produce an outstanding script, are never given a chance because they are new. The point being of course new white writers enter the industry and are almost aways given a chance. So the question remains even if, at a stretch, there was no qualified person of colour to write a script or participate in a writing room, why can't a new writer of colour who produces an outstanding script be given the chance. As you can see the excuse falls down with a little interrogation. Given how closed the industry appears to be to Black people, it appears that Black writers do not remain in the industry long enough to get a substantial amount of work and experience in order to become experienced and senior writers.

In the report it was suggested that the Black people who were hired were often tokenistic or hired as cultural consultants. The interviewees felt that this was a back-covering exercise and that there was no intention to genuinely listen to a Black voice. Two examples were given: one, the refusal to take racist lines out of a script and two, a producer refusing to listen to a writer of colour and refusing to hire them. The writing room was made up of white writers. The project was subsequently greenlit and then regarded as racist.

Discrimination takes various forms in the industry and has an impact on the mental health of people of colour. Additionally, people of colour feel it necessary to leave the industry either for self-preservation purposes or because they come to the realisation that they have come to the end of the road because their path and progression are blocked.

The report revealed the following instances of racism:

- A Black female assistant director being refused a director position and told she should shadow a director. The male white director she shadowed had less experience than her.
- Victims of racism being labelled as troublemakers.
- Perpetrators of racism being celebrated and promoted.
- Racism excused or brushed off with responses such as: 'They probably didn't mean it,' or 'No, I don't think that happens anymore.'
- Being told to 'man up' when complaining about racism.

- Racism and microaggressions being a regular occurrence.
- Being gaslit about the experience of racism.
- Colourism: mixed-Asians and Indians fare better than Black people.

The report highlights that there is no accountability for racism within the industry and that when people of colour try to raise issues, they are often met with fragility.

The 2022 Bectu report, Race to be heard[41] by Marcus Ryder, highlights systemic racist practices such as (all three compared to their white counterparts):

- Over-scrutiny of non-white employees' work.
- Over-disciplining of non-white people's mistakes.
- Unequal terms of trade experienced by 'BAME-led' indies.

The reports clearly demonstrate the systemic nature of racism and how the white racial frame operates. That talented Black people and people of colour are consistently unable to progress in comparison to their white counterparts speaks volumes. It is also a sorry state of affairs that white people with no lived experience of the Black or Asian experience get permission and the funding to tell such stories. That is the epitome of white privilege, it is also cultural appropriation. It is once again demonstrative of the socialisation process that perpetuates the false concept of white supremacy that benefits white people. In the Think Piece Report, Sasha Salmon states: *'I was struck by how normalised it is to exclude people of colour both from telling their own stories and from helping find meaningful solutions to anti-racism in the industry.'*

EXPERIENCES

In some of the chapters I have sought to interview Black and mixed-race people about their experiences in the sector they work in. The reports, reviews and statistics often speak volumes but the human story should always be considered, reminding us that behind the numbers, findings and statistics are real people.

I am most grateful to the three well-known actors who were willing to be interviewed by me and kindly gave up their time to talk and share their experiences. The interviews were on the basis of anonymity. Given the findings in respect of blacklisting and the lack of progression for many Black actors, it is understandable. Thank you to all three of you, it is much appreciated.

ACTOR 1

Actor 1 is a British mixed-race woman who is well known in British television. Actor 1 got her break in the early part of the twenty-first century. She had a few roles in quick succession but then the work ceased. One issue was casting requiring the role to be Caucasian. Eventually there was some move towards race blind casting and contemporary roles did not need the character to be white.

She did not feel that she was discriminated against on set directly or indirectly. From her experience, actors were generally open, anti-racist and seeking diversity. Actor 1 did not feel stereotyped but did get typecast as 'assertive woman'. While she has not had negative experiences, she did feel that predominantly white stories were portrayed.

Actor 1 recognised that there were still issues in respect of representation behind the camera and that darker people, i.e. Black people, fared less well. She is always surprised to see a person of colour behind the camera. She has never worked with a Black producer and only worked with one Black director. In respect of colourism she said: *'I'm aware that there is a more palatable version of blackness. Certain educated Black actors and mixed-race actors are more acceptable than darker Black women, although it has never been overtly said.'*

I asked Actor 1 how things could be improved in the industry and she said there needs to be a concerted and conscious effort to make and give opportunities to write and to be creative. She did not believe that there should be positive discrimination. She said that there has been some improvement in the industry since the BLM movement, but it needs to diversify more. Actor 1 felt that things are shifting but not fast enough.

There was a feeling that racism had been at play when she was in a television series. Other actors were receiving calls for other work, but she received none and wondered if race was a factor as they were all stars of the show. Another experience was being erased from a poster because it was being sold abroad to a country that did not accept non-white people.

I asked Actor 1 how the entertainment model of drama compared to the reality of life and she said: *'It could be more accurate.'*

ACTOR 2

Actor 2 is a Black British man in his 30s who is well known in television and has had some success in the United States. Actor 2 had very positive experiences while studying drama and he felt supported and believed his educational institution was a meritocracy. When asked about stereotyping and roles, he said he was made aware of a specific role written for a Black male character in a London theatre; the only purpose of the Black character was to be aggressive and to push an old lady over.

In respect of experiences of racism, there have been incidences of being called 'bruv', being confused for other people and not being regarded as a lead. There were occasions where assumptions about him had been made. He was left questioning the situation. As a lead in a TV show, he has felt he has had more agency and therefore more confidence in being able to challenge racism. On occasions he has raised issues, he has felt listened to, but he is aware that it is a sensitive topic and people of colour can be blacklisted.

In respect of being behind the screen, there were no Black people. He's aware that colourism is an issue and that people have chosen not to audition him because the depth of his melanin was not what they were looking for. Historically, the industry appears to have been looking for light-skinned Black or Asian people.

I asked if the USA had better opportunities for Black people than in Britain. Actor 2 said not better, just more by virtue of quantity.

Because there is more, it can be better. Actor 2 did state that the USA had more diverse executives and more diverse writers.

ACTOR 3

Actor 3 is a mixed-race woman in her 40s who is well known in British television. In respect of opportunities Actor 3 said she found it hard to get decent, chunky roles; although she is not saying it was necessarily because of race, she is sure that some opportunities have not come her way because of it. She did mention that there may be an issue with the advertising of roles. Sometimes when the role has not specified an age or race and she has auditioned, she has been told *'you are not what we are looking for'*.

For Actor 3 one of the biggest issues was hair. She said that nine out of ten times she will sit down and be met with an exasperated expression and gesture from the make-up artist indicating a *'What am I supposed to do with this?'* look in respect of her hair. Some have suggested cutting her hair off. There have been shows where she has ended up having to do her own hair. She indicated that a lot of make-up artists do not have the skills to deal with Black hair, but the industry is not doing anything about it.

In respect of racism and stereotyping, Actor 3 stated that *'I've had a few jobs where I've not been treated the way I wanted to be treated,'* but couldn't say what the reasons were for the said treatment. Early in her career she was given stereotypical roles such as prisoner or prostitute and decent roles were not there for her when she started. She stated that in terms of challenging racism in a script, as an actor you don't really have any control. That's the script you're going in to deliver and you don't get to divert from the script.

In respect of racism she gave an example of being in a production that was a Black story but the entire crew was white; ironically there were only a few Black performers and they were treated horrendously. Actor 3 stated that in the last ten years things have improved and there was also some improvement with the BLM movement. I asked what would facilitate improvement; Actor 3 indicated that education for the gatekeepers and people in power was needed. She said

'There needs to be a consideration of who is in power and change needs to filter down from the top.' I asked about the lack of diversity and Actor 3 stated: 'there could be better signposting, and that socio-economic circumstances were a factor'. In order to rectify that Actor 3 suggested that there could be more effort on getting information into diverse schools, getting people into roles and more effort getting into communities and informing those communities of the route in.

Actor 3 had worked in America and said there were better opportunities. She said that Black and white people out there had been willing to help. I asked why Black people were making it in America and not here and Actor 3 suggested that British drama training had an excellent reputation, so regardless of whether you were Black or white, America saw excellence in the training and welcomed British talent.

The experience of the actors is in alignment with the seminal reports on race within the industry. Racism was occurring in various forms, whether through lack of opportunity, colourism, inappropriate language, inadequate hair and make-up professionals and/or stereotyping. There was also the issue of power. Actor 2 felt able to challenge racism at times, but all sought to remain anonymous for fear of reprisals and blacklisting.

BEHIND THE CAMERA

I spoke to Ryan Francis, a young Black man, who had tried to get into the entertainment industry. His experience is set out below.

Ryan Francis is a producer and videographer. He grew up in Bristol and at school acquired an interest in television and production. His teacher, Mrs Hughes, had faith in him and pushed him. He said that he felt safe growing up in Bristol but he was aware that gangs, drugs and knife crime were an issue; he was lucky by virtue of the fact that he was the only

Black kid who had both parents together and they kept him on the straight and narrow. He went to City Academy and studied media; the film that he made for the course won in the 16–18-year-old category at the Bristol International Film Festival. He left school and started his own comedy show called TheLittleRyanShow.

Ryan has been in the entertainment industry for 10 years now. He received some mentoring from the BFI and joined the watershed group which created a platform funded by the council to allow under-represented people to post their content every six months. He described being pushed out of the organisation, after which he spent time as a freelancer gaining experience.

He then tried to get work as a runner only to be told in interviews that they couldn't hire him because he was too ambitious. He recalls going to every single production company in Bristol asking to be a runner but nobody was interested. At times they would ask him to come and work for free for three weeks. However, he stated he was a young Black person with no money and so it wasn't financially viable to do so.

Ryan raised the issue of class in relation to breaking into the industry. People are given opportunities to go and work on sets and to become runners but they are expected to do so for free. As such this excludes a lot of people who are from low income or impoverished backgrounds.

He found that when he was applying for jobs in the industry he would be turned down either on the basis of his ambition or because he didn't have the requisite experience. However, on occasions he learned that where he had been told that he did not have the requisite experience, a white person had been given the job who did not have the experience either.

After years of struggling and trying to break into the industry he gave up. He admits that it did affect his mental health. He eventually found a job with a robotics company which had a marketing department that utilised video and social media for its marketing. He was there for two years and feels that he became his true self. He would film ads for Apple, Amazon, and other big corporations. He taught himself to use the cameras and other aspects of production. After some time he made a huge sacrifice and bought his own camera equipment.

He recalls that after George Floyd was murdered the television industry realised that 'they didn't have any Black people' and needed some. From that moment he says that his phone was ringing non-stop. There were opportunities to work as a runner or a researcher and he did work with David Olusoga. He says that one broadcasting corporation came to Bristol indicating that they were there to help under-represented people and shoehorn them into the industry. Ryan indicates that in reality they did nothing. They didn't hire anyone – it was just a publicity stunt.

Ryan subsequently formed Latent Pictures and now takes people on and teaches them about the industry. He said he had to take all of his hatred and turn it into something positive. The company engages in video marketing production and teaches people from all walks of life about the industry. Today he deals with young people who are truly under-represented and he deals with real working-class people. He states that there is a race and gender problem within the industry; however, he believes there is more of a class issue. He indicated that he knew so many white working-class people who won't get the opportunity to work in the industry even though they have the advantage of being white.

His experience in the industry sounded very distressing and soul destroying. He thinks that no one should have to go through what he went through. On his journey through the industry he had no one to help him or represent him.

I asked him about possible solutions to the lack of representation and he suggested that there is a need for the under-represented to create their own companies and that those who create those companies should have selfless motives.

CULTURAL APPROPRIATION

Before I leave this chapter, I wanted to briefly address the issue of cultural appropriation. This occurs when something is culturally non-white but is then shamelessly appropriated and whitewashed. It goes beyond an all-white writing room writing the Black or character of colour, or experience. It's casting white actors in roles that are non-European and setting them in a non-white country. It's beyond whitewashing and, let's be honest, it's dishonest appropriation and exploitation.

If you set a story in Ancient Egypt, the characters in truth are going to be Black. If it's in Persia, the characters should be Iranian. The same reasoning should be applied for China, Japan and other non-white nations. Yet there are films and television series set in those places in ancient times that have an all-white or predominantly white cast playing characters of a different race, or pretending that the white race were there. That they were in the majority and the heroes of the time. That is a clear example of the white racial frame and concepts of white supremacy being acted upon. Now, first of all, that's just nonsense. Second, it is racially offensive and it's dishonest. People may say, well we need to sell the product, but that's just weak. Are you honestly saying that there are no Black or actors of colour who can carry a film or a television series? I really hope not. That's just a myth and later on I will consider myth-busting. If your script is not set in a white Western country and is in ancient times – and to a degree modern times too – then it should have the appropriate cast and characters with the right racial make-up. Otherwise that's just cultural appropriation and you're perpetuating racism.

CONCLUSION

As this chapter has – I hope – demonstrated, there clearly is systemic and institutional racism in the industry. It is up to all of us as individuals to deconstruct it and eradicate. I will address it in my later chapter in respect of why Black actors are heading to America, but in a nutshell it is because of the opportunity to play complex characters unrelated to race and the following two pieces of work are shining examples of that. The first is the television series *Loki*, where the antagonists and their villainy have absolutely nothing to do with their race. This was also apparent in the 2023 film *The Hunger Games: The Ballad of Songbirds & Snakes*. Viola Davis plays the disturbingly evil scientist and Head Game Maker Dr Gaul. Once again, her villainy has nothing to do with race. It is worth pointing out that the first step in the process is the script. So ask yourself, have you written:

    i. An Asian/Muslim terrorist?
    ii. A geisha?
    iii. A Black man who is a criminal, dangerous, or a gangster?
    iv. A Black woman who is a drug addict or prostitute?

If you have, have you written anything else about them? Have you humanised them? Have you given them depth or layers? Have you even given them a name? Or have you simply reduced them to a trope? If you have, my advice is to rip it up and start again or delete them from your script.

'We have seen communities cry out in pain, generation after generation, because of racism and police brutality.'

Jaime Harrison

CHAPTER 7

LAW AND ORDER – PART 1: **THE POLICE**

In Britain and America police procedurals and legal dramas are a staple of mainstream television. In Britain, there are at least ten police procedurals on per week. There is also a smattering of legal drama at home and in the United States. Such dramas have been a staple of television for decades. With the exception of *Line of Duty*, I have often questioned the veracity of British police procedurals over the years.

As I was growing up in the 1980s through to the present day, British police procedural shows have almost always consisted of a white lead, usually male. They are usually non-bigoted and fair-minded. The general feel of the shows is: we have a fair system, we always get our man or woman, and overall police forces are well-run ships with a few bad apples. I do not believe this is a realistic assessment and will discuss why in this chapter. While some shows are getting better at diversity and portraying issues of race and racism, it is worth briefly looking at the actual system of policing and how it relates to race.

The issue of racism within the British police force is an unresolved matter that has been ongoing since the inception of a police force. According to Williams[42] the first police force in Britain was established during the slave trade. As a result of an abundance of cargo being brought to British docks – most notably the Thames – at the time of the slave trade, organised criminals appeared and soon theft of cargo became a problem. Thus the first police force was created to protect the criminal gains of slavery from other criminals.

Racism is not new in British policing but over the last five decades it has come to the attention of the general public. Issues surrounding deaths in custody, disproportionate stop and search, racial violence, racial abuse and failures to investigate have all been examples of the pernicious effects of institutional and individual racism from the police. This is not a problem peculiar to Britain, rather it is a factor of the Western world.

Despite the constant failures and negative impacts of the police as regards ethnic minorities, particularly in relation to Black men, and despite the Metropolitan Police being identified as institutionally racist, the police as an organisation are still in denial about racism among its members and about its prevalence.

If you're going to tackle a procedural drama involving the police then it is worth reading the three seminal reports (Scarman, Macpherson, INQUEST report) on deaths in custody two of which relate to the Metropolitan Police.

THE SCARMAN REPORT 1981[43]

The Scarman Report arose out of the riots that occurred in Brixton in 1981 and subsequently spread to Liverpool and Manchester. The riots were sparked by a number of issues but for the most part they stemmed from anger and resentment at the police because of their treatment of Black people. As Lord Scarman noted, the London Borough of Lambeth had conducted an inquiry at the behest of the Council for Community Relations in Lambeth. Having received 275 submissions of evidence, the report was published in November 1981.

The report was damning and described the police as *'an army of occupation'* and referred to operations as *'attacks on the people of Lambeth'*. It also stated that the police intimidated, harassed and misused the law. All aspects of the police were under scrutiny and harshly criticised. The main criticism of the police involved accusations of racial prejudice, harassment, and inflexible and unimaginative policing.

Lord Scarman did not find the policies and direction of the police racist but put it down to *'some officers, who lapse into unthinking assumptions about Black people'*. In the report Lord Scarman addressed the issue of racism generally and found it started, was taught and manifested in children as young as five. There was recognition that the effect of racism in society was high unemployment among Black people, that racism needed to be eradicated and a number of recommendations were made in regard to the police.

THE 1999 MACPHERSON REPORT[44]

On the evening of 22 April 1993 18-year-old Stephen Lawrence and his friend Duwayne Brooks were waiting for a bus at Well Hall Road, in Eltham. Stephen had gone to see if the bus was coming and had approached Dickson Road, when a group of racists began chasing after them and hurling racist abuse at the pair. One of them armed with a knife stabbed Stephen Lawrence to death.

It must be and it is every parent's worst nightmare to outlive their child, particularly when that life has been snuffed out so violently and so needlessly. One would hope in that darkest time that the police would be sensitive, compassionate, and competent, and that they would take such a murder seriously. Unfortunately, as the Lawrence family found out, being Black meant that didn't happen and like many Black families who have lost a loved one to murder, they had to endure the unendurable as they fought to get justice for their child and hold the police to account, while facing institutional racism and incompetence.

The Macpherson Report which was commissioned as a result of the Metropolitan Police's handling of the case and treatment of the

Lawrence family was a shocking indictment of the organisation. The Macpherson Report laid bare the breath-taking incompetence of senior officers. As a result of racism, the police didn't even bother to try and administer first aid or administer any words of comfort to a dying young man. The incompetence included failure to secure the scene, failure to secure evidence, chase leads or make arrests in good time and investigate appropriately. The investigation was a far cry from the slick procedurals you will see on television.

The Macpherson Report came to the conclusion that the Metropolitan Police was institutionally racist. It is a deserved and justified term but one they have refused to acknowledge – perhaps because it is as a result of collective white fragility. In respect of Duwayne Brooks who had seen his friend murdered, the police treated him as a suspect. The report found that the police had stereotyped him and failed to treat him as a victim and that he was inadequately dealt with.

It found officers engaging in racism would deny that they were racist. There were times when officers were not even aware they were using racially offensive language. The police were grossly insensitive when breaking the news of Stephen's death to his father. As the family sought answers, they were either dismissed or treated inappropriately.

The Macpherson Report roundly criticised the reviews the police had done of themselves. One police review failed to criticise any investigative decisions, even though the investigation was wholly incompetent and deserved severe criticism.

Institutional racism is a term the police, particularly the Metropolitan Police, are doing their utmost to escape from, but as the numbers will show, nothing has really changed and that is evidenced by the Baroness Casey Review of March 2023[45] which is quite damning. In my opinion the police are constantly engaging in typical white fragility and consistently failing to acknowledge the level of racism within their ranks and as an organisation.

Obviously I am not saying that every police officer is a racist. I am saying they have a serious problem with racism on an individual, collective and institutional level and they are in denial about it.

In respect of the Stephen Lawrence investigation, by Friday 23 April 1993, the day after the murder, the killers had been named and there was evidence of their previous violent and racist behaviour. Despite having this information, the police failed to act and did not arrest any of the suspects.

The 1999 Macpherson Report is some 389 pages. Although it is over twenty years old, it is worth a read as it highlights the catalogue of failures, incompetence and casual racism, as well as the stereotyping that beset the police. It lays bare the understandable distress of the Lawrence family and their treatment during the worst time of their lives. It exposed the prevalence of racism and racial violence in the country and again, as per the Scarman Report, recognised the problem of racism within young children.

The Macpherson Report called on the government to address racism in children and to adopt anti-racist policies. In 2022 the police announced they were going to adopt anti-racist policies. That's twenty-three years on from the Macpherson Report.

It begs the question then, why, knowing that racism is a social evil, knowing that Black people are being adversely affected by police racism – having been caught out numerous times engaging in overt racism and having been found to be institutionally racist – are they only now adopting anti-racist policies some twenty-three years later?

I'd say it is for a number of reasons: a) they've been engaging in white fragility b) they never took racism seriously and c) they refused to acknowledge their own prejudices and behaviour. There's also an issue of a lack of professional ethics. Officers may well see racism at play, but many will not object or intervene to stop it when it occurs.

If you're white and you're reading this, you might be thinking, surely it's not that bad. I'd say check your white privilege right about now and remember Nicole Smallman and Bibaa Henry and read the Casey Review of March 2023.

From 1960 to 2020 institutional racism within the police, particularly within the Metropolitan Police, is as potent then as it is now. Areas that have been of concern are:

i. Deaths in custody
ii. Failure to investigate
iii. Stop and Search
iv. Abuse and hostility based on race
v. Police violence.

All of the above have been occurring because of institutional and individual racism within the police and as yet have not been adequately addressed and are not even close to being remedied. During the time it has taken to write and edit this book there have been a catalogue of news reports about racism in the Metropolitan Police with various text messages being uncovered highlighting extremely racially offensive language. These officers, who are clearly racist or allowing racism to happen, are policing our streets. I would ask you to question how you think their encounters with Black people and ethnic minorities go...

DEATHS IN CUSTODY

According to INQUEST[46] (a charity providing expertise on state-related deaths and their investigation to bereaved people, lawyers, advice and support agencies, the media and parliamentarians) '...people with Black, Asian and minoritised ethnicities (BAME) die disproportionately as a result of use of force, or restraint by the police, raising serious questions of institutional racism as a contributory factor in their deaths'. Deborah Coles, Director of INQUEST asserts that there is: 'irrefutable evidence of structural racism embedded in policing practices'.

On 27 April 2018 there was a press release from the United Nations Human Rights Commission, which stated, 'UN human rights experts have expressed serious concerns over the deaths of a disproportionate number of people of African descent and of ethnic minorities in the United Kingdom as a result of excessive force by State security.' It then went on to say, 'The deaths reinforce the experiences of structural racism, over-policing and criminalisation of people of African descent and other minorities in the UK[47].'

The UN press release also revealed that *'Data disclosed by the Metropolitan Police in 2017 found that people of African descent and of ethnic minority background, in particular young African and Caribbean men, subject to deadly use of force by restraint and restraint equipment, were twice as likely to die after the use of force by police officers, and the subsequent lack or insufficiency of access to appropriate healthcare. ... This points to the lack of accountability and the impunity with which law enforcement and State agencies operate'*.

The 2017 Angiolini Review[48] observed that there were disproportionate deaths of BAME people. Furthermore, despite the many reviews into police use of force and subsequent enquiries and reports, there appeared to be a failure to learn lessons. There also appeared to be a lack of training and a lack of understanding of how deadly the use of force can be. I wonder how many dead Black men it takes for the police to realise their use of force will most likely prove fatal to Black men. I also wonder how many dead Black men it will take for the police to realise that neglecting a person purporting to have a medical emergency can end in a fatality.

There have been a number of needless deaths of Black men in police custody and it is key to remember that each death was once a living, breathing human being with their life ahead of them and a family who loved them. Those loved ones are not only having to grieve a devastating loss, they also have to do battle with the police to get answers and fight for justice at the worst time of their lives.

I had been thinking about this chapter all day, about the victims and families who have had to deal with such loss and then fight for justice, and I realised that in these cases, we – I mean Black people – are often not treated as human beings. We are treated as lesser beings. We are not seen as human, or we are regarded as less than human, and from that view stems either hatred or indifference and consistent ill-treatment.

When I decided to write this chapter, I was determined to humanise the people whose lives had been cut so brutally short at the hands of the police with breath-taking impunity, often aided by the media and government.

Christopher Alder (37)
Died 1 April 1998 – Kingston Upon Hull Police Station
Christopher Alder was an army veteran who had served in Northern Ireland and the Falklands War. As a result of being an assault victim, he was conveyed to the hospital. It was suspected that he had sustained a head injury which resulted in what hospital staff regarded as *'troublesome behaviour'*.

He was subsequently taken to the Kingston Upon Hull police station. The custody footage which I have had the misfortune of watching shows him being dragged into the custody area, unconscious and handcuffed with his hands behind his back. He was then put face down on the floor. Despite being motionless and unresponsive, five white male officers stand around him discussing him, not checking his airway, not checking if he is alright. The officers then go on to say *'He's right as rain,'* and *'He's just acting now.'* In the footage you can hear gargling sounds that clearly indicate something is wrong. Still the officers remain convinced he is acting. The footage fast forwards and 8 minutes and 30 seconds later, one of the officers checks on him. It is apparent he has stopped breathing and has no pulse.

It later transpires in the inquest that the officers were making racial jokes and monkey noises while he was dying on the floor. The inquest found serious neglect and that Christopher Alder had been unlawfully killed. All police officers were acquitted of manslaughter and went on to receive payouts on early retirement. The funeral for Christopher was held in 2000. In 2011, the family discovered that they had not in fact buried Christopher because the body that had been released was that of a 77-year-old woman.

Kingsley Burnell (29)
Died 31 March 2011 – Sutton Coldfield Police Station
On 30 March 2011, police attended a hospital where Kingsley Burnell appeared to be suffering from mental health problems. Police restrained Kingsley by using rear cuffs, leg strips and the threat of tasers. En-route to another facility, an ambulance worker placed a blanket over Kingsley's head while he lay chest down on a

trolley, during which time he was subjected to various baton blows and strikes by the police.

The police then left him face down in a locked seclusion room, motionless, the blanket over his head and trousers down by his knees. When someone eventually entered the room to check on him, he had suffered a cardiac arrest and died the next day.

Despite the inquest finding unreasonable force by the police contributed to his death and two officers standing trial for perjury, no officer was convicted of his death or for any kind of assault.

Olaseni Lewis (23)
Died 3 September 2010, likely as a result of excessive force used by the police three days earlier at Bethlem Royal Hospital.
Olaseni Lewis was suffering from an acute psychotic illness. He was admitted to Mayday University Hospital in Croydon and then transferred to the Maudsley Hospital and then on to Bethlem Royal Hospital, a well-known psychiatric unit in London, commonly referred to as Bedlam.

Despite being admitted as a voluntary patient, when Olaseni tried to leave, the staff prevented him from doing so. When matters escalated, instead of calling his parents – as had been agreed – the staff called the police.

Police officers subsequently restrained him for approximately 30–40 minutes. After another attempt to leave, police restrained him for a further 20 minutes. Two sets of handcuffs were applied with the left arm locked in front of his head and his right arm behind his back. One set of restraints was around his ankle and one on his legs. The techniques used were against police practice and held to be dangerous. While in the aforementioned restrained position, the police struck him with a police baton.

Olaseni Lewis was left in that position for twenty minutes – a position that restricted his breathing and subsequently rendered him unconscious. The police left the room believing he was faking his unconsciousness. Medical staff then injected him with anti-psychotic medication.

One officer noticed that Olaseni had stopped breathing and officers then attempted CPR. Olaseni was transferred back to Mayday Hospital but tests on 3 and 4 September showed he had suffered brain stem death. His cause of death was cerebral hypoxia likely brought on by restraint.

The Coroner Selena Lynch opined that: *'there is a risk of future deaths unless action is taken'*. She highlighted the lack of training and understanding of officers in relation to procedures and restraint. It is a three-page report and it does not mention the role racism played but her concerns were justified because there have been more Black deaths in police custody in similar circumstances.

The following Black men are just some in a long list of Black people who died while in the custody of the police. It is worth looking at: www.blacklivesmatter.uk/deaths-in-custody/

21/06/2017 – Edson Da Costa (25)
19/07/2017 – Darren Cumberbatch (32)
22/07/2017 – Rashan Charles (20)
24/11/2017 – Nuno Cardoso (25)
09/03/2018 – Kevin Clarke (35)
29/06/2019 – Ian Taylor (54)

Ian Taylor (54)
Died 29 June 2019 having suffered a cardiac arrest while detained by police on Coldharbour Lane, Brixton.
In May 2022, the inquest into Ian Taylor's case had been concluded and featured prominently in the news. Ian Taylor was an asthmatic and on 29 June 2019, one of the hottest days of the year, he had been arrested by the police. He had repeatedly told the all-white group of police officers that he could not breathe and was asking for help.

The police response was to tell him to: *'grow up,'* and *'stop acting up,'* and called his pleas for help a load of nonsense. The police left him lying on the street. No effort was made to bring him water, or an inhaler, or to drive him to the hospital. He was moved to the police car and suffered a cardiac arrest and died later that evening. Cause of death was a heart attack caused by acute asthma, alongside underlying health conditions and dehydration.

Unfortunately, the list goes on. Black people's encounters with the police in Britain and America can often be a brutal and/or fatal one for them. If a white person had been lying in the street having been stabbed, the police would have undoubtedly tried to assist them and rendered first aid, or offered words of comfort. If a white person had said they were unwell, again I have no doubt the police would have enquired as to their welfare and provided appropriate assistance. In the case of Ian Taylor and Christopher Alder, they were gravely unwell and yet the police response was hostile and inhumane. Despite brutalising Olaseni Lewis and Kingsley Burrell while restrained, those officers remained in their jobs. It is doubtful that those men would have been treated in that way or met such fates had they been white.

FAILURE TO INVESTIGATE

While the police are all too willing to stop, search, harass, arrest, abuse, brutalise and fatally restrain Black people and people of colour, far too often there is an apparent unwillingness to do their jobs. As this chapter will demonstrate, there is frequently an acute lack of interest in investigating when people of colour are victims of crime, even when it comes to murder. I will cite a few examples below, but bear in mind the attitudes and behaviours have been replicated across the country.

The New Cross Massacre (1981)
On the morning of Sunday 18 January 1981 a fire broke out at 439 New Cross Road, London killing thirteen young Black people. The police initially blamed the fire on the far-right group the National Front. It is worthy of note that at the time in that area there was a history of racist arson attacks and on the morning in question

eye witnesses had seen a white man drive away from the house moments after the fire began.

Despite their initial suspicions, police turned their focus on the victims and blamed them for the fire instead of investigating properly. At the inquest the coroner largely ignored the theory of the fire being a racially motivated attack and unlawfully refused to take notes of the hearing. An open verdict was subsequently returned. To date the fire has never been properly investigated, no suspects have ever been apprehended. When the Black community organised a day of action, the press erroneously labelled the relatively peaceful protest a violent one.

The Stephen Lawrence Murder (1993)
On 22 April 1993 Stephen Lawrence was brutally murdered by a number of white racists. The investigation was incompetent and it took longer than Stephen lived to bring two of the killers to justice. As a result of the Macpherson Report into the murder, the police were labelled as institutionally racist.

The Chohan Family Murders (2003)
In February 2003, journalist Onkar Verma was living in New Zealand. He was growing increasingly concerned about his sister Nancy Chohan, his mother Charanjit Kaur, his two nephews aged 18 months and two months old at the time and Nancy's husband Amarjit Chohan. Amarjit Chohan was a successful businessman who lived in Hounslow, London with his family.

Onkar spoke to his mother and sister every day, but at this stage he had not heard from them in days and no one was picking up the phone. Despite repeated requests from Onkar Verma to investigate, the police refused. In stereotypical lazy fashion, they suggested that the family had probably gone back to India because they were having trouble assimilating into the country.

As a result of the police's indifference (and I will say racism) and being concerned for his family, Onkar Verma flew to England and began investigating himself. Eventually Amarjit Chohan's body washed up at sea; in his sock was a letter he had written mentioning the murderer's name. I refuse to give publicity or print to murderers, so I will not name them.

It transpired that the murderer had lured Mr Chohan to Wiltshire, kidnapped him and taken him to his home. While there Mr Chohan was brutally tortured and forced to sign blank documents. The plan was to make it look like Amarjit Chohan had signed his business over and fled to India.

In order to make the plan work, the murderer and his accomplices realised they would have to kill the whole family, so, having killed Amarjit Chohan, they went to his house and murdered his wife, the two babies and his mother-in-law.

The Nicole Smallman and Bibaa Henry Murders (2020)
On 5 June 2020 and into the early hours of 6 June, Bibaa Henry was celebrating her birthday with her sister Nicole Smallman at Fryant Country Park, north-west London.

When the family reported the sisters missing the next day, the police refused to act and did nothing for 36 hours. As a result of the police inaction, on 7 June, Nicole's boyfriend Adam Smith went looking for the sisters and discovered their bodies – they had been brutally murdered.

While on duty and guarding the bodies of the two women, PC Deniz Jaffer and PC Jamie Lewis took photos of the dead women's bodies and shared them on WhatsApp groups, with messages. One message said: *'dead birds'*, and another said *'covid c*nts'*.

THE MORE THINGS CHANGE, THE MORE THEY STAY THE SAME

In respect of the Chohans it seems clear to me that racism was a factor in the decision-making. If you are white and you went to the police and reported your whole family missing, I am sure the police would be taking a statement from you and launching an investigation. That two babies under two were missing should have triggered alarms in relation to child protection. That there was such indifference and inaction in respect of two missing babies demonstrates the level of racism being practised. Again, if Nicole Smallman and Bibaa Henry had been white, I'm of the view that the family would not have been dismissed with such indifference.

The above cases run from the 1980s through to the 2020s. Even though they are high-profile murder cases, they serve to highlight that there can be a clear lack of interest in investigating properly when Black people or people of colour are victims of crime. While the police claim to have changed, the facts tend to discredit that assertion. The Baroness Casey Review of 2023 found that not only was the Metropolitan Police institutionally racist, it was also sexist, misogynistic and homophobic. The Review found that there was poor management, that the Met has failed to ensure the integrity of its officers, and that predatory and unacceptable behaviour has been allowed to flourish (p16). At page 16 of the Review it went on to say that *'Discrimination is tolerated, not dealt with and has become baked into the system.'* It then goes on to give examples of the racism and racist bullying of Black and Asian staff.

The review went on to say at page 17:

> *There are people in the Met with racist attitudes, and Black, Asian and ethnic minority officers and staff are more likely to experience racism, discrimination and bullying at their hands. Discrimination is often ignored, and complaints are likely to be turned against Black, Asian and ethnic minority officers. Many do not think it is worth reporting. Black officers are 81% more likely to be in the misconduct system than their white counterparts.*

STOP AND SEARCH

The use of police powers to stop and search people has been an issue for the police since the Windrush generation arrived in the

United Kingdom. From then and up to now, Black people – particularly Black men – are disproportionately stopped and searched by police compared to their white counterparts.

As at 7 May 2022 the government reported that between April 2020 and March 2021 there were 697,405 stop and searches in England and Wales of which 7.5 stops per 1000 were for white and 52.6 stops per 1000 for Black people. That means that in the year 2020–2021 Black people were 7.5 times more likely to be stopped and searched than their white counterparts, despite being only 3% of the population[49].

In March 2020 the Equality and Human Rights Commission published: *'Stop and Think: A critical review of the use of stop and search powers in England and Wales*[50]'. The review found that if you were Black you were at least six times more likely than a white person to be stopped and searched by police in England and Wales. If you were Asian you were twice as likely to be stopped.

The EHRC review also found that *'the current police use of PACE stop and search powers may be unlawful, disproportionate, discriminatory and damaging to relations within and between communities'*. They found that the highest disproportionate ratios for Black people were in Dorset, Hampshire and Leicestershire and the biggest impact in terms of numbers was in London.

In 2001 a BBC report[51] referred to the Home Office statistics that showed that Black people were five times more likely to be stopped and searched than their white counterparts and one year later, the figure had jumped to eight times more likely. In 2010 the *Guardian* found that Black people were 26 times more likely to be stopped and searched in England and Wales[52].

The Police and Criminal Evidence Act 1984 (PACE) is the main legislation that governs the police. Section 1 of PACE sets out the grounds on which a police officer may stop a person. The section should also be read in conjunction with Code A of PACE 1984. Under section 1 a police officer may search any person or vehicle for stolen or prohibited articles or corrosive items. Section 23 of the Misuse of Drugs Act 1971 allows officers to search people for prohibited drugs.

In accordance with Code A, in order to stop and search a person under section 1 of PACE 1984 or section 23 of the MDA 1971, officers need to have reasonable grounds to suspect that person is in possession of the s1 items or the s23 drugs. In accordance with Code A the officer should have regard to the Equality Act 2010 and *'must have regard to the need to* eliminate *unlawful discrimination, harassment and victimisation'.* Even though there is a prohibition of racial discrimination and harassment, the evidence suggests that the prohibition is ignored and racial discrimination is still widely practised by the police. The plethora of reports, data and reviews indicate that the disproportionate use of stop and search is not justified. In effect the police are not finding a larger degree of stolen and prohibited items on Black people. As the EHRC Review pointed out: *'One common explanation, that Black people are generally more often involved in crime, is not supported by robust evidence.'*

ABUSE AND HARASSMENT

Basingstoke Police Station, Hampshire

In April 2018 a recording device was placed in a police station in Basingstoke, Hampshire following complaints about the police officers working there. Over a period of twenty-four days, six officers were recorded making offensive racist, sexist and homophobic remarks. Two police sergeants and a constable who were still serving were dismissed without notice. An inspector and a constable were informed they would have been dismissed if they were still serving. The sixth, a detective constable, was given a final written warning. Some of the remarks made included describing a Black officer as a 'pavement special' which means a mixed-breed dog. A part of the area where a Black officer worked was known as 'The African Corner', and a Black police officer was referred to as being *'a colonial overseer running a plantation of white people'.*

Charing Cross Police Station, London

For two years, officers in Charing Cross Police Station would casually use highly offensive racist and sexist language. In respect of the racist language, according to the *Metro* newspaper, the language relating to African children, Somali people and Auschwitz was too offensive to publish. The IOPC Report, called Operation Hotton[53] highlighted that the behaviours were not isolated incidents or just a few bad apples, as is so often espoused by senior officers. On paragraph 17, page 7 the report stated: *'Too often banter was used to excuse offensive and discriminatory behaviour.'* Racially offensive messages included those such as: *'My dad kidnapped some African children and made some dog food.'* Somalians were referred to as rats and in the case of an image of a Black man sent to a colleague who sought clarification, the response was: *'Never mind the robber, I like the shirt.'*

British Transport Police

A BBC article dated 5 November 2021[54] states: *'The British Transport Police has apologised to the British African community for "systemic racism" and a corrupt officer in the 1970s.'* This pertains to corrupt officer Derek Ridgewell who committed perjury in the trials of at least ten Black men who were wrongfully convicted and imprisoned for thefts they did not commit.

Child Q

In December 2020 Child Q was fifteen years old and at school. She was wrongly accused of smelling of cannabis. When teachers did not find any drugs on Child Q, they called the police. Child Q was pulled out of an exam, taken to a room and unlawfully strip-searched. Child Q, who was on her period at the time, was forced to remove her clothes, remove her sanitary pad and spread her buttocks. No drugs were found.

The school and the police did not inform Child Q's parents of what was happening and they failed to have an appropriate adult present. It goes without saying that Child Q was Black. As a result of the search Child Q required psychological help and her treatment at the hands of the police and the school triggered a safeguarding review[55] by the London Borough of Hackney who found that racism was an influencing factor in deciding whether to undertake the strip-search. The review highlighted that Child Q's family believed she was doing exceptionally well at school which appears to have caused the teachers to single her out repeatedly. It was also said that after the traumatic strip search, Child Q was told to return to her exam and no one bothered to ask whether she was alright.

It is clear that the police in Britian and America have problems of systemic racism, institutional racism and white supremacy; unfortunately, they are ill equipped and often unwilling to take a long, hard look at themselves, understand what racism is and take steps to reform and root racism out. That may seem harsh but as each decade goes by the same problems arise. In the Casey Review they quote the 1972 Police Commissioner Robert Mark who said: *'he had never experienced... blindness, arrogance and prejudice on anything like the scale accepted as routine in the Met'*. Then you have the 1981 Scarman Report, the 1999 Macpherson Report and the 2023 Casey Review. Despite the issue of institutional racism being highlighted decade after decade, and being reviewed and investigated nothing changes. You may disagree, but I started writing this book in 2022 and in that year alone there have been: the shooting of an unarmed Black man Chris Kaba; numerous reports about disproportionate stop and search; and the Children's Commissioner raising concerns about the disproportionate use of strip-search of ethnic minority children, most of whom were innocent. There is the inquest into the death of seriously asthmatic Ian Taylor, whose medical emergency was callously ignored by the police while he was in their custody; and the death of Oladeji Omishore who was tasered on Chelsea Bridge – he ended up climbing over the bridge, falling and dying. The footage of his last moments is utterly disturbing. Nothing has changed.

The number of deaths in police custody of Black people from the 1960s to the present day is appalling, not to mention the consistent failure to investigate such deaths which is often marred by racism. The New Cross Massacre in 1981, the murder of Stephen Lawrence in 1993, the Chohan family murders in 2003 and the murders of Nicole Smallman and Bibaa Henry in 2020 demonstrate that there is often a lack of interest as a result of racial prejudice in investigating crimes perpetrated against ethnic minorities.

Despite the cries of *'We're not racist,'* and *'We've changed,'* the evidence is overwhelmingly clear that they are racist and they haven't changed – not in any significant way at least. In 2022 the Metropolitan Police were doing their darndest to shake the institutionally racist label. I'd say it was an exercise in futility. The issue is systemic, and further expanded upon by Sharon Walker[56]. She suggests that *'England has a parallel legacy that has emerged from an oppressive, colonial mindset passed through generations, institutions, organisations… via a combination of racial bias… [and] racism'*.

It is worth bearing in mind that some of the deaths in custody of Black men began with the medical professionals calling the police and, in some cases, those medical professionals helping to brutalise those Black men, or ignoring the police brutality that they see being perpetrated against their patients. Eberhardt and DiAngelo refer to the system or societal structure as anti-Black and nowhere is that more apparent than in American and British police forces.

Racism starts with the individual officer. The one who holds racists views. The one who is allowed to express those views to their colleagues with impunity. Views that are shared in conversations and social media groups. Now imagine those individuals policing our streets. Who are they most likely to stop and search for no apparent reason? Who are they most likely to disrespect and strip-search for no apparent reason? And who are they likely to brutalise and kill? It is clear that stop and search disproportionately affects Black people and the reports demonstrate that the disproportionality is not justified. The basis then for many stops is racial bias and racism. This demonstrates not just individual racism but institutional racism.

The encounters between the police and Black people are often negative. Most complaints relate to harassment, abuse and excessive force. Eberhardt referred to two studies of note, which were done in the United States but had similar findings in the United Kingdom. Between 2015 and 2017 Eberhardt and her team analysed the traffic stops of 245 officers in Oakland. College students were then asked to rate 414 utterances using a four-point scale to measure the degree of respect, politeness, friendliness, formality and impartiality the officer conveyed. The students found the officers were professional overall but when the officers were speaking to Black drivers, they were *'less respectful, less polite, less friendly, less formal and less impartial'* when compared to speaking with white people.

From the data gathered from the students, they went through 500,000 words from transcripts and found that officers – both white and Black – *'were significantly more respectful to white drivers than Black drivers'* and that there was a respect deficit when it came to Black drivers. Having practised criminal law in England since 2005 and with the inception of body-worn video, I have seen so many times the difference in interactions between the police and Black people, particularly Black men, and I have to say there is more aggression, more force and less respect.

Now, I am not saying every police officer is a racist. There are some kind and decent dedicated professionals who are doing a difficult, dangerous and thankless job in the face of societal breakdown and savage unsustainable cuts. On the other hand there are officers who are clearly overtly hostile to Black people – even if I am the prosecutor – who go on to engage with Black people in a hostile manner. When dealing with white people it's *'excuse me, sir or madam'*; when dealing with Black people it's often cuffs slapped on, sometimes with no words or introduction, followed by being told they are being detained. I have watched hundreds of hours of body-worn videos and the difference is palpable.

Unfortunately, encounters with the police can be fatal for Black people. Sharon Walker's 2020 article Systemic Racism: Big, Black, Mad and Dangerous in the Criminal Justice System, refers to the continual negative stereotyping of Black men by agencies, particularly the police, as 'big, bad and dangerous', which leads to excessive force being used. The obvious result as we have seen time and again is a fatal encounter.

Walker suggests that more than institutional racism is at play as expounded by the Macpherson report and that systemic racism plays a part. Systemic racism as defined by Feagin (2000) is anti-Blackness which he further elaborates on in 2006:

> '...systemic racism becomes embedded in each aspect of society and perpetuated by social processes that reproduce not only racial inequality but also the fundamental racist relationship between the racially oppressed and the racial oppressors'.

Walker suggests that Britain has a parallel legacy that maintains the system of white privilege and power. She argues that the 'Big, bad and dangerous or superhuman' description is used overtly to justify the excessive use of force and it is in fact, simply a demonstration of white power, the devaluation of human life, i.e. Black life.

I have mentioned Black civilian encounters with the police, but it is worthy of note that Black and ethnic minority officers also have to face racism within the force. There are a number of Black and Asian officers who have written books about their experience of racism within the force which are worth reading if you are going to make your police character Black. It is also worth reading the 2020 House of Lords Library report[57] which highlighted that ethnic minority officers were more likely to be subjected to disciplinary proceedings than their white counterparts, and the Casey Review. There is also reference to anecdotal evidence provided by three officers, who gave their accounts to British newspapers. The first is from Kevin Maxwell, writing in the *Independent*[58], who seeks to disabuse former Commissioner Cressida Dick of her notion that the Met is no longer institutionally racist. In his opening address, Kevin Maxwell indicates that during a decade of service in the Met there was open racism and discrimination and *'no real intention to stamp out racism'*, and he disagrees entirely with her assessment.

The second article is by Shabnam Chaudri[59] who recalls her thirty years of experience in the Met as being marred with racism and then victimisation when she complained of racism. Finally, there is the 2020 anonymous report of a serving Black woman in the Met who writes in the *Guardian*[60] about her experience of racism within the Met and says of her difficulties working in an environment where biases are used against her: *'bias cultivated by an organisation that refuses to truthfully acknowledge its history and persistent racism – makes it hard to feel safe'*. Now, if police officers do not feel safe among their colleagues, then what hope is there for ethnic minority communities?

I interviewed a former Black police sergeant on the condition of anonymity and his experiences were of racism, being on the end of sexually inappropriate behaviour and witnessing the disparities in the promotion prospects of Black officers.

Former Police Sergeant X

Having arrived at the police station on his first day and accessing his locker, he was met with hostility and questions about what he was doing there and if he was lost. He indicated that if anyone tried to complain about bullying and racism, the consequences could be dangerous; also that when an officer requires urgent assistance over the radio, if they are deemed to have complained then fellow officers will simply ignore the call and carry on with their coffee.

There was an element of sexual harassment from white officers who were gay, who would engage in inappropriate language and say things like: *'Is it true what they say about Black men?'*

His experience of promotion was that white officers were given time and opportunity to go on courses and activities that would build their portfolio and then be recommended for the sergeants' exam. Furthermore, Black and Asian officers would not make the first sift, which he believed was as a result of discrimination. He recalls one woman officer who didn't make the sift changing her name to a more European one on the next application and getting through.

The sergeant then helped to create schemes whereby ethnic minority officers could gain the skill and experience necessary to enter for the exam. He recalled that when minority officers got through the sift or were promoted, white officers would tap their skin to suggest to their colleagues that the officer was only getting promoted because of their skin colour and not because of merit. As such, minority officers were discouraged from entering any schemes that would provide them with the requisite opportunities, skills and experience to make the sift, because many white colleagues were resentful and held it against them and reduced it down to race.

Now consider the information above: the reports, the reviews, the data, the deaths and the Black experience. Now consider the plethora of British and American police procedurals that have been or are on television. From a race perspective are they realistic?

Many police procedurals fail to portray the systemic and structural racism that occurs within police forces. In Racist America[61] Feagin states: *'European American institutions were racially hierarchical, white supremacists, and undemocratic. For the most part, they remain so today.'* Feagin refers to W.E.B. Dubois' previous works and explains that systems embed racism at their core. Unfortunately this reality is rarely seen. The *Law & Order* franchise has been repeatedly criticised for failing to address the problems of structural racism within the NYPD.

COLOR OF CHANGE REPORT AND AMERICAN SHOWS

Color of Change is a racial justice organisation in the United States and produced the 2020 report, Normalizing Injustice: The Dangerous Misrepresentations that Define Television's Scripted Crime Genre[62]. The report states that it is *'A comprehensive study of how television's most popular genre excludes writers of color, miseducates people about the criminal justice system and makes racial injustice acceptable.'*

The report studied 26 crime related television series on network and streaming services and 353 randomly selected episodes, which was approximately 70–80% of episodes per series. The series studied were:

- The Blacklist
- Blindspot
- Blue Bloods
- Bosch
- Brooklyn Nine-Nine
- Bull
- Chicago P.D
- Criminal Minds
- Elementary
- Goliath
- Hawaii Five-O
- How to Get Away with Murder
- Law & Order SVU
- Lethal Weapon
- Luke Cage
- Mindhunter
- Narcos
- NCIS
- NCIS Los Angeles
- NCIS New Orleans
- Orange is the New Black
- Seven Seconds
- Shades of Blue
- Sneaky Pete
- S.W.A.T
- 9-1-1

The Normalizing Injustice report stated at page 30 that *'The great majority of series that represented Criminal Justice Professionals (CJP's) committing wrongful actions, did so in a way that normalized them.'* The exceptions were *Seven Seconds* and *Goliath*. The report also found that series also go as far as to make wrongful actions seem good or justified and fail to portray the actions as wrong, or portray the real impact such wrongful actions have on the people who are on the receiving end of such behaviours.

The Normalizing Injustice report explains that wrongful actions in such dramas are generally committed by a 'Good Guy', giving the impression that the Good Guy needed to engage in wrongful action to catch the bad guys. It listed the wrongful actions as:

- Coercion and intimidation
- Corruption
- Lying and tampering
- Violence and abuse
- Overt racism
- Illegal searches

- Rules violations
- Illegal actions
- Wrongful actions

The report asserted that excessive force is rarely portrayed and when it is, it is regarded as not harmful. Alarmingly, the report referred to the Person of Color Endorser. This is where a person of colour's character is used to justify or endorse the wrongful actions being perpetrated by the police. In respect of the need to change, the report states the drama's viewed tended to regard the need for change in terms of requiring more power and authority and more money and manpower. The programmes rarely, if ever, addressed the need for systemic change or real reform, particularly in respect of race.

RENDERING RACISM INVISIBLE

The Normalizing Injustice report found that the majority of shows rendered racism invisible. The exception being *Seven Seconds*. Furthermore there was an absence of depictions of racial bias, racial profiling and excessive use of force against people of colour and the harm that excessive force does. The exception to the use of force depiction – albeit not against a person of colour – was *Goliath*.

The Normalizing Injustice report also looked at the make-up of the writers' room in the genre and found it to be predominantly white and male and tended to exclude people of colour and women, and particularly women of colour.

Be in no doubt that most often a Black person's view of and experience with the police is going to be completely different to that of a white person, particularly that of a middle- or upper-class white person. As American paediatrician Dr Benjamin Spock once said in the 1960s: *'Most middle-class whites have no idea what it feels like to be subjected to police who are routinely suspicious, rude, belligerent and brutal.'* It is a shocking indictment of our society that that statement could just as well have applied to this country and still holds true today.

RIGHT OF REPLY

I provided an earlier copy of this chapter to the Metropolitan Police omitting the questionnaires and exercises below. The original chapter did not contain the Baroness Casey Review comments or the Color of Change report. I invited them to respond. I also provided a summary of what the chapter contained. Their response was as follows:

> This is not the same Met as it was 20–25 years ago. We have improved how we investigate and respond to crimes; how we engage and work with our communities; how we develop and support our own staff and have made huge improvements in becoming a more representative workforce. We now provide mandatory diversity training for all officers and staff which promotes respect and understanding towards all communities and have introduced body-warn [sic] cameras so that the encounters our officers have with the public are recorded and are accountable.
>
> Policing is complex and challenging and we strive to ensure we are fair and just. Where we get it wrong we welcome scrutiny and where there are complaints we take these incredibly seriously and expect to be held to account for our actions, including through independent investigations by the Independent Office for Police Conduct.
>
> New Commissioner Sir Mark Rowley has announced a raft of reforms including an uplift in detectives and new technology to overhaul the Met's work to identify police officers and police staff who corrupt the integrity of the Met through misogyny, homophobia, sexism and other abuse.
>
> At the heart of this reform is the new Anti-Corruption and Abuse Command and a new focus on proactively rooting out criminal colleagues.

> It will use the same tactics used to target those engaged in corrupt relationships with criminals, or those whose behaviour corrupts public trust and the Met's integrity. This includes through abuse such as racism and misogyny.
>
> Metropolitan Police Spokesperson

I also wrote to the Cabinet Office as a result of their denials in respect of the existence of institutional racism and they responded as follows:

> The Government takes all forms of racism seriously. The Commission on Race and Ethnic Disparities' report found evidence that outright racism does exist in the UK and made strong recommendations to tackle the issue in this country. The Commission did not doubt the existence of institutional racism within certain organisations – particularly historically. They also recognised that there are wider structural factors which drive racial inequality. Their report highlights many positive examples of cases where ethnic minority groups are succeeding at higher rates – particularly in schools and through higher education. However, they did find evidence that racism and discrimination continue to exist and affect many people's lives. We cannot rule out that some organisations in the UK may be institutionally racist – and that is why we are funding the Equality and Human Rights Commission to strengthen its investigative work. But the Government also believes the term should be applied based on evidence; often the causes of racial disparities are complex and not actually rooted in discrimination or prejudice. The UK is an open, tolerant, and welcoming country with a proud history. We believe in the strength and resilience of our institutions and that we must preserve, strengthen and entrust them to future generations. We trust individuals to use common sense, shared values and rigorous evidence and to encourage

diversity of opinion when discussing race. That is why we published the ambitious Inclusive Britain action plan in March 2022, which sets out a ground breaking strategy to tackle negative racial disparities, promote unity and build a fairer Britain for all. Inclusive Britain sets out a new and positive agenda for change on race and ethnicity in the UK and the actions within it will put us on course towards a more inclusive and integrated society.

Let us consider the entertainment model of the police procedural in Britain:

i.   Usually a male lead detective/officer.
ii. Sometimes a female lead detective/officer.
iii. Almost always white.
iv. Almost always regarded as fair-minded and non-bigoted.
v.   Overall attitude of the drama is: 'We have a great system with a few bad apples.'
vi. Racism rarely addressed.
vii. Corruption rarely addressed (except *Line of Duty*).

....

EXERCISE 9

1. Consider the above; is the summary an accurate reflection of what you have watched?
2. In light of the summary, if you were writing a police procedural what would you consider?
3. If you have written a police procedural, does your drama fit in with the entertainment model or the reality?
4. If you have written a police procedural, are any of your characters stereotypical?
5. If you have characters of colour, have you humanised them?

....

PORTRAYAL

<u>WHAT AREN'T WE SEEING?</u>

→   Institutional racism
→   Everyday casual racism and racist abuse
→   Overpolicing of minority areas
→   Excessive use of force
→   Negative confrontations
→   Negative racial attitudes
→   Brutality
→   Deaths in custody
→   Discriminatory stop and search
→   Failures to investigate
→   Failures in investigations

WHY NOT?

ENTERTAINING RACISM

By now you will be aware of the problems of racism within the British and American police forces. In respect of British policing I would like to refer to two quotes from the 2023 Casey Review. The first is *'some of the worst cultures, behaviours and practices... have been found in specialist firearms units'*. And it went on to recommend that they be disbanded and reset. The second quote comes from page 238: *'We have found racism, misogyny and homophobia in plain sight.'*

The evidence is clear and overwhelming, that police forces in Britain and America are institutionally racist. This is not surprising considering their creation was based on white supremacy and run by white people. In Britain they were created to protect cargo produced from slave labour and in the United States they were created to catch runaway slaves. Brutality and injustice are at their core and remain so today. Yet these organisations are rarely portrayed in that way

137

on television. It is worth reading the Normalizing Injustice report, but also consider British television police dramas that you have watched. Were they shows that rendered racism invisible? Was the force regarded as a great institution with a couple of bad apples? Were wrongful actions committed by the good guy? Think back to the scenes where the officer 'roughed a person up,' or assaulted them, or entered property without a warrant. Were they portrayed as a good guy? Were their actions portrayed as necessary to get the bad guy? Were you shown the real impact of wrongful, criminal and violent behaviour by the police? Was the prevalence of racism portrayed?

There have been exceptional shows in the United States that have portrayed the realities of racism and/or corruption in the police force such as *Black and Blue*, with Naomie Harris, *Seven Seconds* and *Goliath*. Whilst they are not police dramas, *Grey's Anatomy* and more notably *Station 19* have portrayed police racism with real emotional heart.

In Britain there have been some great shows that have portrayed racism and corruption such as *Line of Duty*, *DI Ray* and *Criminal Record*. Worthy of note is *Endeavour,* which has also tackled racism and fascism within its series. What the above shows demonstrate is that the realities of racism can be portrayed and still provide excellent drama.

It is clear that television influences us. It can enter deep into our psyche and have an impact on our beliefs and, as such, our behaviours and that is quite evident when it comes to race and the police. The Casey review stated that people from Black and mixed ethnic groups have lower trust and confidence in the Met, but does accept that white Londoners are losing trust and confidence. The Color of Change report found that 74% of white Americans think that the criminal justice system treats people of colour the same as it treats white people, or even less harshly than white people. 55% of white Americans believe that the criminal justice system is devoid of racial disparities. I would argue that the reasons for the disparities in view are twofold. One is that Black and Asian people are on the receiving end of mistreatment and two, that mistreatment is rarely portrayed in crime dramas. The effect is that many police dramas are simply entertaining racism.

CONCLUSION

I will leave this chapter asking you to spend some time considering the very last question. Why not? Why aren't we seeing the realities of policing? Why aren't we seeing the racism, the corruption and the incompetence? Why is the officer almost always fair-minded, non-bigoted and always successful in apprehending the suspect? Does it have anything to do with maintaining the white racial frame and the notion that white institutions are the best and therefore cannot be flawed or failures? One reason may be because white middle- and upper-class people will probably have completely different notions as to how the police can operate and how they treat Black people and ethnic minorities.

We are all aware of the phrase *'You have to see it to believe it.'* I would say that the realities of policing are not being seen by the wider public because they are not being shown. If it is not being seen then often police misconduct and racism are not going to be believed. If the realities of British police were shown on screen, perhaps it would provide impetus for them to change in a meaningful way.

'Law is not law if it violates the principles of eternal justice.'

Lydia Maria Child

CHAPTER 8

LAW AND ORDER –
PART 2: **THE LEGAL SYSTEM**

INTRODUCTION

A quick and superficial internet search on British law and slavery will undoubtedly take you to a number of links that highlight Britain's role as abolitionists of the slave trade. However, further and in-depth research shows that slavery was enshrined and baked into law via the various monarchs, parliament and common law.

As early as the 1560s Queen Elizabeth I granted licences to and was funding John Hawkyns to trade in slaves. In 1660 Charles II granted a charter to the Royal Adventurer Company. The Charter gave the RAC the monopoly on British trade with West Africa which included trading in slaves. Indeed Holly Brewer[63] asserts at page 766 *'Charles II helped to make buying and selling of people as slaves both fully legal and enforceable across the empire.'* Brewer explains that Charles II used his judges to not only legalise slavery but to have slaves classed as goods or absolute property. Thus the monarch through the courts was able to create and spread a most evil and pernicious lie that human beings could be chattels, property or assets.

In the 1660s the West Indies and North America were colonies of Britain. Whilst they were able to make laws themselves, they answered to Britain and the authority of the British courts and the monarch. In *The Sugar Barons*[64], Matthew Parker points out that enslaved Africans outnumbered the slave owning whites and they feared that *'black slaves would unite with the poor, downtrodden whites and indentured servants to turn the whole system upside down[65]'*. As a result of this danger, Parker explains that the ruling class began to codify and legislate in the hopes that poor whites would choose race over class. This appears to have been the case in the West Indies and the Americas. Laws were introduced to regulate slavery along racial lines. With the inception of that legislation came murder and rape with impunity, brutalisation, torture and systemic racism that would last for hundreds of years. Britain, the Americas and Europe all had legal systems that purported to espouse democratic ideals and the principle of equality, but that was for equality among white people. The US Constitution was created during the time of slavery by and for white men. The UK Parliament operated with a view to keeping power in check and democratising the nation, but again it was for and by white men; women not being allowed to vote and the nation partaking in the Atlantic Slave Trade. Racism then is inherent in western legal systems.

Feagin points out *'Slavery's impact extended well beyond the economy. Each institutional arena in the nation was controlled by whites and was closely linked to other major arenas... Likewise, the religious, legal, educational, and media systems were interlinked with slavery economy... Woven through each institutional area was a broad racist ideology... centred on rationalizing white-on-black domination and creating positive views of whiteness[66]'*. What has that got to do with my script and the modern legal systems we see today, you may ask. Below are some of the issues that surround the justice system.

THE COURTS – REMAND IN CUSTODY AND SENTENCING

The British and American court systems are subject to racial bias and disproportionality. For decades there has been a discrepancy between Black and white defendants in respect of remand in custody and sentence imposed. In the United Kingdom it has long been a critique of the criminal justice system that Black defendants were more likely to receive a custodial sentence than their white counterparts who were convicted of the same or similar offences.

The United States criminal justice system and sentencing practices have decimated the Black community and their families. It is a land that holds itself out to be a bastion of liberty and democracy but it appears to be anything but for its Black citizens when it comes to the criminal justice system. In England and Wales, the maximum time a person can be held in custody before their trial starts is 182 days, extended to 234 during Covid. Those 182 days only extend to cases that are to be tried in the Crown Court. It is 56 days if your trial is going to be heard in the Magistrates' Court. That means the prosecution has 182 days to get its case together and provide all the evidence.

However, in the United States, there doesn't seem to be a time limit. That means you can be held in custody on a charge of shoplifting for five years and the prosecution don't have to have prepared for trial. That means they get to destroy your life with impunity. It also means that if you're innocent you have to choose being wrongly convicted or holding out in the hope justice will be served. Let us humanise this situation. You are a human being, with a family. You have rent or a mortgage to pay and kids to feed. If you are remanded into custody for a long period of time, you are denied full access to your family. You lose your job. If you lose your job then there is a good chance you are losing your home. If you lose your job and your home – and if you ever get out – you will likely not have the funds to get accommodation. You and your family are now destitute and homeless.

That is not liberty and that is not democracy. How can a so-called free country hold someone in detention for years on end without bringing them to trial? Well, the answer is – because the majority of people held that way are Black. It is a different form of slavery.

Kalief Browder, a young Black man age 17, was arrested and charged with theft offences based on sketchy evidence and held in custody for three years. The prosecution asked for a number of continuances. Eventually the charges were dismissed as there was not enough evidence at trial. Browder, having being subjected to constant violence in Rikers Island jail from officers and inmates, committed suicide two years after his release. In Texas, Jerry Hartfield had his conviction overturned in 1980 while in prison. A retrial was ordered but he remained in prison for another thirty-five years before his release was ordered.

In a 2021 article by CalMatters[67] they found that in California 1300 people had been remanded in custody for longer than three years awaiting trial and 330 people had been remanded in custody for five years awaiting trial. The majority of prisoners on remand were Black and Latino. That's five years of incarceration. Of life standing still. Of being brutalised. Of losing your job, your prospects and potentially your good mental health – not to mention your family. At this stage, take a minute to think about their predicament. They are not numbers, they are human beings with feelings, and needs and families and lives and those lives are being trampled upon by the state and that trampling is being done along racial lines.

The Prison Policy Initiative was set up with a view to ending mass incarceration in the United States. On their website (prisonpolicy.org) they say the following: *'From arrest to sentencing, racial and ethnic disparities are a defining characteristic of our criminal justice system... Black Americans in particular are disproportionately likely to be incarcerated and receive the harshest sentences, including death sentences[68]'*. The PPI have produced a number of reports to try and track the incarceration rates. One report of note relating to incarceration in America is the geography of the prison system. In The Racial Geography of Mass Incarceration[69] it states that Black people are incarcerated at a rate five times higher than whites and that prisons are built in white areas. Ethnic minorities are transported to prisons in predominantly white rural areas. The issue is threefold then: first, if white areas are the recipients of prisons that are then filled with Black people, it is clear that the benefits of a job and job security are being awarded to whites only. Second, if whites are only seeing Black people in prison this is only going to entrench racism even further. Finally, if Black people are being incarcerated far away from home or in another state, they will not be able to have support and visitations.

JOINT ENTERPRISE

The law on joint enterprise in the United Kingdom has seen many miscarriages of justice. In effect, people who were present at the scene of a crime and/or were involved in it but not the principal offender have found themselves convicted and facing significant terms of imprisonment. LIBERTY are currently taking the Crown Prosecution Service and the Ministry of Justice to court because they assert that the law on joint enterprise is disproportionately affecting Black men and that racist stereotypes and gang narratives are leading to Black men being unfairly prosecuted. In their 2016 report entitled 'Dangerous Associations: Joint enterprise, gangs and racism[70]', Williams and Clarke found the following:

i. Prosecutors regularly rely on racial stereotypes in relation to Black defendants using a range of signifiers to direct juries to increase the likelihood of conviction of secondary parties.
ii. The gang label is disproportionately attributed to BAME people.
iii. While the gang label is particularly attributed to Black men, very few Black individuals are located within the serious youth violence cohorts.
iv. The gangs discourse was significantly more likely to be cited in the prosecution of BAME joint enterprise defendants.

As the socialisation process of white supremacy and racism is steeped into the criminal system, you could find yourself convicted and spending 14 to 30 years in prison for a crime you did not commit. So, if you are a young Black man or boy and you are an innocent bystander, you could find yourself on trial for murder or grievous bodily harm. That injustice is being meted out to young Black boys and men across the United Kingdom. Even though the case of *Jogee [2016] UKSC 8* found that the criminal courts had taken a misstep in the law relating to joint enterprise because the prosecutions were potentially in error, and judicial directions were definitely in error, one would have thought that the cases resulting in convictions pre the decision in *Jogee [2016]* would be rendered unsafe and overturned. Unfortunately, in the case of *Johnson [2016] EWCA Crim 1613* which consolidated six cases, the Court of Appeal held that a misdirection in law does not render a conviction unsafe. In effect an injustice occurred due to errors of law. Those errors affected Black people and despite the errors, there is still no justice or remedy for many young Black people languishing in jail. In joint enterprise cases the law, facts and state of mind of the defendant are inextricably linked. Thus, if the law was wrong in respect of the defendant's state of mind, and their involvement, then the conviction cannot be safe.

A snapshot of the issues above demonstrates that in Britain and America, Black people – particularly Black men – are being disproportionately incarcerated compared to their white counterparts. Furthermore, that incarceration is often wrong or unjust.

JURIES

Being tried by an all-white jury is problematic for a defendant of colour. The starting point to bear in mind is that you are innocent until you are proven guilty and that requires the presenting and testing of the evidence to a jury who must decide on the evidence alone. If you are Black you have to hope that none of the twelve men and women on the jury are racist.

This has long been an issue in Britain and America. In Britain there have been reports by fellow jurors reporting that members of the jury are making racist remarks about the Black defendants. With a stern warning, those trials have been allowed to continue and, unsurprisingly, the defendants have been convicted. How can it be regarded as a fair trial? Particularly if the jury are influenced by and come to their verdict based on racism as opposed to evidence? Article 6 of the European Convention on Human Rights, which entered into force as a result of the Human Rights Act 1998, is supposed to guarantee the right to a fair trial, but often trials are not stopped when racism on the part of the jury is brought to the court's attention. It cannot be a fair trial when racism comes into play and the defendant is convicted. It does, however, demonstrate white privilege and a lack of understanding of how racism operates and a lack of will to seriously challenge it.

THE COURTS – COURT USERS

One issue is how Black people and people of colour who use the court system are treated by the court and its staff. There have been far too many instances of Black lawyers – particularly Black men – who have been assumed to be the defendant. My own experiences of racism in the court system have been fairly numerous.

On one occasion, the usher assumed my client was the prosecutor. I've entered court rooms and greeted the legal adviser and usher with a hello or good morning, only to be met with stony silence. I've also witnessed those same staff respond to white lawyers with a hello or greeting. *'Perhaps they didn't hear you,'* or *'Maybe they didn't mean it.'* I would hope by now at Chapter 8 in this book you would know that they did hear me, they did mean it and the reason for the stony silence was because of race.

Two years ago in 2022 I was prosecuting in a London court and the Black police officer who was a victim of racial abuse was being cross-examined by a white defence lawyer. The defence solicitor from a London firm said to the officer *'And you didn't think, by golly...'* Now, golly is an offensive word. It is short for gollywog. I know to some white people who say it it means something else and they try to defend the indefensible but honestly, you're just defending racism

147

by defending the use of that word. Anyway, I said in open court, *'You can't use that word it's racially offensive.'*

There is silence in court. The defence solicitor is clearly embarassed. The Chair of the Magistrates Bench, having clearly heard the racially offensive word and my challenge of it, asks the defence solicitor if he is okay. At this stage, I'm gobsmacked. She hasn't called it out, she hasn't asked the Black people on the receiving end if they are okay and she hasn't asked him to apologise. She then asks the defence solicitor if he would like a break at which he says yes. The court rises to give the solicitor who has been racially offensive a break and doesn't bother to ask the Black court users if they are okay.

I raise this with the legal adviser and she says she will raise it with the Bench. The case resumes. At no stage during the day did the Bench say that what happened was inappropriate. They don't say that racism will not be tolerated. Neither do they ask the defence solicitor to apologise nor do they apologise for failing to enquire about the welfare of the Black court users.

Now those three magistrates might not go around using the N word (but who knows), but on that day they certainly engaged in racial discrimination and they certainly engaged in white preference at the expense of Black people and that is one of the issues. Racism is tolerated and even ignored. There was no recognition, no calling it out and no addressing their own role.

On this occasion I called it out but I was the prosecutor and I was in a position of power to do so. Can a Black defendant do that? Can a Black parent in court do that? What would happen to them if they did? If their raising this issue was ignored would the response be to remove them from the court room? If you're Black and a defendant or a junior court user or member of staff, you might not have the power to call it out.

In that same court another colleague lamented a trial where the defendant was caught on video repeatedly calling a Black bus driver monkey. It was there to be heard loudly, clearly and repeatedly. The all-white Bench acquitted on the basis that they couldn't be sure of what was being said and he could have been saying Moon-Key.

Another issue is the constant massacring of ethnic minority names, mine included. It is Lubimbi. LU-BIM-BI. It's not hard by any stretch. I've had judges and members of the Bench call me something completely different, despite me spelling it out and constantly reminding them of how to say it. Now, it is just downright rude and disrespectful to not call someone by their name. I appreciate we all make mistakes sometimes and get things wrong but I'm talking about the constant mispronounciation or coming up with a completely different name. At worst it is racially offensive, at best it is racially insensitive. There is a long history of white people during slavery and colonisation deciding that a person's name was too complicated, or they just couldn't be bothered to say it, so they gave the person of colour another name. And so, making names up because you can't be bothered to say it is just more white colonialism and entitlement. If you are a member of the judiciary, you can't claim it is due to a lack of intellect because you are in a position that is the epitome of the intelligentsia.

PROSECUTIONS

The Lammy Review has suggested that the Crown Prosecution Service is strides ahead in respect of racism, but I would suggest it is going to vary depending on the locality. London CPS and major cities are going to have a more diverse workforce and thus may be in a better position to reflect society and try to address inequalities. There are of course codes of conduct for Crown Prosecutors which must be considered and adhered to when deciding whether or not to bring a prosecution.

There is a two-stage test in determining whether or not to commence prosecution. The first stage is to consider whether there is sufficient evidence to provide a realistic prospect of conviction. If there isn't then a prosecution should not be brought. If there is sufficient evidence then prosecutors must consider the second stage and that is whether or not it is in the public interest to proceed with a prosecution. While there is a list of examples given to demonstrate when it is or is not in the public interest, there is a certain amount of discretion that can be applied and this can be problematic in racial terms as per the section on joint enterprise.

DISCRIMINATION

In Law and Order, individuals are making decisions every day. Now, that decision maker may not hate or dislike a race of people different from their own, but sometimes the issue is one of preference. There will be circumstances where the decision maker prefers to give the benefit of the doubt to the white suspect, despite the evidence. Or the decision maker prefers to believe the white suspect over a person of colour. That is still racism because you are treating another person less favourably, or disadvantaging another person based on colour. That preference can affect decision making in investigations, prosecutions and court proceedings.

The choices you make are based on racial preference or racial discrimination and that is how the White Racial Frame works and the socialisation process of the false notion of white supremacy. Preference is given to white people because deep down the socialisation process has ingrained the idea into many white people that they are better; that they are more deserving of breaks and benefits and Black people are not. There is overt racism and hostility (as per the reports) and then there is racial preference, or discrimination. All of which is having an adverse effect on Black people and ethnic minorities who utilise the system, whether that be as victims, defendants or lawyers.

THE LEGAL PROFESSION

I attended an Equality, Diversity and Inclusion Seminar held by Lincoln's Inn in 2022. As one of 473 Black barristers in the country, I was interested in the findings in relation to race – they were depressing but not surprising.

One salient finding was that Black women earn on average £18,700 less than their white male counterparts. There were three studies completed across the commercial Bar. Again the findings were depressing.

To my mind the session seemed to focus on *'how can we help you (Black people)?'* I didn't hear the word racism used once. This lecture troubled me. The tone was about what can be done to help minorities. Quotas, mentoring, practice management and suchlike were mentioned, together with various schemes. Now, I appreciate that the desire to redress inequality is genuine but the problem I have is that it sees ethnic minorities as a problem group, as a group to be helped, as a group who need a hand up.

We don't need help. We need racism to be eradicated. We need equality of opportunity and that problem lies at the door of white people in the profession. There needs to be education about what racism is and how it manifests, how it came about and how to dismantle the false notion of white supremacy. Not just of white barristers but of clerks too, for they are the ones who decide whom to allocate work to and what fees to charge. There needs to be education on anti-racism and how to combat it in the workplace.

Without facing racism head on and dismantling the white racial frame of white supremacy nothing will change. I can attend a lecture on the same topic in 10 or 20 years time and without addressing racism, without anti-racism education, we will still be having the same conversations.

There are three reports worthy of note. They are the 2021 Race at the Bar: A Snapshot Report[71] which recognises racial disparities and inequalities at the Bar, particularly for Black and Asian women. It also recognises occurrences of bullying, harassment and discrimination and that Black and Asian women were four times more likely to be subjected to bullying and harassment than white men. The second report is the 2022 The Specialist Commercial Bar and Black Inclusion – First Steps[72] which was commissioned by three specialist bar associations, namely the Chancery Bar, the Commercial Bar, and the Technology and Construction Bar. The summary states (page

6) that their work *'points to a culture experienced by Black barristers characterised by profound levels of isolation, dislocation and not belonging'*. The Specialist Bar Report utilised reports and data, they held meetings, had interviews and round table discussions. The report considered all aspects of life at the Specialist Bar including the current practice retention in the context of race and racism. There was clearly a racial disparity when it came to Black students trying to get in. And there was also a recognition of the need for excellence for Black barristers to survive. Indeed one quote was: *'If you are going to come to the Commercial Bar and you have a certain degree of melanin, you need to be exceptional. You cannot just be good. You need to be absolutely phenomenal and even then you are going to have to work four times as hard.'* The report found that there was overt racism from other barristers, clerks, solicitors, the judiciary and lay clients.

I've had experiences of racism at the Bar too. I recall one set of chambers where the senior clerk mostly refused to speak to me or acknowledge my existence for the period I was there. Good morning, hello, goodnight were all met with stony silence.

I've been lucky to have found most of my opposing colleagues to be friendly, professional and courteous. There have been occasions when I have been met with hostility on sight and aggression throughout the whole hearing by a few white men. Now, they don't know me and they've never met me. The only two things they can see are my race and my gender. Having observed them being perfectly nice and civil to white women, I can only conclude the issue was with my race.

Other experiences include being mistaken for the defendant at court – going into a law enforcement building to meet another lawyer in my suit, only to be asked if I'm here for the cleaning job. Being made redundant in a law enforcement position even though I had been in the position longer than my white male counterpart, was more productive than him and held a professional qualification which he didn't. When I sought to challenge the situation I was offered a significant demotion.

I've been at dinner at Lincoln's Inn when a white man spilt a drink all over me. He just walked off. No apology, no assistance, nothing. Was I not worthy of an apology? Again at my Inn when I took my three white guests to dinner, a white male barrister came over and told my white male guest to put his robes on. My guest politely informed him that he wasn't the barrister. Awkward. It got even more awkward as he turned to the white women in turn and asked if they were the barristers. When it came to me there was silence. This man did not appear to be able to accept that a Black woman could be intelligent, educated and, above all, be a barrister. I've had white defendants who have refused to be represented by a Black person.

These are snapshots of my experiences, but I would wager that racism, discrimination, hostility and microaggressions are replicated across the country for Black lawyers.

I also interviewed a Black barrister who had been called to the Bar in the 1980s. She had experienced racism throughout her education and career, and her experiences are summarised below.

Barrister X

Barrister X is a Black woman who practises criminal law in a reputable set of London chambers. She had decided at the age of 14 that she wanted to become a barrister. At secondary school her teachers did not believe she would be able to become a barrister and would say things like *'Would you like to try something else?'* or *'You might not achieve it.'* However, barrister X was clear that at that age her mind was already made up.

Barrister X went on to do her A levels. She said that she was fortunate enough to have a Black history teacher who inspired her and told her that if she aimed high she would achieve it. She subsequently attended a London polytechnic and described the teachers as being strange towards Black students and more helpful to the white students.

She qualified as a barrister in the 1980s and says that trying to get pupillage was a nightmare. I asked her why.

'I had the grades. My face simply didn't fit, but ultimately I achieved a fantastic pupillage.'

Barrister X did not experience racism in her first set of chambers but she did from clients. She recalls going to represent a client in a London court who had been remanded in custody. When she went to visit his cell he said, *'I don't want to be represented by a nig-nog.'* She stated that he wasn't the last person to be racist towards her, but now such behaviour is water off a duck's back. However, it is exhausting. She recalls attending Camberwell Magistrates Court. She was wearing her suit and had her counsel's blue notebook and the brief (identifiable by pink string for criminal briefs tied around the papers); despite clearly being identifiable as a barrister the list caller still assumed that she was a defendant waiting for her representative. She does recall an incidence of bullying from a male barrister at court; however, she is not sure if it was racism, or sexism or both.

Although Barrister X is successful, she says it is a fact that she would be further along in her career if she had been white. She says that she hasn't been clerked as well as other people have been and recalls the set of chambers where the clerk did not like Black people or women and so after a year she left. Two years later that set of chambers accepted that the clerk was engaging in sexism but they still couldn't accept that racism was taking place.

Barrister X explained the clerks could make or break your career as they are responsible for work and contacts. Barrister X realised she had to make her own contacts and states that is how she survived.

In respect of representing young Black men and boys, she said there is always an assumption that they are in a gang. You have to establish and prove they are not in a gang first. She also said that Black people are more likely to go to prison than white people. She recalls two cases that struck her in particular. One involving a Black woman, the other a white woman. Their offending was similar on facts but the Black woman went to prison and the white woman didn't.

I asked Barrister X how the entertainment model compared to the reality of practising law and whether she had any observations. She said in 2017 she suddenly started to see Black people in positions of power in films. One had a Black chief inspector and also a Black DCI. To her it was unreal. Over the last two and a half years there are Black people everywhere in adverts. That is unrealistic. She said they're going to the opposite extreme. They can't seem to get it right. She said a balance is required and that people are asking for representation but she felt the number of Black people appearing in adverts had gone over the top. Barrister X preferred American television to British and made reference to *Suits*. The Black woman who was the lead of the firm was effective and she knew her stuff. That appeared to be the kind of television that barrister X enjoyed.

THE JUDICIARY

Crucial to the justice system in any democracy is the judiciary. In order for a justice system to be fair – and of course for justice to be done – it needs judges who will be fair, independent and unbiased. Unfortunately, when it comes to race and racism this isn't always the case as the evidence suggests.

There have been a number of reviews, research reports, articles and findings in respect of racial bias within the judiciary and in respect of recruitment and retention. Most recently there have been two reports worthy of note. One was the November 2022 report 'Racial Bias and the Bench: A response to the Judicial Diversity and Inclusion Strategy 2020–2025'. The second was the July 2022 *Times* article which highlighted that there was a secret report which had found evidence of widespread judicial bullying and racism by the judiciary, but that the report was not going to be disclosed to the public.

The Judicial Diversity and Inclusion Strategy (JDIS) was launched on 5 November 2020 by Lord Burnett of Maldon, the then Lord Chief

Justice, and he set out four core aims to achieve between 2020 and 2025. Those aims are:

1. Creating an environment in which there is greater responsibility for and reporting on progress in achieving diversity and inclusion.
2. Supporting and building a more inclusive and respectful culture and working environment within the judiciary.
3. Supporting and developing the career potential of existing judges.
4. Supporting greater understanding of judicial roles and achieving greater diversity in the pool of applicants for judicial roles.

The introduction to the JDIS begins by implying that Britain has an internationally renowned judiciary which is the envy of the world. It also states: *'Judicial office holders are appointed on merit following a fair and open competition from the widest range of elligible candidates.'* The JDIS indicates that it is working to improve diversity and that it is taking an anti-discriminatory approach and seeking to promote positive behaviour. Additionally, the JDIS states that in 2020 8% of all court judges were BAME and 4% of High Court Judges and above were BAME; this is in contrast to the Racial Bias and the Bench Report (RBB) 2022.

The RBB report takes issue with the JDIS and the *Equal Treatment Bench Book* (ETBB) – the latter is provided to all members of the judiciary. In respect of the JDIS, it highlighted that there was no mention of racism within the strategy. The report looked at a number of issues within the judiciary namely:

- Racism affecting Black defendants and litigants.
- Racism affecting Black lawyers.
- Judicial appointments and the lack of diversity.

Having considered the above they critiqued the JDIS. The RBB report surveyed legal professionals in May 2022 and received 373 responses. The breakdown of responses by race was as follows:

- Asian – 48 = 12.9%
- Black – 48 = 12.9%
- Mixed – 32 = 8.5%
- White – 214 = 57.4%
- Other – 23 = 6.2%
- Prefer not to say – 8 = 2.1%

The responses suggest that racism within the judiciary is prevalent. The respondents' comments as stated at page 13 were as follows:

'In relation to judges acting in a racially biased way, there have been many and repeated examples.'

'I have seen many instances where the pain and suffering of Black people at the hands of the state is trivialised by judges.'

'I would have to write for pages and pages to express the racism I have seen.'

'Too [sic] many incidents to describe. Main thing is racist sentencing of young Black males.'

'I have seen it in tone, facial expressions and demeanour, as well as explicitly ("you people").'

The respondents also indicated that they had seen racial bias towards court users by the judiciary in the following way as per page 14:

- applicants 44.5%
- defendants 55.6%
- legal professionals 47.9%
- rulings 51.9%

The RBB report indicated that in the criminal justice system there is a problematic disparity in sentencing, particularly against Black men. White men in education are seen as needing to be given a second chance, whereas for Black men in education it is seen as an aggravating feature. Black people were punished more severely and were more likely to be imprisoned, while white people engaging in similar offending were given repeated chances and spared jail. Legal professionals also highlighted the hostility and negative demeanour some of the judiciary engaged in towards Black defendants, resulting in convictions and in harsher sentencing. They also raised particular concern about anti-Black racism, and that Black and Asian court users were more likely to be subjected to racism.

I do recall a number of occasions where I've had to deal with racism from the bench. The first was when I was defending a Black man for possession of drugs at a sentencing hearing. While mitigating on his behalf it was clear that the old white magistrates were completely uninterested in anything I had to say. They had absolutely no regard for his situation and from their body language they were openly hostile to him. He was as we both expected sent to prison for possession of small amounts of Class A drugs.

Another example of racism from the judiciary that I have faced has been in terms of address. Normally I would be addressed as Miss Lubimbi or Madam Prosecutor, or be referred to as the prosecutor. I have been in courts where some judges have simply refused to call me by my name when speaking to my opposing counsel and instead of referring to me as the prosecutor, Madam Prosecutor or Miss Lubimbi it has simply been a very hostile 'she' or 'her'. Another occasion I witnessed was when I was a litigant in person lodging an employment tribunal claim for racial discrimination. I had the first hearing before a judge and I was seeking answers to a race relations questionnaire as I believed I had been discriminated against by a government department. They had refused to answer my initial questions as to why I hadn't been called to an interview when I was more than qualified. The judge said to me *'Well, Miss Lubimbi, anyone can claim racism these days, can't they!'* It was quite clear that she was hostile to me and my case and refused to consider any notion of racism. The government department refused to answer the race relations questionnaire and the judge acceded to the government body's request and ordered me to put a sum of money down if I wanted to continue with the case. At the material time I did not have the funds to do so and the case was dismissed.

Another aspect of judicial racism highlighted in the RBB 2022 report was the judicial bullying and racism towards Black and Asian lawyers. There was evidence of judges refusing to listen, interrupting, or believing that the Black or Asian lawyer was the defendant even when they were robed.

Clearly, this results in a different system if you are Black or Asian. As the report notes at page 8: *'people from ethnic minorities are simply not consistently able to access the same fair-trial rights as white people'*. It also goes on to say that: *'judicial racism is still very much with us, and still influences the fate of the many Black and ethnic minority people who come before the courts as criminal defendants, civil litigants, victims of crimes and bereaved families and survivors'*.

The RBB report also highlights that judicial recruitment and appointment is problematic. They're critical of the JDIS because it points out that only 1% of the judiciary is Black despite Black people being 3% of the population and that there are no Black judges in the Court of Appeal, the High Court, or Supreme Court. It also refers to the JUSTICE reports of 1972 and 1991 regarding racism at the Bench – after 50 years and despite the recommendations, very little appears to have changed. The report suggests that the judiciary appears to be self-congratulatory; that there is no meaningful effort made to combat racism; that there are no steps to engage in anti-racism; and that from an academic point of view, the subject of racism and the Bench is off limits.

The RBB report came up with ten recommendations which I have set out below:

1. Acknowledge institutional racism in the justice system.
2. Organise compulsory and ongoing high-quality racial bias and anti-racist training for all judges and key workers in the justice system.
3. Overhaul the whole process of judicial appointments.
4. Create a critical mass of diverse judges reflective of society rather than occasional and isolated appointments.
5. Publish all judicial research.
6. Revise the *Equal Treatment Bench Book*.

7. Revamp the process for making complaints and ensure all hearings are recorded and easily accessible.
8. Encourage a culture shift towards anti-racist practice by judges.
9. Adopt a multi-pronged approach that sees each of the above recommendations as interrelated and inadequate in isolation or without the support of the other interventions.
10. Institute a robust accountability and implementation strategy to ensure that 'progress' is substantive rather than merely procedural and performative.

Now I would ask you to consider the British legal dramas that you have watched.

....

EXERCISE 10

1. Are they an accurate reflection of what the evidence suggests?
2. How is the legal sytem portrayed in the context of systemic racism?
3. How are the lawyers and judiciary portrayed?
4. Are all the defendants usually Black and impoverished?
5. Following the decision-making of the lawyers, judges and juries – in such dramas are those decisions ever portrayed as flawed or discriminatory?
6. Are a Black or person of colour's view and experience portrayed?

....

So, you want to write a legal drama? If your character is Black and they are a judge, lawyer, litigant or defendant, they are going to be having a completely different experience to that of their white counterparts. I have to say that one of my worst fears (if I was innocent) would be to be tried by an all-white jury. I'm not saying that every juror on the panel is going to be a racist but it only takes one or two to have racist views to sway the rest resulting in them delivering a wrongful verdict of guilty, and this has been demonstrated to have happened. It is also worthy of note that in those cases when racism in the jury has been brought to the attention of the judge, the response has been a direction to not engage in racism instead of ordering a retrial. If a verdict is based on racism it cannot be a fair or correct one.

SO WHAT AREN'T WE SEEING?

→ Innocent Black people being caught up in the system and the impact of that.
→ Racist stereotyping by police and certain prosecutors disproportionately affecting Black people.
→ Lawyers acting in a racist manner.
→ The judiciary and court users engaging in racism through stereotyping, bullying and harassment.
→ Juries having racist views and convicting people of colour.
→ Black lawyers being subjected to racism in various forms.
→ Black parents losing their child to the system.
→ Black people not having their cases investigated when they are victims of crime.

WHY NOT?

Now, I'm not saying your legal drama should always show racism in every episode. I'm saying that it is not realistic or authentic to have a series which never shows racism occurring, or its effects, when it is so prevalent and so damaging. It's not realistic to have a Black barrister or solicitor who never experiences racism inside or outside court.

It is now February 2024 and I am on the final edits of this book. I've had two very similar experiences of racism this month. The first was in a Scandinavian vegan café. There were three tables in use. The first were already eating. The white waitress took the order of the second table and I was on the third. She saw me. Saw me as she took the order of table two. Saw me as she walked back to the counter and saw me from her position behind the counter which was less than ten feet away. I know she saw me because we made eye contact. I sit and wait for at least five minutes, my order has not been taken. I wait a few minutes more and still no order. Minutes later a white woman enters and sits down. The same white waitress goes to her table in under a minute to take her order. I challenge this. She lies and says *'I'm sorry I didn't see you there.'* I challenge her lies and speak to the manager, who immediately takes her side. Ethical when it comes to animals perhaps, but clearly not when it comes to the treatment of Black people.

The same thing happens in another café a couple of weeks later. Four tables. Two have already been served. I am less than eight feet away from the counter. The white and Asian counter staff behind the counter see me. They know I've been waiting nearly ten minutes. A white couple enters and two minutes later the Asian counter staff member takes the white couple's order. I go to the counter and challenge him. He tells me he was told to take their order first. The white woman behind the counter tells me she didn't see me – she did. I leave both establishments. I refuse to be treated like a second-class citizen. I refuse to spend my money in establishments that are engaging in blatant racism and then gaslighting me about it.

Like I said in chapter 1, rain and racism appear out of nowhere and happen frequently. A great example of everyday racism was portrayed in the gripping and glossy UK legal drama *Showtrial*. In one of the episodes Black duty solicitor Cleo Roberts appears to have established a rapport with her white client Talitha Campbell. Talitha makes a racist comment and the shock, hurt and anger is palpable.

In America some great legal dramas have also explored racism in a legal and everyday context. *How to Get Away with Murder* starring Viola Davis explores issues of race in her personal life and in the criminal justice system and disproportionate sentencing. *The Good Wife* did some great scenes with Cush Jumbo who joins the firm and every time she is introduced to a white member of staff, the staff member refers to another Black colleague and say that *'she will like her'.* Assuming that just because the colleagues are Black, they will like each other. *The Good Fight* saw Diane Lockhart lose her fortune and job and join the predominantly Black firm Reddick, Boseman & Kolstad. The firm is frequently harassed by state power as it takes on a number of cases relating to police racism and brutality. Finally *Seven Seconds* portrayed how inherent racism and white privilege are in the US criminal justice system when it came to bail and sentencing.

It is not realistic to live in a racist society made up of people from all walks of life, yet put one section of society on a pedestal and claim that they are above racism and that racism is not happening. Unfortunately this seems to happen quite a lot in legal dramas. Racism is often rendered invisible. The courts are seen as neutral and dispensing justice and the structural inequalities are not portrayed. Having read through this chapter, if you are writing a legal drama consider what you have written so far and ask if it is credible in respect of race, or is it maintaining the illusion that all is well from a racial perspective?

'Racism has never been put in a critical context by the media in this country. When it comes to fighting racism, the media are part of the problem. They perpetuate myths and stereotypes about Black people. They lie by omission, distortion and selection. They give racists respectability.'

Stuart Hall, Cultural Theorist,
Open Door – It Ain't Half Racist Mum **(BBC, 1979)**

CHAPTER 9

THE MEDIA

The above quote was made in 1979 but in many respects still holds true in 2024. Consider the hateful and divisive headlines that have furnished the front pages of many British tabloids over the last decade. This chapter will examine racism within the press and compare it to their portrayal in film and television and how the media portray themselves. I will briefly consider how the media covers war, missing people, celebrities and royalty, Black people as victims of state killings, and the fight for racial justice. Having considered each topic, I would suggest that the media not only has a problem with racism, but that it is hostile to racial justice.

Most people turn to the mainstream media for information relating to news and current affairs on a national and international level. It won't be in dispute that most media outlets are regarded as having a political leaning. In Britain for example it is left, right or centre. Some regard themselves as wholly independent of any political bias.

Each media outlet has a specific format. In television news there is a presenter in the studio presenting. The lead story is portrayed first and there is almost always a journalist at the location of the incident telling the viewer what has happened and then giving their opinion on the circumstances and predictions of what will happen next. Various people are interviewed and shocking images follow. In the printed press there is always a headline article which dominates the front page. The remaining publication is filled with a number of other stories and then opinion pieces on the current and pressing issues and stories of the day.

Western media organisations often regard themselves as the gold standard in journalism. Praise such as *'fiercely independent'*, and *'fair-minded'* are often bandied about; indeed in elite circles some may even agree with this analysis. The press regard themselves – and indeed are often portrayed – as institutions that are a vanguard of democracy. They tell you that they bring truth to power, that they work tirelessly and fearlessly to expose corruption, often at great personal sacrifice, and sometimes they pay the ultimate price with their lives. The press are regarded as an institution that represents the underdog. In some circumstances that may well be true but the media as a whole is far from independent and in many ways maintains the status quo; that is one of the social constructs of white supremacy, and the media often perpetuates if not increases the racism that exists in our society today.

WAR

When I started writing this book in 2022 the Russia/Ukraine war was in progress, and dominating television and print news. Western reporters were reporting from the Ukraine. Below are some examples of modern-day media racism that can be seen in the reporting of the Ukraine war quotes for example:

> *'Now the unthinkable has happened to them. And this is not a developing Third World nation. This is Europe.'*
> Lucy Watson – ITV

'But this isn't a place, with all due respect, like Iraq or Afghanistan
that has seen conflict raging for decades. You know, this is a
relatively civilised, relatively European – I have to choose those
words carefully, too – city where you wouldn't expect that or
hope it's not going to happen.'
Charlie D'Agata – CBC (reporting from Kyiv)

'Just to put it bluntly, these are not refugees from Syria... They
are Christians, they are white.'
Kelly Kobella – NBC

And on it went, the constant reminder of white supremacist views.
Europe is civilised because it is full of white people unlike those 'non-
white' countries that are, by virtue of these statements, uncivilised.
Nations they regard as 'third world' which have 'failed to develop'.
What is breath-taking is the sincerity with which they believe their
false narratives and that they fundamentally failed to know their
history. What is also breath-taking is the unchecked racism that is
wrapped up in so-called reporting.

First and foremost it would behove the journalist to know that
Iraq's conflicts are as a result of American and Western intervention.
Saddam Hussein was a puppet of the West. His rise to power
came about through Western backing. During his reign of terror he
oversaw and was responsible for mass murder, mass incarceration
and brutalisation. Why was he supported or tolerated by the West?
Because he was in direct opposition to Iran. Oh wait, Iran: a country
whose leader was overthrown by the CIA and MI6 and another dictator
inserted. Once Saddam Hussain was no longer a useful puppet
that could be controlled, the West set about ensuring the country's
destruction, not to mention stealing its wealth. Despite being told
that sanctions would harm both child and civilian populations and
should not be imposed, Britain and America under Thatcher and
Reagan imposed them. As a result, it is estimated that half a million
children under five perished. Two wars systematically destroyed the
country, society and, as a result of war crimes committed by British
and American troops (the latter setting up rape camps), ultimately

167

led to civil war and the creation of ISIS. So when this reporter says Iraq has been warring for decades the glaring omission is that the warring has been created by America and Britain. But of course, he's not going to say that because there is the notion of white civility to maintain. Again, Afghanistan with its complicated history has not been helped by Western intervention from the outset. Twenty years and a trillion dollars later the British abandoned the interpreters to die as a thank-you for their assistance. They were able to send a plane and rescue the dogs though!

Civilised Ukraine on the other hand, which has a neo-Nazi problem, is the cause célèbre of the white Western media. The media messages are loud and clear: *'Now that the other side is white, we should be appalled that they are dying in a war – unlike brown people.'* Here the suggestion is that Europe is civilised and, with the exception of America, everywhere else isn't. The racist statements expressed are as pernicious as they are disturbing and false, but this is the issue with the white racial frame. Statements such as these are often agreed with. They are very rarely interrogated by the mainstream. Many Europeans and Americans will agree with the statement and not see anything wrong with what has been said and that is because of the socialisation process of white supremacy.

But let us interrogate this 'civilised Europe equals peaceful' narrative. I couldn't begin to list the number of wars that Europeans have fought between themselves save to say:

Hundred Years' War	Anglo-Spanish War
World War One	Thirty Years' War
World War Two	Seven Years' War
Crimean War	Napoleonic Wars
Anglo-French War	Albigensian Crusade

They are just a few of the wars fought on European soil between Europeans. There were a number of brutal and bloody wars fought by Europeans in the West Indies, America and South America. The depravity of the Crimean War led to the initiation of the Geneva

Convention. Then we have the barbarism and genocides that Europe engaged in on the African, Asian and American continents. It is worth taking the time to research how many brutal and bloody coups the Americans, the British and the French have orchestrated. It is worth researching how many murderous tyrants they have supported and the crimes against humanity that took place.

If the Europeans were not warring with each other, they were committing genocide and stealing land in Africa, Asia and the Americas. Only in the late twentieth century did some African nations achieve independence from their European colonisers and the African fight for independence was met with barbarous and depraved violence from their European oppressors. In *Imperial Reckoning* Caroline Elkins writes about the Kenya Emergency. She gives a gripping and forensic account of the British interning hundreds of thousands of Kenyans, engaging in mass rape, mass murder, mass torture, brutalisation and medical experimentation – all the while denying in parliament that it was taking place.

In Kenya, Elkins explains, British racism was systematic and overt. The indigenous people were systematically incarcerated and tortured, women systematically raped in front of husbands and fathers. Children were subjected to medical experiments. The prisoners were beaten and made to work. Despite the Universal Declaration of Human Rights being drafted with significant input from the British, it was deemed not to apply to Black people and so the aforementioned happened.

Kenya is just one snapshot of the British colonising a country, but that brutal colonisation was replicated across the African and the Asian continents. Other countries engaging in colonisation were the Italians, the French, the Germans and the Belgians and they were all committing atrocities for over one hundred years. Yet these atrocities are rarely talked about, and even when European colonisation in Africa and Asia is, it is regarded as a civilising mission in the consciousness of Western minds. The horrors of colonisation are not part of the mainstream consciousness and have in many ways been erased from the history books. So, it is a dark and humorous irony when reporters talk about European or Western civilisation for it is a lie. So, when the media says this is Europe, it is civilised, any informed Black person or person of colour will, I suspect, be raising a bemused eyebrow because Europe has been anything but civilised to other nations and to each other for many years.

The concept of calling nations developing countries or Third World is also problematic. Not just because Third World is offensive, but because it suggests that these nations have been unable to develop. There are various charters and conventions in international law that espouse the principles of national sovereignty and self-determination. But this right to self-determination is a lie. Ask some of the African nations or South American or Middle Eastern countries if they have had the right to self-determination. The answer will be no. Through colonisation, unfair trading, wars and coups those countries have been destabilised and destroyed. The West, particularly America, will not let any nation prosper if it is in conflict with its own economic interests, even if it means funding a coup and putting in place a mass-murdering tyrant.

The concept of civilised Europe and developing countries are views from a white racial frame with white supremacy at the heart of its ideology. The issue with the WRF is that untruths and distortions are used to support it. These are the messages that are conveyed around the world through Western media thus perpetuating the same ideology.

MISSING WHITE WOMEN SYNDROME

Nothing drives the press into a frenzy – after war and shootings – more than a missing white woman. Watch the news in the United Kingdom and you'd think only white women ever go missing. Not particularly white men and never Black people. In respect of the missing white woman, it does attract attention and headlines for days. In some cases it seems it's a story stuck in the consciousness.

Let me start by saying that anyone going missing is a cause for concern. It is a parent's and loved one's worst nightmare but if you break it down statistically you will see that white women are not the majority of people who go missing. So why do they attract so much attention? Or, alternatively, why do boys aged 12–17, the largest group of missing people, not attract so much attention? Why do Black people, who disproportionately go missing, also not attract any attention?

FACTS AND FIGURES TAKEN FROM MISSINGPEOPLE.ORG.UK

By the end of March 2020, 5300 people had been missing for over a year; roughly 1700 of them were children. They had been abused, trafficked or sexually exploited. The starting point has to be the police (see Chapter 6). Their lack of interest in investigating people of colour going missing has already been discussed. If you are worthy of police attention they will engage the help of the press.

In an article dated 24 October 2016[73] the Liverpool Echo stated that *'Around 250,000 people go missing in the UK every year.'* Quoting Paul Joseph, Manager at Missing People, the article goes on to say *'Around 97% of missing people either come home or are found dead within a week. And around 99% have come home, or been found dead within a year.'*

UK MISSING PERSONS UNIT 2020/21 – MISSING INCIDENTS

Below is a breakdown from page 9 of the missing people during 2020 and 2021 in England and Wales taken from the Statistical Tables for the Missing Persons Data Report.

Female	Male	Trans	Unknown
73,389	87,862	206	2,078
44.9%	53.7%	0.1%	1.3%

A statistical breakdown of missing incidents in England and Wales by age is to be found at page 11 and is as follows:

Age	Number	%
0–11	3,770	2.3
12–17	89,397	55.5
18–39	42,303	26.3
40–59	17,754	11
60+	7,521	4.7
Unknown	256	0.2

In respect of race, the 2020/21 figures are set out below:

Race	Number	%
White N. European	107,644	60.5
White S. European	2,996	1.7
Black	16,602	9.3
Asian	6,809	3.8
Chinese, Japanese, S.E. Asian	423	0.2
Middle Eastern	1,153	0.6
Unknown	42,197	23.7

N.B. The above numbers in respect of race are taken from page 12 of the statistics, add up to 99.8%. The statistics say 100%, so it is not clear who makes up the missing 0.2%.

In 2019/20 some of the missing figures were significantly higher and the snapshot is set out below:

Female	Male	Trans	Unknown
131,062	170,757	319	24,017
40.2%	52.4%	0.1%	7.4%

N.B. The above numbers in respect of gender are taken from page 8 of the statistics, add up to 100.1%. The statistics say 100%, so it is not clear who makes up the additional 0.1%.

Age				Number		%
0–11				7,992		2.4
12–17				168,629		51.7
18–39				64,696		19.8
40–59				26,541		8.1
60+				13,235		4.1
Unknown				45,32		13.8

Age	0–11	12–17	18–39	40–59	60+	Unkn.
Female	2,337	75,896	23,586	8,416	4,376	119
Male	5,092	83,378	36,979	16,522	8,165	168
Trans	0	185	108	23	3	0
Unkn.	123	548	494	224	138	4,225
Total	7,552	160,007	61,167	25,185	12,682	4,512
%	2.8	59.0	22.6	9.3	4.7	1.7

N.B. The above two tables are taken from pages 11 and 13 of the statistical data. Table 1 provides different missing figures for people in England and Wales to Table 2. The percentages in Table 1 total 99.9% and the percentages in Table 2 total 100.1%; both are marked as 100% in the statistical data.

Ethnicity	Female	Male	Trans	Unknown	Total E&W
White N. European	72,995	91,082	225	673	164,975
White S. European	2,642	3,522	9	19	6,192
Black	11,703	19,499	33	66	31,301
Asian	4,902	6,413	9	55	11,379
Chinese, Japanese, S.E. Asian	321	359	0	9	689

Middle Eastern	713	1,762	0	14	2,489
Unknown	21,454	27,667	43	4,916	54,080

The data above clearly shows that the majority of missing people are men and that boys aged 12 to 17 years of age are the highest category of missing people.

In all data sets there were more men than women who went missing, and it is clear that the most at risk group are boys aged 12–17 years of age. The 2019/20 report showed that in London there were 18,676 missing Black people which was 36.1% of the Metropolitan Police missing person statistics. However, according to the UK government's own census data[74], Black people were only 13.5% of London's population. In the 2021 report, Black Londoners made up 31.3% of the missing statistics, which again demonstrates an over-representation of missing Black people.

According to official data, in 2019/20 96% of missing cases resulted in no harm. There were 955 fatal outcomes and by 31 March 2020 there were 4,543 long-term missing people, of which 1,687 were children. Of the unidentified bodies there were 33 men and 8 women. So why is it that missing boys and over-represented missing Black people have not made news?

Gwen Ifill, an American journalist, suggested that the mainstream media (MSM) covers missing white women more than missing women of colour, the latter being rarely covered. In Taylor Ardrey's article at Insider.com dated 23 September 2021[75] *'Experts say the "Missing White Woman Syndrome" leaves girls of color disproportionately out of news coverage.'* Ardrey points out racial disparities when it comes to the US media's reporting of missing white women who are given significantly more coverage than missing women of colour, who are rarely ever covered by the mainstream. Citing Dr Kaye Wise Whitehead, she states: *'women of colour are not seen as damsels in distress. There are tropes around the "angry Black woman", "the strong Hispanic woman" that we don't have to be lifted up, protected and centred'.* Of those who went missing in the United Sates in

2020, nearly 40% were people of colour. In Wyoming 700 indigenous people, 85% of them children, were reported missing over the last decade – they did not get the coverage given to the disappearance of Gabby Petito (a young white female), who went missing in that same state in August 2021.

It appears to be a phenomenon of the European and North American press. Zach Sommers states that Missing White Women Syndrome exists and considers the threshold and intensity of coverage in his article 'Missing White Woman Syndrome: An Empirical Analysis of Race and Gender Disparities in Online News Coverage of Missing Persons (2016)[76]'. Having studied official statistics and analysed the data, he found that MWWS existed and that Black women were under-represented in the media.

Given that boys aged 12–17 years make up the majority of missing people in the United Kingdom, with the exception of the Moors murder victims, when was the last time you saw a television or national newspaper article about a missing boy? Given that Black people are 3% of the population yet 14% of missing person statistics, has the media ever brought this to your attention?

BLACK PEOPLE AS VICTIMS OF CRIME AND THE MEDIA

In his article, Ryan Erfani-Ghettani[77] asserts that the right-wing media has a hostile attitude towards anti-racism. This is evidenced by their reporting of events that involved either Black people dying at the hands of the police, or Black people engaging in marches and anti-racist activism.

THE MEDIA COVERAGE OF BLACK DEATHS

Erfani-Ghettani suggests that the media has a role in denying justice for the bereaved of those who have been unlawfully killed by the state. Rather than the focus being on scrutinising police wrongdoing Erfani-Ghettani says Black victims are smeared as *'too strong'* or 'too volatile' or 'too clever for their own good and so have brought their deaths upon themselves'. He refers to the police shooting of Jermaine Baker in 2015 who was shot while possibly asleep at the wheel of his car. Erfani-Ghettani states that the *Daily Mail* erroneously stated that Baker was linked to the Bloodline Gang. He also points to *The Sun*'s Kelvin MacKenzie's statement when he declared, 'He cared not one jot that Baker had been shot and I'm quite pleased he is dead.'

Erfani-Ghettani also cites the 1985 reporting of Cynthia Jarrett at Broadwater Farm as another example of press hostility. Having illegally entered Cynthia Jarrett's home, the police allegedly pushed her to the ground and she suffered a heart attack and died. According to Erfani-Ghettani, the police pushed a narrative that the fault lay at Miss Jarrett's daughter's door as she had an anti-police and aggressive attitude, which in turn led to negative portrayals of the victim.

A further incident referred to by Erfani-Ghettani is Joy Gardner's fatal encounter with the police in 1993 in Tottenham, London. The police shackled Miss Gardner and then wrapped thirteen feet of tape around her nose and mouth. Bernie Grant, MP for Tottenham, had become involved in both cases and was lambasted by the press. *The Sun* ran the headline: 'Don't call me barmy Bernie' and described him as peeling a banana and juggling an orange.

Peaceful protests have been portrayed as 'a gospel of violence'. Secondary to the issue of negative portrayal is the immediate response to any criticism of the police in the context of racial injustice being perpetuated by them against the Black community. Erfani-Ghettani asserts that it is often politicians and the media who openly question – despite the unlawful and fatal encounters – whether the police have enough powers. It is, in my opinion, a frightening mindset and ideology to perpetuate. An executive armed force being able to act unlawfully and with no accountability affects all citizens, not just Black ones and the force in that circumstance is illegitimate and anathema to democracy. It is worth going through some of the deaths of Black people at the hands of the police and examining the media's response. Then ask yourself the question: if a white person had been killed in such a way, would the response from the press be the same?

BLACK PEOPLE AS VICTIMS OF CRIME

With the New Cross Massacre unsolved as a result of a woeful investigation and the police's decision to blame the victims, there was a day of action and a march. Rather than focus on the purpose of the march, i.e. police incompetence and structural racism, the press chose to focus on the small minority of people that had caused trouble. The trouble that ensued was minor and yet thousands of people had attended the protest and most marched peacefully. Distortion and untruths are tactics repeated by the police and the press, seemingly in conjunction with each other, and such behaviour was demonstrated in the 1989 Hillsborough disaster where ultimately 97 people lost their lives. The press and the police released a number of untrue statements about the Liverpool fans and chose to defame and vilify the dead victims.

The modus operandi of the press was repeated again when a day of action was organised in respect of the murder of Stephen Lawrence. The *Daily Mail* placed an article about Stephen Lawrence and his family in the centre of an article about violence and riots that were unrelated and had taken place the week before. Neville Lawrence, Stephen's father, had carried out work at Paul Dacre's house and on that occasion was able to speak to him directly and rectify the situation. It was after that that the *Daily Mail* became supporters of the Lawrences and went on to publish the now famous headline naming and showing the murderers. However, if Neville Lawrence had not known Paul Dacre, the story about an innocent Black man who had been brutally murdered would have remained a smearing one.

I draw your attention to Officer Anthony Long who had apparently been dubbed by the Metropolitan Police Chiefs as *'their very own serial killer'* due to his history of shooting suspects dead. Long had shot dead Azelle Rodney who was 24 at the time. Once again, the press falsely claimed Rodney had been carrying a gun. Despite having no lawful reason for shooting Azelle Rodney, Long was cleared of murder. Despite his serial killer tendencies, the press went on to report a narrative in favour of Long as opposed to the victim's.

MISTAKEN IDENTITY OF HIGH PROFILE BLACK PEOPLE AND BLACK CELEBRITIES

This appears to be a constant flow of white television presenters on television in Britain and America and is evident that a lot of white people think that we all look alike. In the alternative, they just don't see us and don't bother to really look. In 2020 the BBC used images of LeBron James instead of Kobe Bryant. They also mistook Dawn Butler MP for Marsha de Cordova. In the United States Samuel Jackson was mistaken for Laurence Fishburne and Octavia Spencer was misidentified as Viola Davis and Seal has been mistaken for Michael Clarke Duncan. The most incredulous was an article posting a photograph of Oprah Winfrey and claiming it was Shonda Rhimes. The examples above are just a small sample of well-known Black people being mistaken for other well-known Black people. I doubt that the media would have dared to interview or post a photo of a white A-List celebrity without at least bothering to ascertain who they were.

FOOTBALLERS

With the possible exception of the Duchess of Sussex, it seems to be rich young Black men who attract most of the ire of the right-wing press, and they are subjected to vitriolic and hateful headlines. Some notable examples are Raheem Sterling, Marcus Rashford and Tosin Adarabioyo. Negative headlines about Raheem Sterling portrayed him as greedy and cheap, referred to his 'long-suffering' girlfriend and, most egregious of all, put a picture of him next to a story about drug dealing that had absolutely nothing to do with him whatsoever. Unsurprisingly, with a campaign of racial hatred against him by the media, Raheem Sterling has been subjected to racist abuse online, in the press and on the street. He has even been the victim of a racially aggravated assault.

Marcus Rashford has also been the victim of media race-baiting. The fact that he bought five properties with his earnings while campaigning for free school meals was clearly dog-whistle racism. Finally, Tosin Adarabioyo was also subjected to negative headlines for buying a house. It is worth comparing the headlines of the three Black footballers to white footballers who were in the same position, particularly Phil Foden and David Beckham. All have bought houses for themselves and their families. The Black footballers are portrayed negatively as flash, bling, or hypocrites, and are subjected to insults and negative portrayals. While the white footballers are portrayed as family men, close knit, successful, good guys.

You may even at this stage of the book wish to make excuses for the media and not believe the differences in treatment are down to race. I would ask you at this stage: why are you so reluctant and unwilling to accept racism was the reason for this adverse treatment? Why, despite the evidence in the last few chapters, are you not willing to accept the scale of the problem? It is often the case that those engaging in racism publicly and perniciously will deny it, even though the headlines are there to be seen as are the comparators. It is not just a right-wing problem, it is a media problem. Many sections of the press run stories that affect Black people in negative ways. One notable victim is Jamelia where the press ran clickbait stories about her step-brother. Having had no link to him for over 30 years, she was yet the focus of the story relating to his actions. The BBC, the *Mail*, the *Mirror*, the *Daily Star* and *The Sun* all ran the story putting her front and centre of a criminal case that had absolutely nothing to do with her. Jamelia spoke publicly about the impact this had on her both financially and emotionally. In the *Guardian*, Jamelia also highlights the different treatment Ferne McCann received by way of comparison. Ferne McCann's ex-boyfriend received twenty years imprisonment for throwing acid at people in a nightclub, causing them various injuries. Ferne was portrayed as a victim and in a sympathetic manner by the media.

MEGHAN MARKLE, THE DUCHESS OF SUSSEX

No one has attracted as much racial hatred and racism from the media as Meghan Markle has. The press will deny to the hilt that they have been racist towards her but the headlines – of which there are many – have been racist, hateful and relentless. They fit into two categories: the racist headlines and the headlines campaign compared to Kate Middleton which clearly show racial discrimination. Below are some of the racist headlines in respect of the Duchess of Sussex:

Harry's girl is (almost) straight outta Compton – Daily Mail (2016)

Harry to marry into gangster royalty? – Daily Star (2016)

Yes, they're joyfully in love. So why do I have a niggling worry… – Daily Mail (2017)

…rich and exotic DNA – Daily Mail (2016)

Tweet comparing baby Archie to a chimpanzee – Danny Baker (2019) (was a BBC presenter at the time)

The real problem with Meghan Markle: she just doesn't speak our language – Telegraph (2020)

When the story topic is exactly the same, Kate is portrayed positively and Meghan negatively by comparison. Ellie Hall in her *BuzzFeed* article dated 13 January 2020 collated a list of twenty stories that highlighted the different treatment – and, I would say, racist double standards. Take a look at the articles below. I would ask you to read and consider it before continuing.

DAILY MAIL – 21 March 2018 Not long to go! Pregnant Kate tenderly cradles her baby bump while wrapping up her royal duties ahead of maternity leave – and William confirms she's due any minute now	*DAILY MAIL* – 26 January 2019 Why can't Meghan Markle keep her hands off her bump? Experts tackle the question that has got the nation talking: Is it pride, vanity, acting – or a new age technique?
EXPRESS – 14 September 2017 Kate's morning sickness cure? Prince William gifted with an avocado for pregnant Duchess	*EXPRESS* – 23 January 2019 Meghan Markle's beloved avocado linked to human rights abuse and drought, millennial shame
DAILY MAIL – 16 December 2016 Carole wins granny war! Duke and Duchess of Cambridge will spend second 'private' Christmas with the Middleton family rather than joining the Queen at Sandringham	*DAILY MAIL* – 13 November 2019 Doesn't the queen deserve better than this baffling festive absence? RICHARD KAY examines the impact of Prince Harry and Meghan Markle's decision not to spend Christmas with the royal family
DAILY MAIL – 17 January 2014 Kate and Wills Inc: Duke and Duchess secretly set up companies to protect their brand – just like the Beckhams	*DAILY MAIL* – 9 January 2020 A right royal cash in! How Prince Harry and Meghan Markle trademarked over 100 items from hoodies to socks SIX MONTHS before split with monarchy – with new empire worth up to £400m
THE SUN – 18 April 2017 STIFF UPPER LIP Prince William blasts monarchy's stiff upper lip tradition and backs Harry's admission of his mental anguish after death of mother Diana	*THE SUN* – 23 October 2019 ROYAL RIFTS Prince Harry and Meghan ditched British stiff upper lip – is this a good thing? Sun parents and kids are torn

DAILY MAIL – 4 May 2011 HOW KATE SCENTED THE ABBEY… It was reported that new Duchess of Cambridge requested her favourite scented candles and toiletries from luxury fragrance brand Jo Malone be delivered to scent the Abbey	*DAILY MAIL* – 30 November 2018 Kicking up a stink: 'Dictatorial bride' Meghan wanted air fresheners for 'musty' 15th-century Chapel… but the Palace said no
DAILY EXPRESS – 29 August 2011 Why you can always say it with flowers	*DAILY EXPRESS* – 13 October 2019 Royal wedding: How Meghan Markle's flowers may have put Princess Charlotte's life at risk

Meghan Markle left the Royal Family in 2020 and after the Netflix documentary *Meghan & Harry*, she has rarely commented to the media and yet the British tabloid press continue to bombard the public with negative headlines about her to the point of obsession. No other Royal appears to attract such negativity even if their behaviour would warrant a measure of opprobrium.

RACISM IN THE MEDIA

While the press may argue that they are not racist, I would argue that articles relating to Black people when they are successful, victims of crime, fighting for racial justice or marrying into royalty suggest differently. This is not surprising. Going back to the quote from 1979 at the beginning of this chapter it still holds true today. The quote came from a documentary called *Open Talk: It Ain't Racist Mum* which was presented by Stuart Hall and Maggie Steed. The documentary is available on YouTube and is well worth watching. The presenters took issue with the racist television shows being broadcast at the time because they were (rightly) concerned that most white people in Britain believed the racist stereotypes that were being portrayed. They also took issue with British documentaries and chat shows. Through various clips they demonstrated that broadcasters and journalists were allowing racism to go unchallenged and that racist assertions and accusations were unsubstantiated. They were also concerned that broadcasters were giving airtime to racists such as Enoch Powell whose views were not challenged. What was clear from the show's clips was that racism within broadcasting and journalism seemed to be commonplace and acceptable from the top of the organisation to the bottom. Today, racism in the media still persists.

In her *Press Gazette* article dated 1 April 2021, Aisha Majid revealed the findings of a survey that had been undertaken in respect of racism and the media[78]. The findings were as follows:

- 2 in 5 (41%) of journalists had personally experienced or witnessed racism or bigotry in the newsroom.
- 55% said the same regarding tabloids.
- 53% said the same of broadsheet press.
- 59% (3 in 5) said the same in broadcast media.
- 74% (534) of Black journalists had personally experienced or witnessed racism.
- 37% of white journalists had witnessed or experienced it.

The report is a shocking indictment of the lack of diversity in newsrooms, the casual and overt racism and the racial prejudice in respect of which stories will be run. The survey suggests that to run a story about a murder victim, the victim should be white. Further, that there was no interest in running stories about the Black community unless, I would add, it is a negative, stereotypical and racist story.

So let's look at how the media industry compares to the reality; in order to do that I will be looking at editors and newspapers and newsrooms. Think back to films about newspapers breaking stories. Consider the journalists and editors who are usually responsible for the paper in films and television.

- They are almost always white.
- They are almost always fair-minded and dogged.
- They are always in pursuit of the truth.
- They put their lives, reputation or career on the line and, despite overwhelming odds, they get the scoop.
- They hold power to account and thanks to them democracy is maintained or restored.

Now ask the question:

WHAT AREN'T WE SEEING?

→ A pressroom with an all-white environment
→ Racism, xenophobia which is casual or overt in press and newsrooms
→ Unethical decision-making leading them to run untrue, racist or clickbait articles
→ Headlines demonising a race, or a person based on their race
→ Ignoring stories because the subject matter relates to racial justice or the victim is Black – remember the missing white woman syndrome
→ Mistaking one Black celebrity for another

WHY NOT?

I'm not saying that all of the media is racist. I'm saying there is a problem with racism in the media and it is prevalent and pervasive. There have been journalists who have been murdered or imprisoned trying to uncover the truth. Journalists who have been murdered when trying to hold the powerful to account. However, there is a large section of the media, particularly the tabloids, who do engage in racism, whether it be in the editing room or in print.

Owen Jones, writing in *The Establishment: And how they get away with it*, indicates that journalists were asked to write negative stories about Muslims that were untrue. Michelle Stanistreet of the *Daily Express* complained about the paper's coverage of asylum seekers and Muslims, but the editor was on the Press Complaints Commission and said no action was to be taken by them.

It seems that where the media is concerned facts can be ignored or distorted, and lies can also be told. The press can at times appear to be an Establishment tool doing the bidding of the government, if it is a government they approve of. For instance, consider the decimation of Neil Kinnock and Jeremy Corbyn who are testament to that fact. There is an unhealthy relationship between the government and media; for instance *The Sun* publishing lies about the Liverpool fans at the Hillsborough disaster. Consider them backing Tony Blair immediately before and during the illegal Gulf War.

CONCLUSION

The British press and the Western media are often portrayed as a paragon of good and a bastion of democracy; however, what is not portrayed is the racism that is all too evident in the articles they publish and the opinions they deliver. Whilst there are hardly any television series about the media in Britain, I would ask you to consider the above and consider how the media are portrayed within other British and American television series and films. Are you shown Black people being misidentified or asked inappropriate questions? Are you shown the TV presenter fawning over the white guest whilst ignoring the Black guest? Do you ever see racialised and racist decision-making in dramatised newsrooms? I'd wager not.

Once again, I refer to American television series, which have at times highlighted the racial biases within the press. A great example was the addictive *Scandal* with Kerry Washington. When Olivia Pope is found to be having an affair with the President, the press machine goes into overdrive. Marcus calls out the press racism and the team go on the offensive to combat the dog whistle racism.

'...in New Orleans, where it was cheaper to use ni**ers than cats, because they were everywhere and [they were] cheap experimental animals – they started to use them, Negroes and patients in hospitals...'

Dr Harry Bailey, psychiatrist

CHAPTER 10

HEALTHCARE AND ENTERTAINMENT

Another staple of dramatic entertainment is the medical drama. Currently, *Grey's Anatomy* is still a global phenomenon and success. In the United Kingdom there's a litany of medical dramas that have graced the screens of British television. So the question is, from a race point of view, do they reflect the reality of Black people and other people of colour, or are they from a white perspective? I'm minded to say that it is the latter.

There are two main issues that arise in healthcare in the United Kingdom and of course in the United States and other Western nations. The first is the treatment of Black people within the system and the second is how the staff are treated.

SHAKEN FOUNDATIONS

I have to say, having completed the research for this chapter, it has shaken me to the core. It disturbed me and shook my foundations. It made me question my belief in God. It made me question God. If I'm honest I'm still shaken. I have thought about the victims of the medical profession. I'm thinking about the Black women slaves who were sold by their masters to the medical professionals. Those women were then forcibly restrained and without anaesthetic they would have their vaginas sliced open and mutilated by doctors who were trying to specialise in gynaecology. There would have been various items inserted into their vaginas to develop tools. Their agony, their pain, their mutilation would be ignored or looked upon with indifference. I'm imagining being in their position. Why don't you imagine being in that position? Imagine being owned. Imagine being sold. Imagine being restrained and having your genitalia mutilated, in full view of a group of white men and without anaesthetic; your screams are ignored as a scalpel slices through the inside and outside of your vagina. The powerlessness that you would feel as well as the pain and the humiliation that you would endure. Now imagine being given morphine *after* your brutal ordeal. Not as pain relief but to get you addicted to it. To ensure obedience and to wipe out your ability to resist any further brutal experimentation. How would you regard the doctor who did that to you? My guess is, you would think he was a monster, right? You'd think he should be in jail or be cast into ignominy and have a similar reputation to Mengele. You would hope he'd have his ability to practise medicine taken away and that the medical establishment would disavow him.

YOU WOULD BE WRONG.

That doctor was James Marion Sims MD and he is regarded as a hero to the medical establishment and to the American establishment. So much so that there were even statues dedicated to him in Central Park not far from the New York Academy of Medicine. His statue read *'His brilliant achievement carried the fame of American surgery throughout the entire world'*. You see, in Western history, Sims is regarded as the grandfather of gynaecology who developed methods to repair fistulas. But the method of his research has been wholly ignored. The victims silenced and then erased. To the Western white world, Sims was a hero. Often, however, your heroes are villains, particularly in the medical and scientific professions.

This chapter will look at the dark past of medical experiments on and abuses of Black people by Western medicine, particularly in the United States, and how the past influences the present: not just the attitudes of the medical professionals, but also how Black people were and are treated within the profession as patients and professionals. The picture today is still dire. It will show how the systemic abuse has been erased by the medical and scientific community and how it has silenced its victims. It will also show how experimentation was covered up through fraud, destruction of records and how the suffering of Black people has been removed from public awareness and consciousness.

In her brilliant but grim book, *Medical Apartheid*, Harriet A Washington sets out the gruesome past of slaves at the hands of doctors through to the earliest years of the twenty-first century where medical professionals and researchers were still experimenting on Black people without their consent and sometimes without their knowledge. She demonstrates how pervasive racism made scientists in various countries seek to develop biological weapons that would only kill Black people.

According to Washington, slave owners in the Deep South of America would sell their slaves who had become old or infirm to doctors, who would then conduct painful and often disabling or deadly experiments on them. Remember that as a slave you had no legal rights or protections, you were property and your owner could do with you what they liked – rape, murder, mutilation, experiments and torture – and all of the above happened daily all across the Deep South and the Caribbean. The medical profession was no exception when it came to engaging in such conduct. The medical profession created scientific myths in order to justify racism, slavery and white barbarism against Black people. As Washington states at page 38: *'physicians discovered many imaginary physical differences in Blacks ... All of which provided scientific racists with ample evidence of Black biological primitivism'*. She and Eberhardt set out the examples of scientific racism that still permeate Western thought today. Below are some examples:

Samuel A Cartwright MD
Asserted that Blacks could not survive without white supervision due to physical and mental defects. In effect Cartwright was advocating

slavery and that white people should remain in charge of them. As a result, Black people trying to escape slavery were often regarded as suffering from some kind of disease or defect and Cartwright called this Drapetomania.

Josiah Nott MD and George Gliddon – *Types of Mankind*

According to Wikipedia[79], Nott claimed *'the Negro achieves his greatest perfection, physical and moral, and also greatest longevity, in a state of slavery'*. Nott was also a slave owner and a scientist, and he used his latter credentials to justify the former. In his book co-written with Gliddon, *Types of Mankind* which was published in 1854, they asserted that races had different ancestral lineages. They created over 700 pages of racist nonsense inspired by fellow racist scientist Samuel Morton. In effect Nott and Gliddon suggested that races took after, or were biologically similar to, certain animals of their continents and they compared Africans to chimpanzees and gorillas. While they did not say that one race was superior to another – that had already been disproved – they disingenuously stated that whites were closer to intelligence and civility, and that Blacks were primitive and lacking intelligence. They were asserting it indirectly. As Eberhardt points out in *Biased*, the association with Black people and apes is one that has persisted to the present day.

Dr W T English

English wrote about *The Negro Problem from the Physician's Point of View*[80] and stated: *'having studied Black bodies they are a mass of imperfections from head to toe'*.

Samuel Morton

Morton started the theory of multi-race creation, i.e. polygenism, and asserted falsely that the white race was superior and Blacks were inferior.

Dr Thomas Hamilton

According to an article by Linda Villarosa in IBW21.org[81], Doctor Thomas Hamilton was the first doctor to create the myth that Black people do not feel pain. As such he went on to conduct various medical experiments on Black slaves. Despite their screams, Hamilton went on to insist that they couldn't feel pain. An insight into Hamilton's barbarism is documented in escaped slave John Brown's autobiography, *Slave Life in Georgia*, in which he gives an account of his life, sufferings and escape. John Brown details the horrific abuses inflicted upon him.

Dr Benjamin Moseley

Moseley's Wikipedia page makes no mention of his views or experiments on Black people and neither does the bio page of him listed on the Royal College of Physicians website. There is a chilling absence from both about the atrocities that Moseley committed. However, Moseley also expounded the theory that Black people could not feel pain. He was a British doctor and slave owner in Jamaica. In the ibw.21 article, they refer to Moseley's 1787 article, 'A Treatise on Tropical Diseases: And on the Climate of the West Indies', in which he claimed: *'What would be the cause of insupportable pain to a white man, a Negro would almost disregard... I have amputated the leg of many Negroes who have held the upper part of the limb themselves'*.

Among the false assertions there were a number of erroneous ideologies created about Black hypersexuality, lasciviousness and aggressiveness. The result of these assertions was simply a licence to rape and mistreat Black people and such treatment was widespread, daily and ongoing for centuries.

EXPERIMENTS

In light of the aforementioned myths, scientists and doctors went on to do unspeakable things to Black people in the name of science and they did so without anaesthesia. Below are just a few examples of what was done to Black people without anaesthetic by slave-owning medical professionals:

- Slicing and mutilating women's vaginas.
- Pouring near boiling water on to bodies.
- Drilling holes into the heads of newborns.
- Caesarean sections.
- Bladder surgery.
- Eye surgery.
- Genito-uro surgery.
- Stripping blood vessels from legs.
- Removing bones and bone fragments.
- Amputations.

They are just a fraction of the brutalities inflicted upon Black people during slavery and Washington provides a long list of the horrors inflicted. She also refers to the systematic use of Black people in the North and South of America for cruel displays and dissections. Black people's bodies were filling up university medical schools for teaching and dissection to the point that graves would be robbed for such bodies. Black bodies were not regarded as human beings in life or in death and they were commonly referred to as 'subject matter'.

Washington describes the fate of Ota Benga. Benga was a pygmy from the Congo. He had come home one day to find his family and village had been slaughtered by the Belgians. He was subsequently sold to William Hornaday in 1906 who then put Benga on display – in Bronx Zoo – with a gorilla and an orangutan. Imagine the thousands if not hundreds of thousands of white people who visited the Bronx to see this 'display'. The association between Black people and apes would be cemented in their minds forever. Similar displays were made in French museums. British naval surgeon Dr Alexander Dunlop bought Khoisan Black woman Saartjie Baartman and also put her on display in various events in Europe. Baartman was displayed naked in public, she was publicly experimented upon by visitors, she was allowed to be physically examined by them, and she was publicly raped. She was not the only one to have suffered that fate. Baartman's abuse and humiliation continued even after her death. As Washington highlights, French zoologist Georges Cuvier, a white supremacist, dissected her body. He preserved her lips, vulva and anus in glass jars and displayed them in the Parisian Musée de l'Homme. One plaque read: *'She had a way of pouting her lips exactly like that we have observed in the orangutan'.*

Again, imagine the thousands of white people visiting those museums, being informed by scientists who have displayed a dissected Black body and compared it to an ape's. These attitudes were inculcated into the white population and they remain prevalent in society and within the medical profession. Fast forward to 2020 and the arrival of COVID-19. The general population is being told to *'trust the science'*. I assume the rationale for this mantra was that the scientists were educated, knowledgeable and ethical and they have our best interests at heart, right? However, racism still persists in the medical profession today.

Washington sets out a number of research experiments that persisted through to the twenty-first century without the person's knowledge or consent and a summary of those is set out below.

The Tuskegee Syphilis Experiment, 1933–1972

The US Public Health Service allowed 399 African American men to believe that they were being treated for syphilis when they were not. Even though effective antibiotics were available in 1943 the government and scientists left the men untreated so they could track the effects of the disease. The men went on to pass it on to their wives and because it is also a congenital disease it was passed on to their children. When the story broke in 1972 the Public Health Service issued a mixture of denials and gaslighting statements.

The Plutonium Experiments

In 1945 in the United States, Ebb Cade was involved in a serious accident and had broken almost every bone in his body. He was conveyed to the Oak Ridge Army Hospital. The doctors there were from the US Atomic Energy Commission (AEC). While incapacitated Doctor Joseph Howland, a military doctor, injected Cade with a lethal dose of plutonium 239, without his knowledge or consent. They had done so to test the effects of plutonium. Cade was not the only Black person to be subjected to plutonium exposure. The AEC conducted such studies over a number of years on predominantly Black people without their consent; the true scale of the experiment is alleged to have been covered up.

Skin
From the 1950s to 1970s Doctor Albert Kligman conducted dangerous experiments on the skin of mostly African American men who were incarcerated at Philadelphia's Holmesburg Prison. The details of the experiments can be found in the book *Acres of Skin*. (Allen Hornblum, Routledge, 1998)

MKUltra, 1952–1972
On behalf of the CIA Kligman also conducted experiments on African Americans by testing mind-altering and mind-control substances. Prisoners reported frightening hallucinations and permanent changes in their personalities after being given various substances. Once again there appears to have been destruction of the evidence or falsification of the records, and there were also denials. Remember the quote at the beginning of this chapter? Dr Bailey was also tasked by the CIA to conduct experiments on Black people as part of MKUltra.

Well, Thandi, that was America, the British didn't do things like that you may think. Yes, they did. Ah, but Thandi, that was then, things are different now you may say. No – they are not. At least children were off limits, you might believe. They were not and often they were subject to even worse horrors. Let us remember that the British were slave owners too. The difference is that their plantations were mostly in the Caribbean, but their medical professionals and scientists also expounded racist ideologies, conducted experiments on slaves and brutalised Black people. The difference is that they were not doing it to Black people on home soil. This means that there was no real scrutiny of the horrific abuses they conducted in the name of science, except for the odd admission. In effect Britain's atrocities are not in the consciousness of the British people because their misdeeds were committed far from home.

After slavery the British, along with the rest of Europe, set about colonising Africa. The French, Germans, Belgians, Italians, and British all entered Africa, stole land, lives, futures, and dehumanised Black people through brutal repression, torture and violence. All of the colonisers were conducting medical experiments on Africans without consent and with impunity. African countries under British colonial rule were: Egypt, Libya, Sudan, Somalia, Kenya, Tanzania, Zimbabwe, Nigeria, South Africa and Sierra Leone.

Honor Smith, a British physician stated[82]: *'It is the almost unlimited field that Africa offers for clinical research that I find so enthralling.'* Here then is a doctor overtly stating that they can experiment on Africans without limits and you can just imagine the horrors that they inflicted on African people. In her article 'Medicine, Empires and Ethics in Colonial Africa', Helen Tilley points out that: *'Through much of the colonial era, there existed no agreed upon ethical standard for human subjects research.'* She goes on to say, *'For some investigators and clinicians, these open-ended conditions in colonial Africa created an ethos, in both treatment and research campaigns, that the ends justified the means.'* In effect nothing was off limits. In Caroline Elkins' book *Imperial Reckoning*, she details the horrors committed by the British government in Kenya. She also makes reference to adults and children being experimented upon, recording that children were given injections one day and dropping dead the next. Many of the records relating to the Kenya atrocities were destroyed by the British, a common response to Western abuses and crimes against Black people. You will be hard pressed to find the history of abuse engaged in by the medical profession and scientists. Simple internet searches will not really assist. You need to scour journals, comb articles and books and chase footnotes. If on the other hand you want to find out about Nazi experiments in the context of Nazi Germany, the internet abounds with information. Simply put, medical crimes against Black or brown people are not acknowledged, recognised or talked about. There is no insight or introspection on the harm done and the mistrust that it has created. There is also absolutely no recognition that Western advances in medicine are due in large part to the suffering of Black people – suffering inflicted for the benefit of whites.

In many ways, things are not really that different now; granted, with the development of drugs and technology and ethics boards governing professionals, you're not going to get public amputations but experimentation on Black people in America and Africa is still taking place without knowledge or the appropriate consent, and sometimes with deadly consequences. In *Medical Apartheid* Washington cites a number of examples of American medical professionals, who, with the backing or complicity of the state or federal government, experimented upon predominantly Black Americans and Africans. Writing in 2006 she starts by saying on page 5, *'The Office for Protection from Research Risks (OPRR) has been busily investigating abuses at more than 60 research centres, including experimentation-related deaths at premier universities, from Colombia to California. Another important subset of human subject abuse has been scientific fraud, wherein scientists from the University of South Carolina to MIT have also been found to have lied through falsified data or fictitious research agendas, often in the service of research that abused Black Americans. Within recent years the OPRR has also suspended research at such revered universities as Alabama, Pennsylvania, Duke, Yale and even John Hopkins.'*

Fake Blood

Medical Apartheid also focuses on another form of experimentation in American hospitals. At least twenty United States emergency rooms were using artificial blood known as Polyheme on seriously ill patients who needed a blood transfusion. This was done on mostly unconscious patients without their knowledge or consent. Statistics showed that the majority of people using emergency rooms in America were Black. It transpired that Polyheme produced more adverse reactions than human blood, being: shock, respiratory failure and pneumonia; there was also a 49% higher death rate.

2007 Cardiac and Trauma Treatments

Washington also points out that in May 2007 the federal government was going to launch more of the same, that is, a $50-million, five-year, eleven-site project to be managed by the Resuscitation Outcomes Consortium. It would subject approximately 21,000 patients to medical experiments without first asking their permission. I appreciate that many patients who have suffered acute trauma or cardiac events may not be in a position to consent due to incapacitation. However, where possible next of kin consent should be obtained. If a treatment is going to be trialled in a hospital or city and the treatment is high risk, I do not see why the residents of the city or town are not given advance notice and the ability to consent or refuse such treatment. Given that we are in a digital age, I do not believe that it would be so difficult to allow people to opt out.

Given that Black Americans are more likely to use emergency care than any other Americans it is a very disturbing picture. America and the West like to boast on the international stage that they are democracies. They are also not shy about criticising other nations for their human rights breaches. Despite the West ignoring the horrors of the slave trade and colonisation and the systematic maiming, torture and murder of Black people in the name of science, they sat up and took notice of the horrors of medical experiments committed against Jewish people. Why? I would wager it's because they were white. Look into any history book about the Holocaust, the mindset indicates that the West was horrified by these events. Why? They had been committing genocide and mutilating Black people and people of colour for centuries. You will also note that the Nazi treatment of Black people in Germany is ignored. In Nazi Germany Blacks were forcefully sterilised. They were forbidden from entering into interracial marriages and they too were sent to prisons and concentration camps. Yet when you read history and watch films or movies and documentaries about Nazi Germany there is no mention of Black people during that time, the treatment they received and their fate. The Universal Declaration of Human Rights and the Nuremberg Code were established as a direct result of the horrors committed during World War Two. The UDHR sets out the minimum human rights a nation should provide its citizens for a just, fair and democratic society. It is not a binding document, it is simply something to aspire to; however, the West does like to spout this document quite a bit so the relevant articles are as follows:

> **Article 2**
> Everyone is entitled to all the rights and freedoms set forth in this declaration, without distinction of any kind such as race, colour...
>
> **Article 3**
> Everyone has the right to life, liberty and security of person.

Therefore the right to life, liberty and security of person cannot be denied to a person or persons on the basis of race. The rights in Article 3, I would suggest, provide a right to bodily autonomy. In reality, if Black people are the predominant users of emergency medicine and medical experiments are being done on them without their knowledge or consent, then they are being denied their human rights and it can be said that the denial is on the basis of race. Apparently, the Americans have a constitution which also is supposed to guarantee some fundamental rights and freedoms but it doesn't appear to be worth the paper it is written on when it comes to Black people. Because, if you have the right to life, liberty and the pursuit of happiness, how is it that your body can be used without your permission? That is not liberty. That is tyranny and the yoke of slavery has clearly not been lifted.

THE NUREMBERG CODE

The Nuremberg Trials are the infamous trials of members of the Nazi regime. As a result of the abhorrent treatment and medical experiments that were conducted during the period of Nazi rule, the Nuremberg Code set out a number of principles that should be adhered to when it comes to medical experiments and consent.

PERMISSIBLE MEDICAL EXPERIMENTS

The great weight of the evidence before us to effect that certain types of medical experiments on human beings, when kept within reasonably well-defined bounds, conform to the ethics of the medical profession generally. The protagonists of the practice of human experimentation justify their views on the basis that such experiments yield results for the good of society that are unprocurable by other methods or means of study. All agree, however, that certain basic principles must be observed in order to satisfy moral, ethical and legal concepts:

1. **The voluntary consent of the human subject is absolutely essential.** This means that the person involved should have legal capacity to give consent; **should be so situated as to be able to exercise free power of choice, without the intervention of any element of force, fraud, deceit, duress, over-reaching, or other ulterior form of constraint or coercion; and should have sufficient knowledge and comprehension of the elements of the subject matter involved as to enable him to make an understanding and enlightened decision.** This latter element requires that before the acceptance of an affirmative decision by the experimental subject there should be made known to him the nature, duration, and purpose of the experiment; the method and means by which it is to be conducted; all inconveniences and hazards reasonably to be expected; and the effects upon his health or person which may possibly come from his participation in the experiment. The duty and responsibility for ascertaining the quality of the consent rests upon each individual who initiates, directs, or engages in the experiment. It is a personal

duty and responsibility which may not be delegated to another with impunity.

2. The experiment should be such as to yield fruitful results for the good of society, unprocurable by other methods or means of study, and not random and unnecessary in nature.

3. The experiment should be so designed and based on the results of animal experimentation and a knowledge of the natural history of the disease or other problem under study that the anticipated results justify the performance of the experiment.

4. The experiment should be so conducted as to avoid all unnecessary physical and mental suffering and injury.

5. No experiment should be conducted where there is an *a priori* reason to believe that death or disabling injury will occur; except, perhaps, in those experiments where the experimental physicians also serve as subjects.

6. The degree of risk to be taken should never exceed that determined by the humanitarian importance of the problem to be solved by the experiment.

7. Proper preparations should be made and adequate facilities provided to protect the experimental subject against even remote possibilities of injury, disability or death.

8. The experiment should be conducted only by scientifically qualified persons. The highest degree of skill and care should be required through all stages of the experiment of those who conduct or engage in the experiment.

9. During the course of the experiment the human subject should be at liberty to bring the experiment to an end if he has reached the physical or mental state where

> continuation of the experiment seems to him to be impossible.
>
> 10. During the course of the experiment the scientist in charge must be prepared to terminate the experiment at any stage, if he has probable cause to believe, in the exercise of good faith, superior skill and careful judgment required of him, that a continuation of the experiment is likely to result in injury, disability or death to the experimental subject.

As you can see the code requires persons to be able to give informed consent and furthermore such consent should not be obtained through coercion or deception. As we have seen, since 1947 Western nations have ignored the Universal Declaration of Human Rights and the Nuremberg Code when it comes to Black people.

OPERATION PAPERCLIP

Despite America's public condemnation of the Nazis and support for the Nuremberg Trials, the American government and American scientists had close links with Nazi scientists and they shared the same ideology in respect of the false notion of white supremacy. As part of Operation Paperclip the US government invited top Nazi scientists to America to work on scientific projects in exchange for immunity and a new identity. As Washington points out some of the Nazi scientists were tasked with continuing their non-consensual research which exploited patients. The US government placed over seven hundred Nazi scientists in hospitals and clinics across America. Because the studies were done in secret and of course without consent, a racial breakdown of those experimented upon is not possible.

Now, consider a Black person going to an American hospital. A hospital where the doctors are Nazis and segregationists. How is that Black person going to be treated? Will they be murdered or mutilated? Will they be experimented upon without their knowledge?

Who knows? If you were Black and you had that knowledge would you enter that hospital?

CHILDREN

Children have not been off limits when it comes to medical experiments. Washington sets out the abuses that were inflicted upon Black children in the United States and in Africa. She asserts that this is for a number of reasons. Racism in science is not new, but it is ongoing. Some of the experiments have sought to prove – and failed – that violence and aggression are racial traits. To be clear, scientific racists have been desperate to prove that violence, aggression and criminality are inherent within the Black population. It is quite audacious considering the brutality that white power inflicted on Africa, the Americas and Asia for hundreds of years. Not to mention that the average school shooter is white, teenage and male and that the average serial killer is white and male but, hey, don't let facts get in the way of scientific racism. In his article 'White Shooters are Most Often Responsible for Mass School Shootings[83]' (2 June 2022), Walter Rhein suggests that politicians and the media largely ignore the race of the shooter because it does not fit in with their anti-Black agenda. Rhein explains that a mass shooting is defined as an incident where *'four or more victims are murdered with at least one of those homicides taking place in a public location and with no connection to underlying criminal activity, such as gangs or drugs'*. He lists a number of school shootings between 1989 and 2018 which show that 11 out of the 13 shooters were white males and 2 out of the 13 were Native American. He highlights the fact that there were no Black shooters.

Malissa N Kekahu[84] points out that in the United States school shootings have mostly been committed by white individuals and that Black and brown individuals are disproportionately killed by, or are victims of, gun violence (Heitzig 2015). Kekahu points out that the topic of whiteness is largely ignored by the mainstream media when it comes to such violence. Having read the FBI Report into school shootings, again it is clear that the topic of race – or should I say whiteness – is largely ignored. The report sets out the characteristics of a school shooter and at pages 16–24 one may read that the shooters seem strikingly similar to angry white teenage boys with white supremacist tendencies. I would suggest this is ignored because, where violence is perpetrated by white people, it doesn't fit into the white racial frame narrative.

In the United Kingdom the vast majority of serial killers in recent years have been known to be white: Harold Shipman, Peter Sutcliffe, Fred West, Rose West, Beverley Allitt, Myra Hindley, Ian Brady, Amelia Dyer, Dennis Nilsen and Lucy Letby.

The construction of white supremacy and racism has gone to great lengths to tell the world that a white society, or Western society, is a civilised society and Black people are uncivilised and dangerous. As such, if the average serial killer is a white male or the average school shooter is a white male, this is clearly going to go against the racist narrative that is so often pushed every day in mainstream media and in institutions. I would say this is why there is an absence of racialisation when it comes to white violence.

Whilst there has been an absence of racialising white violence, some sections of the American scientific community have conducted unethical experiments on Black children in order to link criminality with Black people.

New York State Psychiatric Institute (NYSPI), 1992–1997

As a result of data breaches NYSPI was able to obtain the details of 126 Black boys between the ages of 6 and 10 whose brothers were imprisoned. NYSPI was looking for a link between genetics and violence. They administered the cardiotoxic drug fenfluramine to 34 boys without their or their parents' consent. As a result the children suffered headaches and vomiting. At least one suffered long-term adverse effects. There is a suggestion in Washington's book that the families of the children had been coerced into silence. No white children were subject to this cruel and abusive experiment, so it would have been fundamentally flawed in any event. Defending the study the NYSPI Chair, Doctor Walsh, referred to the spate of school shootings that had occurred. Again, had the doctor bothered to ascertain facts they would have known that all of the shooters had been white teenage boys.

Other experiments that have been conducted on children are set out below.

Covert HIV Testing, 1980s

In the 1980s the state of New York funded covert testing of babies for HIV without the mother's consent and knowledge; 68% were African American. Neither the government nor medical professionals told the mothers that they or their children were HIV positive, so they did not know that they needed to seek treatment. There is also the issue of those infected mothers potentially passing the disease on to a new partner.

EZ Vaccine, 1987–1991

According to Washington[85] *'Between 1987 and 1991, US researchers administered as much as five hundred times the approved dosage of the experimental Edmonton Zagreb (EZ) vaccine to African American and Hispanic babies in Los Angeles.'* The parents were not informed that the drug was experimental, nor that the children were being given excessive doses. Washington also points out that the parents were unaware that the vaccine had had disastrous results for the two thousand Haitian children who had been vaccinated with the same drug.

Kennedy Krieger Institute, 1990s

Scientists trying to study effects of lead poisoning induced Black parents to allow them to study their children. They did not tell the parents about the lead exposure in the buildings. They also encouraged more than 125 landlords with lead-contaminated buildings to rent to Black families with young children so they could study the long-term effects of lead poisoning.

Trovan, 1996

American pharmaceutical company Pfizer issued the experimental drug Trovan (trovafloxacin) to Nigerian children in the village of Kano during a meningitis outbreak. The drug had not been approved by the American FDA and it was later withdrawn by the European Medicines Agency as a result of physical side effects. It is alleged that the drugs were given to the children without the parents' consent. As a result of the experimental drug being administered eleven children died, five having received trovafloxacin and six given ceftriaxone. Countless others were left with permanent disabling conditions such as paralysis, deafness, speech impediments and neurological deficits. After nearly fifteen years of litigation, Pfizer eventually agreed to pay an out of court settlement to some of the families whose children had died or were affected by the vaccine.

THEY REALLY ARE TRYING TO KILL US THROUGH SCIENCE

> *'The development of molecular medicine based on our new understanding of genomics will allow a vast range of new weaponry to be developed. Among that range could be biological weapons specifically targeted at particular ethnic groups.'*
> **Professor Malcolm Dando, University of Bradford, 1999**

The above quote is the start of Chapter 15 in Washington's book *Medical Apartheid*, which she titles 'Aberrant Wars'. In it she details the endeavours of white South African and American scientists who set about engaging in biological and chemical experiments and terrorism against the Black population.

In her paper on British Colonial Violence[86] Dr Michelle Gordon explains that scientific racism was used to justify colonialism and its expansionist policies. They created racial hierarchies and legitimised racism. Colonisation was therefore seen as a civilising mission of *'the natives'* and she asserts that, as a result of scholarly theories, extreme violence was felt to be justified while the British engaged in their colonial endeavours. It was medical professionals during the apartheid regime and in military detention facilities who determined how much torture a person could take. It was medical professionals who experimented on Black people who were interred in concentration camps on the continent of Africa.

One of the many malevolent aspects of scientific racism has been the obsession of preserving the white race. Not just preserving it but ridding it of any flaws. Terms such as 'racial hygiene' or 'racial purity' have often been employed to hide what they really mean – genocide. There have been many American, British, European and white South African scientists and politicians who have supported eugenic and genocidal policies aimed at eliminating Black people and people of colour. Their ideology does not stop there though. They have sought to eliminate or remove from society Jewish people, gay people, the intellectually disabled, the physically disabled and those they regarded as deviant.

South African scientists under the apartheid regime created a department that was working on diseases and biological weapons that would only kill Black people. They also had significant input from American scientists.

EFFORTS TO HALT REPRODUCTION

Another aspect of scientific racism is the issue of Black reproduction. There have been numerous attempts by the white scientific community to sterilise Black people in order to keep the Black population down or to make it extinct. The reason – I would say – is so the white majority can keep oppressive control. There are numerous articles on the forceful sterilisation of women of colour by colonialists in Africa, Asia and the Americas. Western scientists have often supported eugenic theories and in racist societies talked about racial hygiene. White ruling classes in countries have espoused the false notion of racial superiority and oppressive medical measures were enacted. Sterilisation of Black people and people of colour has been part of the oppressive scientific package. In *Medical Apartheid*

Washington refers to the Mississippi Appendectomies of the 1960s. This is where Black women were sterilised without their knowledge or consent during routine surgery.

Margaret Sanger had significant responsibility for making available the contraceptive pill. Sanger is lauded as a radical feminist. However, there are a number of white women who are only feminist for white women and hold racist views. Sanger is one such person and is quoted as saying as regards making contraception available to Blacks:

> 'The most successful educational approach to the Negro is through a religious appeal. We do not want the word to get out that we want to exterminate the Negro population...'

Indeed, such attitudes prevail today. As Washington points out, the pill, Norplant and Depo-Provera were first tested in Africa, Brazil, Puerto Rico and India. Contraceptives were then rolled out in schools across America on Black girls in the next set of trials. The issue could be a book in itself. This is something that is still occurring today in America, Africa, India and South America. Sterilisation can take many forms. Surgery is often done without knowledge or consent, or acquiescence is gained through coercion. Once again this topic could form a book in its own right but if medical violence against women and women of colour is something that is of interest to you then I would urge you to research full sterilisation of people of colour. It will be an illuminating if not disturbing insight into how violent the medical profession can be. Unfortunately, there are often times they have been backed up by the state and regulating bodies which makes their ability to inflict harm even more egregious and even more oppressive.

RACISM AND THE NHS

There have been a number of scandals and findings in the NHS. I am sure that there are competent and dedicated professionals who spend their days saving lives and looking after the sick among us, and they do so with compassion and grace. Unfortunately, some of those professionals do not extend that compassion, care and competence to people of colour – and this is where the envisaged backlash begins! The NHS is an institution and like many British institutions it has a problem with institutional and individual racism. This part of the chapter looks at the adverse findings relating to the treatment of Black people and people of colour in the NHS as patients and staff. I would wager that racism also occurs in the private healthcare sector. I recall attending a private endocrinology appointment. I was sat down and a white receptionist exited the office. She simply glared at me. We don't know each other. The only thing she has is my gender and race. I'm guessing she wasn't glaring at me because I was a woman. My name had been misspelt in a number of places. I corrected the error in those places and pointed it out to the receptionist. When I get the bill, they still haven't bothered to rectify their mistake. I'm sure I'm not the only Black person who has used private healthcare and I'm sure I'm not the only Black person to have had an adverse experience. I also recall a private orthopaedic surgeon using a racially offensive term on Twitter. When it was pointed out, he remained silent. One questions how a surgeon engaging in blatant racism and refusing to apologise for it is going to treat Black patients. What are their outcomes going to be like?

FIVE X MORE

Five X More was a campaign started by Tinuke Awe and Clotilde Abe, who, as a result of their own experiences and the experience of other women of colour, sought to address the racial inequality that Black women face during pregnancy and childbirth. Mothers and Babies: Reducing Risk through Audits and Confidential Enquiries produced a report entitled 'Saving Lives, Improving Mothers' Care' in November 2021. The foreword reveals '...a stark disparity in maternal mortality rates between women from Black and Asian aggregated ethnic groups and White women – more than four times higher for Black women, two times higher for mixed ethnicity women and almost twice as high for Asian women'. Further: 'We remain deeply concerned that Black and Brown peoples' basic human rights to safety, dignity, respect and equality in pregnancy and childbirth are not being protected, respected or upheld.' They highlighted that racist attitudes, microaggressions, dismissal of concerns and breakdown of trust affect maternity services, and they recognise that systemic racism affects maternity care.

In the 2022 Birthrights report, 'Systemic Racism, Not Broken Bodies – An Inquiry into Racial Injustice and Human Rights in Maternity Care', it highlighted research showing that mortality rates for Black and Asian women in NHS maternity care has maintained similar trends for decades. At page two it states: '...with Black, Asian and Mixed ethnicity women also more likely to experience baby loss, become seriously ill and have worse experiences of care in pregnancy and childbirth, compared to white women'. It goes on to say: 'But for too long, explanations for racial inequities in maternal outcomes have focussed on Black and Brown bodies as the problem – regarding them as "defective" and "other", and a risk to be managed ... [However] it is racism, not broken bodies, that is at the root of many inequities in maternity outcomes and experiences'.

The report gives a number of examples of how racism played out in maternity wards where ethnic minority women were ignored when they were trying to raise serious concerns. Examples relate to a Black baby being jaundiced and the health worker refusing to take the mother's concerns seriously; the baby ended up being seriously ill with the condition. Another ethnic minority woman being ignored when she complained of chest pains and she actually had a pulmonary embolism. Another woman's complaints of being unwell being ignored when she had sepsis. Staff being angry at a woman who was in serious pain and returned to hospital much to their ire and upon examination turned out to be dilated between 8 and 9 centimetres. There were numerous accounts of people of colour's pain being dismissed or minimised. The report concluded that there was a failure to listen and that failure was in part a consequence of racism. Evidently the myth that Black people do not feel pain, or have the ability to endure pain, still persists in modern British medicine.

The Birthrights report recognised that racist attitudes and behaviours of caregivers – including stereotypes, microaggressions and assumptions about risk based on race – are having a serious detrimental effect. They stated that there were *'a multitude of accounts where women and staff had heard Asian women being referred to as 'princesses' or 'precious' and Black women as 'aggressive' or 'angry'.* The report stated that *'Black, Brown and Mixed ethnic minority people are subject to dehumanisation in maternity care, manifested by disrespect, rudeness and lack of empathy that breaches basic human rights principles of dignity and respect.'* They acquired their research via a number of stories that had been shared by focus groups and by lawyers and *'[it] demonstrated a pervasive lack of curiosity or empathy, harsh or rough treatment, and even shouting or threats'.* The aspects that the report highlighted were the teaching methods in maternity care and they suggested that teaching is from a colonial perspective. There were also concerns in respect of medical staff failing to obtain proper and informed consent, often as a result of failing to have an interpreter present for pregnant women who cannot speak English.

Birthright also conducted a study on racism in the workforce where the respondents were healthcare professionals, the majority being midwives; 70% were BAME and 24% were white. Almost all of the respondents stated that systemic racism and/or racial discrimination is contributing to maternity outcomes and experiences. There was a disturbing quote extrapolated in their report and it was as follows: *'Yes, I'm still a student midwife. I'm in my second year now and I've experienced quite a lot of overtly racist comments in the short time I've been in my Trust.'* There were accounts of good practice within the report; however, what is of concern is the persistent and pervasive racism that appears to go unchecked within the NHS maternity care system. It is clear that racism and racist ideologies of old still linger. The belief that Black people do not feel pain, or feel pain less than white people, is still a pernicious ideology that is permeating maternity care within the NHS.

In America the survival rate for African American newborns is a shocking indictment of racism within the medical profession. In their

2020 study, Greenwood et al[87] found that there were significant disparities in survival rates between Black and white newborns. They examined 1.8 million hospital births in the state of Florida between 1992 and 2015 and found the following:

i. Mortality among Black infants outstrips medical inequalities in many other health domains.
ii. Bias was exhibited equally towards adults and children.
iii. Under the care of white physicians, Black newborns experience triple the in-hospital mortality rate of white infants.
iv. When a white newborn is cared for by a white doctor, the mortality rate is 290 per 100,000.
v. When a Black newborn is cared for by a white doctor, the mortality rate is 894 per 100,000.
vi. No difference in mortality for white babies if the doctor is Black or white.
vii. Black newborns have an advantage and lower mortality rate when cared for by Black physicians: 173 per 100,000.
viii. White physicians are underperforming in respect of natal care.
ix. Black physicians systemically outperform their colleagues when caring for Black newborns.

The numbers speak for themselves. It is quite clear that race and racism is playing a part on both sides of the Atlantic when it comes to maternal and natal care of Black people, often with fatal consequences.

BLACK PEOPLE IN NHS MENTAL HEALTH SERVICES

In her 2020 article entitled 'Systemic Racism: Big, Black, Mad and Dangerous in the Criminal Justice System', Sharon Walker sets out how systemic and structural racism have led to the over-representation of Black people, particularly Black men, in the mental health system. As she points out (Cummins 2015): *'Psychiatry along with criminal justice agencies has played a key role in creating the racist stereotype of the physically aggressive, violent Black male.'* The consequences are, Walker points out, the over-representation of Black men being diagnosed with schizophrenia and their deaths in state custody, whether that be while in police detention or mental health detention. Walker asserts that this over-representation of Black men dying in police or mental health custody as a result of excessive use of force is systemic racism arising out of slavery and colonisation. Such behaviour is an exercise of white power; it is dehumanising and it devalues Black lives. She equates it to a modern version of lynching. Racism in UK mental health services is also pervasive and persistent; as Walker points out, Black psychiatric patients were on average detained nine years longer than their white counterparts. It has also been established that Black people are four times more likely to be sectioned than their white counterparts.

STAFFING

It is not only patients who are adversely affected by racism within the NHS, so too the Black and ethnic minority staff working within the system. Richard Majors started his paper[88] by pointing out the established findings which were: *'The NHS treat BME staff less favourably than white staff in their recruitment, promotion and career progression.'* He also established that BME staff were significantly more likely to be bullied than white staff and that these behaviours were a predicator to patient care. There is a culture of bullying, harassment, abuse and microaggressions and it is everyday, and he asserted that even referencing is racialised. Of course, racialising references determine your future prospects in your career or lack thereof. Majors goes on to comment on *'discrimination and inequalities, regarding people of colour often perpetuated by white management, academic staff, colleagues and support staff in both overt and covert racist ways'*. Majors highlights the discrepancy in treatment diagnosis and outcomes between Blacks and whites, with Blacks being adversely affected and whites having more positive experiences and outcomes within the mental health services in the NHS. Majors also raises concerns about the over-misdiagnosis of schizophrenia in the Black community particularly in Black males by white mental health professionals. He dates this back to the Black civil rights movement, referring to the article 'The Protest Psychosis: How Schizophrenia Became a Black Disease' (2010). In effect Black men during the civil rights movement were viewed by the American Psychiatric Association, as reflected in its Diagnostic and Statistical Manual of Mental Disorders, as hostile and aggressive and delusional for their participation in protest activities and for belonging to political organisations. Clearly then such diagnoses were politically driven. Majors also identifies the centrality of whiteness and white hegemony which drives racial microaggressions towards Black staff and therapists. He asserts that as a result of racism Black people are more likely to drop out of, or be pushed out of, graduate school.

There have been a number of articles in relation to racism against staff in the NHS. That racism has consisted of bullying, abuse, discrimination, harassment, lack of opportunity to further their careers, via lack of access to training as well as a lack of opportunities for promotion. There is also empirical evidence suggesting that Black nurses are more likely to be disciplined than their white counterparts and less likely to receive a promotion as a result of discrimination. I set out below several reports that have made the headlines:

- Racism embedded in NHS organisational culture and norms prevents progress on healthcare staff inequities – 7 January 2022 https://www.kcl.ac.uk/news/racism-embedded-in-nhs-organisational-culture-and-norms-prevents-progress-on-healthcare-staff-inequities

- Ethnic minority NHS workers suffer 'shocking' racism and unfair treatment – 15 February 2022 https://www.personneltoday.com/hr/ethnic-minority-nhs-workers-racism-university-manchester/

- Review finds nurses enduring 'covert and overt' racial discrimination – 15 February 2022 https://www.

nursingtimes.net/news/research-and-innovation/
review-finds-nhs-nurses-enduring-covert-and-overt-racial-
discrimination-15-02-2022/

- The NHS has a racism problem – to deny this is putting
both patients and staff at risk – 8 September 2022 https://
www.independent.co.uk/voices/nhs-racism-issue-staff-
patient-welfare-b2162770.html

There are a multitude of reports that rely on empirical data, focus groups and reviews that demonstrate that Black staff in particular, along with other ethnic minority staff, are being subjected to racism on a regular if not daily basis. I would suggest you research the topic if it is something that you have interest in but, as I said, there is a plethora of information available.

As part of my research, I interviewed a number of Black doctors in various parts of the country who worked in NHS hospitals. They all had experienced racism. I have set out the accounts below. I have kept them anonymous to save them from any repercussions or adverse outcomes. I will refer to them by a letter but will not reveal if that letter is made up, a first or last name.

Dr X – Surgeon specialising in obstetrics and gynaecology

Dr X is a mixed-race woman who grew up in the South of England. She qualified as a doctor at a London University in 2012 and is a Registrar surgeon who specialises in obstetrics and gynaecology. Growing up she liked science and talking to people; she also liked watching *Casualty* and *Holby City* and this is what inspired her to become a doctor. Overall, school was a positive experience.

At university there was not a lot of overt racism. The racial make-up was 300 white people to six or seven Black people. There was racially inappropriate language such as being referred to as half-caste. There were also occasions where assumptions were made about her on the basis of her race. One example cited was being referred to as African American by the lecturer. She also observed that 60% of the intake were privately educated.

In respect of working in hospitals Dr X stated that she was treated better than Black doctors as she was lighter skinned and it appeared that if you had a British accent you would be treated better. She indicated that, of those who didn't have a British accent, Black and Asian people suffered the most. She and her friends experienced racism. She was aware of a Black friend being the subject of a complaint by a white patient in a hospital in the South East. The white patient had complained about having a Black doctor and the NHS Trust required the said Black doctor to respond to the complaints. She regarded this as unthinking by the NHS trust.

Dr X recalls working in a southern NHS hospital and being subject to microaggressions, one example being of a midwife telling her: *'You're not English. You're not really English. I mean not English, English.'* Another midwife said to her: *'Your English is really good,'* and in another hospital a midwife grabbed her hair and began squeezing and stating that it was *'so poofy'*.

Dr X said the midwives were suspicious of her and *'they always bypassed me to go to a male white doctor'*. The mistrust lasts longer and is more significant if you are Black or Asian and don't have a British accent. As a staff member of colour she found that after 6 to 12 months if they see you are good at your job, they, i.e. the white staff, will start to trust you but she acknowledges that there are some that never will.

Dr X also indicated that white doctors are treated differently even if there is an adverse outcome; if the doctor is white and British, the outcome is regarded as unavoidable. If the doctor is a person of colour, concerns are raised that are generally not founded. She also indicated that doctors of colour from abroad tend to have more experience. She also found that white men can be tactless towards women who have had stillbirths and yet not get into trouble for it.

Another example of a racist microaggression was a member of staff asking the group in front of an Indian woman doctor: *'Why is it that Indians talk so loudly? Is it because the phone lines are so bad?'* In respect of dealing with racism at work, Dr X said that microaggressions would not be taken seriously, it would have to be overt racism.

In respect of patients, Dr X said that stereotypes still persist to this day about Black people having higher pain thresholds, and myths about the African pelvis. Black women are regarded as aggressive and Asian women as princesses.

She recalls a Black woman who had been bleeding internally having a cardiac arrest. She indicated that had the previous shift responded appropriately to that patient it could have been prevented. She believed her care had been deeply inadequate. Rather than accept responsibility the doctor said, *'What is it about Black women?'* Dr X indicated that when Black couples are in hospital for maternity issues, Black men who are understandably concerned about their partners are always deemed to be aggressive and they are the only ones ever threatened with security.

In respect of her personal experiences of racism there have been incidences. On one occasion she was holding her newborn and fell over onto him. She remembers that people just walked past her. No one asked if she was okay and no one offered to help her. When she was relaying the experience to white people they would indicate that it wasn't racism. They would say, *'I'm sure it wasn't that.'* The other incidents related to when she was pregnant. At every appointment she went to she was always asked if she had been a victim of female genital mutilation and believed that this was racial stereotyping. In respect of attitudes, she says that she will get a call from a nurse asking her to look at their patient. A score of 10 is regarded as unwell. The nurse will say she's a 12 but she seems fine. Dr X says whenever she is told that she knows the nurses are referring to a Black woman.

I asked her about the realities of her profession compared to medical dramas and she said that she doesn't think there are as many patients of colour as portrayed. Also, that there aren't that many Black doctors. And that you don't see the treatment of Black doctors on TV.

Dr O

Dr O is a Black woman specialising in general medicine who practises in the North East of England. She qualified in Nigeria in 2008. She has also practised medicine in Scotland. In respect of her treatment, she said the biggest issue was mistrust. She would tell the staff members the treatment plan for the patients and the nurses would immediately run to a white junior colleague and ask them if that was the plan. This happened daily. Doctor O felt that she was being systematically undermined by members of staff.

At the hospital in the North East she said Black doctors were frequently undermined by the staff. Two issues she raised as problematic were the behaviours of the advanced clinical practitioners (ACPs) who are nurses and manage the patients, and the treatment of Black doctors. The ACPs would shout at Black doctors. They would bully them and if a Black doctor had written on the patient's chart the ACP would cross it out. They would not do that to white British doctors.

The NHS Trust also made every Black doctor take another exam even though it was not sanctioned by the General Medical Council. The British Medical Association was written to, and that process was stopped.

In respect of white doctors, she said that some of them were OK but some were downright disrespectful. They would interrupt you during handovers, would talk over you, and sometimes they would repeat exactly what you had just said and get applauded for it by the team. Dr O said not everyone was overtly hostile but there would be a lot of passive aggressive behaviour and passive aggressive emails. Such behaviour was done with impunity.

Dr O indicated that the NHS Trust did not treat Black people well. She stated that the Trust treats Black people like they are only there to fill the rota. She said that there are no or very little career development opportunities for Black doctors. In respect of career development, she said that there are so many obstacles in your way. If a Black doctor asks for a development opportunity, they are told to wait. However, if a white doctor asks for the same thing they are given it two weeks later. Dr O's experience sounded utterly awful and in fact she told me: *'I almost expect to be treated badly by staff and patients and when I am not, I'm pleasantly surprised.'*

Dr O indicated that the Trust does not take racism against Black staff by patients seriously. She said that the less sick a patient is, the worse they behave. She has been called the N word at least three times. She has been referred to as a Nigerian scammer and has been asked where all the British doctors are. She said the Trust never wants to call the police when patients are racially abusive to Black staff even when a patient threw a colostomy bag at a nurse.

Dr O has experienced racism in her personal life as well. She indicated that her neighbours had been racially abusing her. I asked if the police had taken any action and she said they had told her they would have a word.

I asked her about her experiences in NHS hospitals and how it compares to medical dramas. Dr O said that the way they portray Black doctors as being treated as equals and having their opinions respected and being able to contribute is not realistic. She said Black doctors are not always treated with respect and their opinions are not respected. Black doctors in her experience would definitely not be invited to social events. Doctor O also mentioned that it was not portrayed how Black women can be objectified and sexualised in the hospital setting. She referred to colleagues brushing up against her and running into her. She indicated that staff and patients give sexualised looks and behave in a way that objectified and sexualised her.

Dr Y

Dr Y is a Senior Registrar in obstetrics and gynaecology in England. She had wanted to be a doctor since she was a child.

In respect of medical school she recalls one GP examiner who would pull faces when marking Black people. He would mark them low and all Black students had the same experience with him. He was always angry at any Black person.

Dr Y spent two years in a northern hospital and had a good experience with patients and staff. She progressed through training and worked in a London hospital. She regarded it as toxic. She was often dismissed by consultants and there was a lot of eye-rolling. If staff warned her that *'the woman is aggressive'* she knew they were referring to a Black woman. She recalls a particularly racist midwife, evidenced in the way she treated people. She also recalls a time when she was called to an emergency and the midwife in question, who was supposed to gather everyone together to prepare for surgery, was simply sat twiddling her thumbs.

Dr Y said that medicine is not culturally safe and gave two examples of Black women whose concerns had been ignored. One ended up having a cardiac arrest and the other lost her baby to sepsis. In the latter case the midwives never raised their concerns with the consultants.

Dr Y believes that her seniority provides her with some protection against racism. Dr Y indicated that there were more career development opportunities for white people than Black people. The two issues she raises are that they tend to have all gone to private school, and that all the white people had been coached into positions before the time of their interview. Dr Y did not know any person of colour who was on a DPhil or PhD.

Dr Y felt that as a Black person, however qualified, you have to prove yourself before you are believed. You have to work to break down a lot of stereotypes before you are respected.

Dr V

Dr V is a Black man and a general practitioner in England. He had always had a fascination with the human body. He grew up in Nigeria and came to the United Kingdom when he was in his teens. While at college in the UK he said that he informed the head of science of his ambitions and the teacher's response was to ridicule him. The teacher said it was futile of him to try. The same teacher, however, was really encouraging to other students. Dr V did a degree before medical school and obtained a 2:2 in the second year and asked the head of the department to write a reference for medical school. The head of the department said he hadn't done well enough to write a reference but then he went on to help a white student with a 2:2 with her application. Doctor V did get a 2:1 in the final year and the head of department still refused to provide a reference.

Dr V recalled an interview at a London medical school where he was the only Black applicant. The white students had said that the interviewers were really kind and really nice. However, for him it was the worst interview he had ever had. He received what he describes as an absolute grilling. He later learned that the questions put to him were for an advanced year.

During medical school there was a GP educator who had a problem with him. The GP educator failed him on the spot for a prescription assessment, even though he had not seen his sheet or seen what he had written. Despite doing everything right the GP assessor would still fail him.

Dr V recalls his final exams at medical school, consisting of various assessments at different stations. At the end of the exam the results are published. Dr V went to check his results but they were not there. He went to see the staff and they told him that he had scored so highly that they thought he had cheated. He had got the highest score of the year. When the assessors could see his face, his score was low; however, when his face was not seen his score was high. It is highly indicative that his race was a factor when he was being assessed in face-to-face exams. The staff said that while they could not find any evidence he had cheated, he would have to do the whole year again. This left him feeling angry and deflated.

Dr V also did a second-year foundation at a northern hospital. He said certain female consultants were not comfortable with 'our work' and by that he meant in relation to the Black male doctors. He went on to say it was the way they were spoken to such as 'no hellos', being ridiculed and they would say things like 'Am I not speaking English?' if they were asked to repeat something.

Dr V spent some time doing locum work at various hospitals and had a good experience. He then decided to retrain as a GP. During training he was the only Black person in the class and felt picked on. He raised a grievance in confidence about a GP supervisor and the supervisor invited himself into the confidential meeting. Dr V stated that the supervisor would pick on his work and raise issues that were not being raised with other white students. I was made aware that the Royal College of General Practitioners had been taken to court for racial discrimination because they were failing students of colour in face-to-face exams. Dr V was aware of an assessment where all the people of colour were taking an assessment. They were not given any positive feedback and the examiners were picking on anything they could and all the people of colour were failed.

Dr V has been a GP since 2019. He describes people as being surprised to see him as he has a white sounding name. In one GP practice he had more complaints in six months than he had had in three years and he indicated that at that practice the patients had a problem with Black and Asian doctors.

Since 2019 Dr V has been a locum GP. He says overall it has been a positive experience but there have been incidences of racism. He recalls turning up to one GP surgery for a night shift and when he arrived and alerted the staff to his arrival, they ignored him. They did not go to see who he was or enquire what he wanted and they refused to open the door to him. He has also experienced patients not believing he was a doctor.

I spoke at length to the doctors, and it was clear that racism persists in the medical profession, in medical schools, hospitals and GP surgeries. It is also clear that racism is adversely affecting staff and can have an adverse if not deadly consequence for Black women; particularly Black women during pregnancy and childbirth. Each doctor I spoke to had experienced racism, some of it absolutely appalling. I was saddened and horrified about the scale of the problem; unfortunately I was not surprised. As a lawyer what drew my ire was the treatment of Doctor V. Without evidence, the faculty accused him of cheating. The medical professionals and teachers could not accept that a Black man could score so highly. They chose to hold on to their deeply racist beliefs and, adding insult to grave injury, he was denied due process, a fair hearing and representation.

Without any evidence or adverse finding they imposed a sanction on him by making him repeat the year. Educated professionals in a training environment should surely have known that they must have a sense of fair play, and that there should be procedural justice when dealing with allegations and complaints. Here they simply meted out a punishment without due process. And I am of the firm view that abandoning this fairness and justice was done because Doctor V was not white.

In the past and present, healthcare presents a completely different picture and experience for Black patients and staff within learning institutions, hospitals and medical research in Britain, America and Africa. As Washington points out at page 114, *'hospitals and medical schools became firmly cemented into the African American consciousness as places of terror, violence and shame, not of medical care'*. I would go further and say that hospitals developed by the West have been places of violence, terror and shame for Black people across the globe. If you look deep into the history books you will find that American and European scientific racists shared the same racist ideology. They used perverted science to justify slavery, racism and brutality against Blacks and people of colour and any sign of rebellion or protest was met with medical violence. It is clear that those racist ideologies still persist today. Science and medicine have been used to try and link racial genetics to social problems meaning racism, inequality and poverty are not addressed. There has also been the consistent use of fraud in scientific research – falsifying and erasing data, overt denials, and gaslighting the victims of experimentation and medical exploitation. Falsifying data or records in healthcare is something that still goes on today.

In respect of racial discrimination and racism a number of questions arise. How is it that at the time of writing this book (2024) Black men are still being mis- or over-diagnosed with schizophrenia? Why are Black people four times more likely to be sectioned than their white counterparts? Why does their medical incarceration last nine years longer? How is it that our very existence is still threatened by virtue of the attacks on Black reproductive rights, starting with the fact that in Britain Black women are five times more likely to die during pregnancy and childbirth than their white counterparts and in America Black babies are three times more likely to die when cared for by a white doctor?

ERASURE

During my research I was struck by the complete erasure from history of Black people who had made significant contributions to the development of Western medicine. If you consider the prevailing attitudes, one may be led to believe that Western medicine is purely a result of white ingenuity and inventions, but this is clearly not the case. Black people have been removed from the narrative and I would say it was done deliberately.

During slavery, slave owners would often seek treatment for their medical problems and childbirth from the slaves, because many of the slaves were expert herbalists and healers with extensive knowledge. Slave owners often regarded the white doctors as ineffective and expensive. The white doctors in the South, not wanting their profits to be threatened, bid to outlaw treatment being given by anyone but themselves, even if their treatment was ineffective and deadly. In her book *Medical Apartheid*, Washington asserts that white people took advantage of slaves' knowledge of healing and went on to make fortunes, while Black healers were relegated to obscurity. One significant contribution to Western medicine is inoculation. Contrary to popular belief, this was not a Western invention but an African one. According to the Royal Society[89] and Washington, inoculation was a practice that had been carried out in Africa for centuries. There is a suggestion that the slave Onesimus had introduced the process to Cotton Mathers during an outbreak of smallpox in America. The process – having tested it on slaves first – was then implemented and rolled out by Mathers and George Washington.

In chapter three I mentioned other Black scientists who had made major contributions to the development of Western medicine such as

Dr Patricia Bath who invented laser eye surgery. There was Dr Charles Drew who invented the blood bank and established the American Red Cross blood bank. Dr Daniel Hale Williams performed the first open heart surgery in 1893 and Dr Percy Julian developed the treatment for glaucoma and synthesised cortisone. Other Black people who significantly changed the course of Western medicine are Dr Jane Cooke Wright and her father Dr Louis Wright who developed and identified chemotherapy drugs which enabled cancer and leukaemia patients to enter remission, saving millions of lives. There was also Dr William A Hinton who created the blood test for syphilis.

There is of course Mary Seacole, who was erased from the history books for more than a hundred and forty years. According to The Mary Seacole Trust[90], having been refused permission by the British War Office to travel to Crimea and nurse soldiers, Mary funded her own trip. Once there she established the British Hotel with Thomas Day and provided care to sick and wounded British soldiers and even attended the frontline to care for the wounded British. She returned to Britain and received praise from soldiers and officers. The *Times* war correspondent William H Russell, wrote in 1857: *'I trust that England will not forget one who nursed her sick, who sought out her wounded to aid and succour them, and who performed the last offices for some of her illustrious dead.'*

The erasure of Black people's contributions to Western medicine has been – I would suggest – as a result of racism. One scientist being erased from the history books and consciousness of the Western world may be regarded as unfortunate or accidental, but a whole slew of doctors and medical professionals is a concerted and deliberate effort. If you do not believe the erasure was as a result of racism, or done to maintain the socialisation process of the false concept of white supremacy, then what would you say is the reason? Ask yourself on what basis you come to a conclusion if it is not one of racism.

Having read this chapter, I would ask you to consider whether any of what has been said is represented in your viewing of medical films and television dramas. In Britain the staple medical dramas are *Casualty*, *Doctors* and *Holby City*. If you have watched any of those dramas, was systemic racism ever portrayed? Did the experience of the doctors in the dramas correlate with the experiences of the doctors I interviewed? Was there any recognition of the adverse outcomes for Black and Asian patients.

If you watch American and British medical dramas, I would say that you don't often get to see the above-mentioned portrayed. You may watch a drama where the caring, beleaguered doctor is begging a person to be sterilised because of their drug addiction or their dysfunctionality but what you don't see is the oppressive nature of social services and medical professionals in certain countries forcing women into that sterilisation. What you don't see is people being experimented upon without their consent. What you don't see are the fatal consequences and trauma suffered by Black people and people of colour at the hands of the medical profession. Once again, the exception to the norm comes from America and I point out Shonda Rhimes' *Grey's Anatomy* which is now in its 20th season. *Grey's Anatomy* has at times dramatised the racism that Black doctors face in their everyday lives and the structural inequalities that impact Black people.

Consider the medical dramas and films you have seen to date.

....

EXERCISE 11

1. How were the medial professionals portrayed?
2. If you are a regular viewer of medical dramas, did it inform your view of doctors?
3. How did you regard doctors in light of the dramas you have watched?
4. Consider what you have read so far in this chapter and what has not been shown in those dramas.
5. How would you regard the medical profession now in terms of race?

....

WHAT ARE WE NOT SEEING?

OLD MEDICAL DRAMAS

→ Overt use of racism by doctors
→ Cruel and gruesome experiments on Black slaves
→ Grave-robbing of Black bodies to fill hospitals in order to perform dissections
→ Painful surgeries on Black people
→ Sexual exploitation and exhibition of Black bodies on display

CURRENT MEDICAL DRAMAS

→ Overt racism by doctors and other healthcare professionals
→ Bullying harassment and abuse of Black staff by patients, doctors and medical staff
→ Non-consensual drug trials on Blacks and people in Africa
→ Coercive tactics of medical professionals
→ Failure to get consent
→ The Black experience of being a patient
→ The adverse outcomes for Black people as a result of racism

WHY NOT?

I would suggest that the medical and scientific communities are determined to maintain their appearance of being ethical, cutting edge and the epitome of white civilisation; so much so that for the most part they refuse to acknowledge the sins of the past, or accept that their progress was built on the blood, pain, torture and murder of Black people. That is classic maintenance of the white racial frame that Professor Feagin talks about. The medical profession and scientists often like to hold Nazi science up as the worst of their fraternity and to separate them and treat them as a one-off, but Nazi science was not a one-off, it was part of the scientific community: so much so that they were welcomed into America under Operation Paperclip. There also appears to be a refusal to acknowledge some of the pernicious racist attitudes that exist today to the detriment of Black patients and Black staff. If the British medical profession was serious about eliminating racism within its structures it would have committed to anti-racism practices decades ago – but it didn't and as a result Black people are still adversely affected today.

CONCLUSION

I don't leave this chapter with a message of hope. I leave it having laid bare the horrors committed by the scientific and medical professionals against Black people for hundreds of years. I leave it asking you to consider those horrors, that pain, those deaths and those lives so brutally and unjustly taken. Then ask you to consider that not only were those things done to Black people for the sole benefit of white people, but that the method of gain has been erased from Western consciousness and that the falsification of records and destruction of such practices was done to hide such criminal behaviour. So, when you write a medical drama, whether it be set in days of old or today, I would ask you to bear in mind everything that you have read and learned in this chapter.

'It is critical to know our racial history if we are going to understand our racial present.'

Professor Joe R. Feagin

CHAPTER 11

SO, CAN YOU WRITE
A BLACK CHARACTER?

I have to say that I have spent many an afternoon or evening feeling depressed during the writing of this book. If you are white, you might have spent a bit of time feeling triggered. I'll address both. As I stated earlier, this book arose due to a comment from a white script editor and turned into a lecture and was then commissioned to become a book. As a Black woman growing up in the United Kingdom I've faced racism all of my life in varying forms and will continue to face it. I, like every other Black person, know it exists. We experience it, we feel it, we see it and we are adversely affected by it. Sometimes we pay the ultimate price for our colour with our lives. Each chapter has required me to do research. Research into the existence of and the effect of racism. I know it exists, but I also know I won't be believed by many. So, I have looked at the depth and extent of racism. The reviews, the reports, the findings, the impacts, the stories. It's everywhere. It's always. It's not changing and that is what is depressing. What has been discussed in the 60s, 70s, 80s and every decade since up to the present day is racism and its prevalence: individual, institutional, systemic and structural. We know this. Society knows this. And yet nothing has changed in seven decades. In this book I've looked at law and order, healthcare, the media and the entertainment industry. I've also touched on education and employment. Each has hard data showing racism. Each period of research has been a depressing education as I analysed the data. So yes, it is depressing. Depressing because it has not surprised me. Depressing because nothing has changed and depressing because even though the data has been provided I can envisage a barrage of hate at the revelation that this book brings. I can imagine some of the angry responses that I will receive.

> 'She has a chip on her shoulder.'
> 'She's a typical angry Black woman.'
> 'She sees racism everywhere.'

I can imagine a concerted effort to deny racism, its existence in all aspects of society and then an onslaught of gaslighting and hostility. It is depressing because some people may read this but think 'that was interesting' or triggering and then put it down and never have to think about racism again. Those people are undoubtedly going to be white people. And it's depressing because in fifty years – if nothing changes – people will be saying how relevant this book is today.

I realised something else when I was writing this book. I'm tired. I'm tired of being treated like a lesser being. And tired of having to deal with racism and tired of everyday racism that pervades all aspects of my life and the lives of other people of colour. I'm tired because racism is in all aspects of society and it is perpetuated through the media and entertainment and they are in full denial about the extent of their racism and how they continue to perpetuate it.

Now before I address your triggered feelings, I want to ask if you can understand my feelings and experience? Can you understand the weariness? The disillusionment? The depression? Because there is a question I'm going to be asking in this chapter. The title of the chapter is 'So, Can You Write a Black Character?' But at the heart of the question is, 'Do you understand the Black experience?' Do you understand racism and the adverse impact it has on Black, Asian and other people of colour? Going back to you being triggered... I appreciate that this book may not have been an easy read for you and it may have triggered some responses in you, but I hope it has opened your eyes to the realities of racism. I hope it has also opened your heart and mind and let the data in and that it has not allowed you to close them again. I hope this is something you can't unsee. I hope that despite the triggered feelings you realise that if you are white, you are for many reasons still the privileged one. I say that because it's a simple truth that white people benefit from racism in various ways. First and foremost, you are not on the receiving end of it. You do not have to adjust your thoughts and behaviours accordingly when a situation of racism arises, and you are not adversely affected by it. Your life chances, your success, your aspirations, they are not impeded because of the colour of your skin.

Going back to one of the potential responses I may receive in regard to this book, of *'she sees racism everywhere'*; well, that is because racism is everywhere. That is not an embittered cry, that is a fact of life. It is everywhere because, as DiAngelo points out: *'white supremacy is a socialisation process',* so of course it is everywhere. It is in every institution. It is in many individuals. It is in decision-making, it is all day, every day and people of colour are all too aware of it. Even the hard-line right-wing politicians of colour who appear to promote racist and xenophobic policies are aware of it. They would have experienced racism in their lives. They may be in denial about it or they may even use it, i.e. their experience of racism, to deflect from the racist policies of the government that they are looking to implement.

I say, rather than be triggered and angry or deny the existence of racism, try to accept the truth of the position. If you don't, I would suggest that you go and do some further research of your own. I have provided you with a number of reports and reviews and articles and you can do a lot more research into any topic. In fact just type in your area of research and the word racism next to it and there will be a plethora of information, reviews and reports for you to study.

So yes, accept the real state of our society and in fact the world, because from that place you will gain a deeper understanding of race and racism. I do not write this chapter as a harbinger of doom,

I write it to reveal the truth. I write it with a hope. Racism, as I have said, is a social construct, so logic dictates that if something was constructed it can be deconstructed. We are all pieces of the jigsaw puzzle. One piece of the puzzle does not a picture make, but all of us coming together can create a better picture; each one of us is a creation; each one of us adds to the picture; what we add is a matter for each of us. As such, I would ask you to add something positive to repaint the picture. So, the starting point in answering the question to this chapter is set out below.

EXERCISE 12

1. Have you written a Black character?
2. Have you written a character who is a person of colour?
3. What did you write them as?
4. Did you humanise them, or simply refer to them as a trope such as drug dealer, terrorist, geisha, etc?
5. Before you wrote your character had you done any research?
6. In light of what you have read in this book, is the character you have written portrayed in a racist or stereotypical way?
7. In respect of the character that you have written, have you made any assumptions in respect of the character's race?
8. Is the character you have written authentic and well-rounded?
9. If you have written a Black character or character of colour, what would you do differently in light of what you have learned?
10. Before you wrote your Black character or person of colour, had you spoken with a person who is the same race as your character about what you were writing?
11. If not, why not?
12. If so, what was the reaction?
13. If you have written a Black character for a television series, have they had any experiences of racism in any of the episodes that you have outlined?
14. In light of what you have read and learned about racism, would any of your plots or dialogue change?
15. If so, what would you change?

'Let excellence be your brand... When you are excellent you become unforgettable.'

Oprah Winfrey

CHAPTER 12

WHY ARE BLACK BRITONS **HEADING TO AMERICA**

It appears to be a common story that Black and mixed-race actors struggle to get a break in the United Kingdom, but then have success in the United States. Time and time again an actor will not be given the roles or opportunities their white counterparts are, so the question is why?

In 2013 the then shadow business secretary Chuka Umunna delivered a speech on social mobility at Herbert Smith Freehills in London, lamenting the fact that Black British actors were having to go to America to achieve success in their careers. His speech, which was transcribed in *The New Black Magazine*[91], said:

> *'...broadcast and film media have a tendency to stereotype Black people: to present an image of Black British people that suggests we can succeed in sport, entertainment and music, but not necessarily in other fields. If I am wrong about this, then why do so many Black British actors have to leave the UK for the US to get decent film and television roles that fall outside the stereotypes? Too many in the British film and television industries simply don't cast Black British actors in certain roles that fall outside those stereotypes'.*

Below are examples of five men and five women who are Black or mixed-race and have succeeded in America when they couldn't in the first instance at home.

1. IDRIS ELBA

According to IMDb Idris Elba was born in 1972 in London. He became interested in acting while at school, and went on to gain a place at the National Youth Music Theatre thanks to a £1,500 grant from the Prince's Trust. He had some roles in Britain, namely in *Family Affairs* (1997), *Ultraviolet* (1998) and *Dangerfield* (1999). Idris Elba got his big break in the United States playing Russell 'Stringer' Bell in HBO's series *The Wire* which ran for six years until 2008. Idris Elba then played the titular character DCI John Luther in British police drama *Luther* as well as going on to have film success in America.

In 2016 Idris Elba addressed parliament and said as follows:

> 'The Britain I come from is the most successfully diverse multicultural country on earth. But here's my point: you wouldn't know it if you turned on the TV. There is a disconnect between the real world and the TV world. When you don't reflect the real world, too much talent is actually crushed. Talent is everywhere but opportunity isn't. We haven't done enough to nurture our diverse talent.'

He indicated that the scripts that he generally got were the Black male athletic types and that was just *Crimewatch*! He saw the glass ceiling. Furthermore, he didn't see himself or his culture in TV so he literally stopped watching it. He said that scripts were not describing a character, they were describing a skin colour. He got lots of work but could only play so many best friends or gang leaders. He knew he wasn't going to land a leading role and knew that if he wanted to star in a leading role, he would have to go to America. Idris Elba talked about America's most famous diversity policy – the American Dream. Where if you're talented and you work hard you can succeed and in his speech to Parliament, he was saying that he wanted the same in Britain for Black actors, for them to stay. However, he indicated that statistics past and present show that is not occurring in Britain. He pointed to the fact that 1.5% of BAMEs are represented in the industry but they make up 4% of the nation. He called for a change in mindset of commissioners and he also lamented the lack of commitment to transparency and accountability from people who are at the top in the industry. Writing in the *Sunday Times* in 2020, he made calls for the UK film industry to improve its diversity.

2. DAVID HAREWOOD

According to IMDb Black British actor David Harewood was born in 1965 in Birmingham and raised there. He studied at the Royal Academy of Dramatic Art in London. On 27 July 2020 David was a guest on Joe Wicks' podcast and he talked about his experience of racism and working in Britain. He stated that it had been tough in the UK and that he hadn't worked for nine months in England. That he was done and that he hadn't had success. He had an American agent who sent him the *Homeland* script and he was down to his last £80 at that stage. In effect he had to leave the UK in order to work. He also pointed out that the last four major roles he'd had all came out of America. Despite not getting any work in the UK he always had faith that he had talent and he realised that it wasn't him, it was the industry. He also stated that, *'Most Black actors leave the UK because there just isn't the industry to support them here.'* And he referred to David Oyelowo, John Boyega and Daniel Kaluuya. David pointed out that if you turned the TV on in America, there is a range of shows with Black leading actors and actresses and he also indicated that racism and its effects aren't really understood in the United Kingdom.

David Harewood has raised issues of racism earlier. On 31 January 2012 in an interview with the *Belfast Telegraph*[92] he stated, *'Unfortunately there really aren't that many roles for authoritative,* strong *Black characters in this country. We just don't write those characters that's a fact.'* And in 2021 in the *Guardian* he was quoted as saying, *'The path to global recognition is clearer than the path to national recognition. Here we're still dealing with people's perceptions of what Black can be.'*

3. JOHN BOYEGA

John Boyega's IMDb profile reveals that he was born in 1992 in London. He received his big break in British horror comedy film *Attack the Block* about a group of young kids and a young woman trying to defend their home from an alien invasion. He was also cast in British Nigerian collaboration *Half of a Yellow Sun*. In *Vibe Magazine*[93] in 2018 John Boyega stated that being typecast in England prompted him to move to America. John received his big break in the 'Star Wars' franchise, namely Episode VII *The Force Awakens*. He also appeared in the rebooted *24* series as well as the films *Imperial Dreams* (2014), *The Circle* (2017) and *Detroit* (2017).

4. DANIEL KALUUYA

Daniel Kaluuya's IMDb profile reveals he was born in 1989 in London. In a YouTube video he states in relation to racism in America, that racism is more pronounced. The disease (racism) is still there but it manifests in a different way. He suggested that the reason a lot of Black British actors are in America is because racism in Britain is not seen but it is felt and it's oppressive and at times stops you from becoming your best you. In an article in the *Independent*[94] dated 12 January 2020 he stated he works more in the US after struggling to land roles in the UK due to the colour of his skin, and that he became frustrated with producers' apparent prejudice in favour of white actors. That article appeared in the same year that the BAFTAs snubbed actors of colour – only white people won awards that year. Daniel found major success in the United States and starred in the hit film *Get Out* (2017). He has also appeared in *Sicario* (2015), *Black Panther* (2018) and *Judas and the Black Messiah* (2021).

5. DAVID OYELOWO

David Oyelowo's IMDB profile reveals he was born in Oxford in 1976. He was classically trained at the London Academy of Music and Dramatic Art. David had notable success in theatre and television, playing a spy in the hit television series *Spooks* and he was also in the BBC television movie *Born Equal*. However, David still needed to leave the UK for America in order to further his career.

In a 2015 interview with *Radio Times*[95] he said *'We make dramas [in Britain], but there are almost never Black people in them, even though we've been on these shores for hundreds of years. I remember taking a historical drama with a Black figure at its centre to a British executive with greenlight power, and what they said was that if it's not Jane Austen or Dickens, the audience don't understand. And I thought OK, you are stopping people having a context for the country they live in and you are marginalising me. I can't live with that. So I've got to get out.'*

David went on to find stellar success in the United States and has starred in three Oscar nominated films: *The Help* (2011), *Lincoln* (2012) and *Selma* (2014).

The above five men are not the only Black men to have had success in America: Delroy Lindo, Chiwetel Ejiofor, Ricky Whittle, Regé-Jean Page and Lucien Laviscount are just a selection of those who have succeeded in the United States.

Black British women have also found themselves having to leave Britain's shores for America in order to establish or further their careers. It is interesting to note that many of these women have had to deal with gender as an issue in the form of sexual harassment or abuse.

1. THANDIWE NEWTON

The IMDb profile of Thandiwe Newton states that she was born in 1972 in London to a Zimbabwean mother and British father. In a 2008 interview with the *Guardian* Thandiwe agreed with David Harewood's assertion that in order for Black Britons to succeed they needed to go to America. Indeed, Thandiwe Newton has had significant success in the United States having been cast in various films including *Interview with the Vampire*, *Mission: Impossible II*, *The Chronicles of Riddick*, *Crash* and *W*. She has also appeared in high-profile television shows such as *ER* and most notably *Westworld*.

Thandiwe Newton has talked candidly about her experiences of sexual abuse and being groomed in the early years of her career and while the term intersectionality was coined sometime later, Thandiwe's experience speaks to the issue of being Black and a woman in the industry. In her *Vulture*[96] interview, she talks about the *'couldn't care less'* attitude towards Black women who were being abused. She also talked about how in interviews the media tried to reframe her ordeal of sexual abuse as an affair. Ironically it took Twitter and a white woman to complain about sexual harassment, abuse and assault in the industry for the Western population to take notice, leading to the formation of the MeToo movement.

2. SOPHIE OKONEDO

According to IMDb Sophie Okonedo was born in London in 1968 and trained at the Royal Academy of Dramatic Art. She made her film debut in *Young Soul Rebels* (1991) and has gone on to star in *The Governor* (1991) and a *Doctor Who* spin-off. Sophie went on to have success in America, and featured in *Ace Ventura: When Nature Calls*, *Dirty Pretty Things* and *Aeon Flux*. She is a prolific actress who has appeared in British and American film and television. However, in 2014, she recognised that she was not getting the same opportunities in Britain as her white counterparts.

In a 2014 *Guardian*[97] article Mark Lawson starts a piece with a statement and a question, and it is as follows: *'Sophie Okonedo is one of Britain's most accomplished and acclaimed actors – but most of her job offers come from the US, where last month she won a coveted Tony Award for a Broadway role. So why is the UK neglecting its Black stars?'* Lawson describes her as *'a standout talent among a generation of British performers who left drama school in the 1990s'.*

Sophie Okonedo responds in the article by saying: *'I do notice that – over the last year – I've had maybe two scripts from England and tens and tens, from America. The balance is ridiculous. I'm still struggling [in the UK] in a way that my white counterparts at the same level wouldn't have quite the same struggle. People who started with me would have their own series by now and I'm still fighting to get the second lead...'* She didn't concede that it was down to racism but did acknowledge that to get work she had to go across the Atlantic.

3. NAOMIE HARRIS

According to IMDb Naomie Harris was born in 1976 in London. She attended the Anna Scher Theatre School and had success as a child actor, appearing in *Simon and the Witch* (1987) and *The Tomorrow People* (1992). She went on to study social and political sciences at Cambridge University. Naomie then trained at the Bristol Old Vic Theatre School. Naomie did have success in the United Kingdom and has often expressed gratitude to Danny Boyle for giving her the role in the hit UK film *28 Days Later* in 2002.

Naomie's other major breakthroughs came via the United States and she appeared in *Miami Vice* (2006), two of the *Pirates of the Caribbean* films, *Dead Man's Chest* in 2006 and *At World's End* in 2007. She also appeared in *Skyfall* (2012) and was nominated for an Oscar in *Moonlight*. In an interview with *Glamour*[98] magazine Naomie talked openly about her experience of racism and sexism. Despite not having any money she was adamant she was not going to take on stereotypical roles, which appeared to have been numerous, and was determined to play roles that portrayed Black women in a positive light.

Naomie experienced racism while at university and race also appears to have been a factor in her career, evidenced by the lack of meaningful roles or abundance of stereotypical roles for Black women. In *Glamour* magazine she also recalls '...*going to an audition and having a very famous actor put his hand up my skirt during the audition. And having the casting director there, and the director of the movie there, and nobody saying anything at all – and feeling like I couldn't say anything as well*'. Although the MeToo movement started Naomi admits that it is still a challenge to speak up, and constantly reminds herself that she has the right to do so.

4. NATHALIE EMMANUEL

According to IMDb Nathalie Emmanuel was born in March 1989 in Southend-on-Sea. At the age of 10 she appeared in the West End production of *The Lion King*. According to Wikipedia she appeared in *Hollyoaks* from 2006 to 2010. Nathalie also had UK film success and appeared in crime thriller *Twenty8k*. Once again Nathalie achieved stellar success in America starring in the American HBO production *Game of Thrones*. She also went on to play a hacker in the *Fast and Furious* franchise.

In an interview with *ESSENCE* magazine Nathalie stated: '*The British industry hasn't always embraced us. ... So many Black mixed people like myself have come out to America because the opportunities just weren't here for us. What's happened is a lot of talent has been lost to the States.*' She also recognises that because the industry is bigger in the US there is more opportunity.

5. GUGU MBATHA-RAW

Gugu Mbatha-Raw's IMDb profile states that she was born in 1983 in Oxford. She joined the local acting group Dramascope, followed by the Oxford Youth Music Theatre, before going on to win a scholarship to the Royal Academy of Dramatic Art in London. Gugu has had notable successes in British television and theatre. Appearing in *Bad Girls* (1999), *Doctor Who* (2005) and *Marple* (2004). She also appeared in British film *Belle* (2013). She received her American break in the TV series *Touch* in 2012 with Kiefer Sutherland.

In an interview with *Tatler*[99] in 2022 Gugu stated that she did not believe she had been a victim of discrimination, but she did recognise that structural racism was still an issue and signed the open letter to the UK screen industry calling on it to tackle structural and systemic racism.

The above women of colour are not the only ones to have found success or improved their careers in America. Marianne Jean-Baptiste, Carmen Ejogo, Cynthia Erivo, Lashana Lynch, Antonia Thomas and Ruth Negga are just a few of the Black women who have been welcomed in America and succeeded. Given the success of the aforementioned Black men and women, what cannot be in doubt is their skill, their talent and their star quality. So the question remains: why are talented British and Irish Black actors going to America to find success? I would suggest that there are a number of factors.

STRUCTURAL AND SYSTEMIC RACISM

The issue of racial discrimination in the British entertainment industry clearly appears to have been going on for decades. If you look at the actors mentioned their careers range from the 1990s to the present day. It is an indictment of the entertainment industry that the issue of racism has clearly not been dealt with despite the drain of talent, the economic loss and, of course, despite Black people and people of colour raising this issue time and time again over the last three decades and being ignored.

It cannot be in doubt that the British entertainment industry has a problem with systemic and structural racism. Exacerbating the problem is the issue of class and power. That is, that power in the industry is held by the white middle and upper classes of society and they are perpetuating the status quo. Coupled with that power and privilege is the socialisation process known as white supremacy. It bleeds into everything: power, resources, views, employment, writing and creating. So unless the structure and system of racism are meaningfully challenged, racism will continue to manifest and people of colour will continue to be locked out of the industry despite their talents. According to a report by McKinsey & Co[100] it is estimated that racial inequalities, resulting in the exclusion of talent of people of colour, cost the industry approximately $10 billion per year. As actors of colour have joked, in the report, the industry would rather lose $10 billion than hire us!

POWER

This is linked to the above but expands on the issue further. In the UK the people with greenlight power and producing power are predominantly white, if not exclusively so. In the United States there are more Black executives and more Black people with the ability to influence networks and get things made; people such as Shonda Rhimes, Tyler Perry, Oprah Winfrey and Will Smith; they all have production companies and are all able to produce and executive produce.

THE WRITING

This is where the problems begin. If the writers are all white and are the only ones being given the opportunity to have their content made at the expense of Black people and people of colour, then the industry will never change. As Idris Elba pointed out in 2016, he wasn't being offered a human role, he was being offered a skin colour. And clearly a stereotype was attached to that skin colour. In a 2021 *Guardian*[101] article, Ricardo P Lloyd expressed his disappointment and heartache at being typecast and having to pin down such roles. As he stated in the article: *'I've got two degrees, I've done Shakespeare, but I'm still the roadman saying:* "Man's gonna stab you up" *with a spliff in my mouth.'*

I recently had a friend stay at my flat for a catch-up and we talked about race and racism. As a white woman, she was struggling to understand racism and how and why it manifested. I sat with this for a while and I explained that some people do not see me as human. They don't see me as an equal. To them I am a lesser being; they will see only my skin colour and based on that they will hate me. They will not believe I have an intellect, humanity, or complexity. The statement appeared to blow her mind. I could see the shock on her face. The sad fact is we both know it to be true. I see it, I feel it, I live it every day and do so in various ways.

Sadly, there are those in the entertainment industry who share those views. If they didn't, racism in all its forms would not continue to be perpetuated. So if you are going to write a Black person, write them as a complex human who is flawed, just as you would a white character. Don't write a stereotype. I can't emphasise this enough: to stereotype is to dehumanise.

And if you are writing a Black character who is not a human being but a stereotype you are a person who is consciously or unconsciously engaging in racism. Yes, you are, and you are dehumanising Black people, or people of colour. You are perpetuating racism and stereotypes and I urge you to stop doing so. We are human beings, we are also complex characters. We experience the human condition and we are not a stereotype.

THE CONTENT

In American film and television the Black character can be a family man or woman, a doctor, a nurse, lawyer, a hacker, a scientist or a geek. They can be anything. That is the American Dream and yes, America has serious problems when it comes to race but at least they are portraying Black people in human and complex roles and in that respect there is potentially more room to dismantle racism.

Scandal was an American drama series created by Shonda Rhimes and starring Kerry Washington as the formidable Olivia Pope, a fixer in DC and former director of communications for a Republican President, whom she was also having an affair with. *Scandal* ran for seven seasons and was compulsive viewing. It showed a powerful and successful Black woman who was clearly flawed. It dispelled the myth that a Black woman could not draw in audiences in a prime time slot.

Suits is an American legal drama created by Aaron Korsh, starring Gabriel Macht and Patrick J Adams. It is a legal drama about successful commercial lawyers. It is set in New York and has had nine seasons. I found myself binge watching *Suits* and I loved the characters. Gina Torres' character Jessica Pearson was great as the effective powerhouse and Meghan Markle was also great as the ambitious Rachel Zane.

Worth a special mention is *Station 19* created by Stacy McKee for Shondaland. *Station 19* follows Seattle's firefighters based at Station 19 and follows the story of Andrea Herrera who is looking to follow in her father's footsteps and become Captain of the station. The seventh and final season is due to air in 2024. *Station 19* has a diverse cast and has really delved into the issues of race and racism in America, in regards to police brutality, racial violence and Black girls going missing. There were some truly moving, harrowing and gripping storylines. I remember watching a touching scene between firefighters Ben and Dean and thinking *'we have been humanised'*. It was a profound moment for me. What struck me about the aforementioned shows are that they are portraying Black people in all walks of life, as complex and humanised characters.

OPPORTUNITY AND SIZE

One factor that leads to Black British actors heading to America is opportunity. Clearly the American entertainment industry is bigger and thus there is more opportunity available for more people, but the issue in the UK is that Black people are not being given the opportunity. In the UK a Black person or person of colour is regarded as being a risk. It is a difficult argument to sustain particularly when certain white people have been allowed to fail repeatedly, and yet are given more opportunity and more funding. Surely two, or three, or more failed projects is a bigger risk than the newcomer who is Black or a person of colour, but who has substantial credentials. If you regard a Black person or person of colour's project as a risk perhaps it is worth asking yourself the question why? It is also worth trying to adopt objective criteria when using the word risk.

SOCIETY

America, despite all its flaws, has diversity in all areas of life. They have elected a Black president, there are Black generals in the military, Black moguls, and Black executives, and that is portrayed in television and film. In Britain systemic racism prevents many ethnic minorities from rising to the highest echelons of society. In British television and film think about the last time – if ever – you saw the following:

- A Black senior officer above the rank of colonel or other military equivalent
- A Black scientist
- A Black CEO of a legitimate business
- A Black engineer
- A Black politician

You can do a specific recall or a general one. And in your general recall how were the Black characters portrayed? Remember that the inequality of opportunity is costing the entertainment industry $10 billion a year.

They say that life imitates art. Well, make beautiful art. Art that is diverse, complex, inclusive, that breaks down barriers and is also entertaining.

I will leave this chapter on a note I got from a script editor. I had written a fantasy script that specified the race of the characters. The note I got back was that I shouldn't put the race of the character in the script. It appeared problematic that the lead character was Black. The advice was that it is up to the producer or director what race the character would be. At this stage I had given up watching British television. It didn't reflect anything about me or my life. Now I'm not saying television is all about me, but if there are no positive portrayals of Black people, if we cannot appear in everyday settings in all walks of life, if educated Black people are anathema to the British entertainment industry, then why on earth should I watch it? The answer is I shouldn't and so I stopped. I only watched American programmes. So when this script editor said let the producer pick, my initial response was well they are probably just going to make the character white. That was seven years ago. Given the aforementioned reports and insights that I've gained since, I do not think that my assertion was wrong. Black talent has been flocking to America for over 30 years. It is time to produce content in Britain that will enable Black people and people of colour to stay on these shores. It is time to diversify British storytelling. We should all be striving for excellence and excellence comes from all walks of life, from all races, all genders, all colours and all abilities.

'Be certain that you do not die without having done something wonderful for humanity.'

Maya Angelou

CHAPTER 13

MYTH BUSTING

Having read a number of articles about racism and discrimination in the entertainment industry, one aspect that hinders Black people and people of colour are the myths that surround any project with a Black lead or a Black cast. And so I dedicate this chapter to myth busting. When it comes to it there are four main myths that the industry engages in and perpetuates which prevent other projects being made and they are as follows:

1. It's a Black film.
2. Black actors won't sell.
3. Black actors can't lead.
4. Black actors are a risk.

Often in the entertainment industry there is a reticence on the part of executives to cast a Black actor in a lead role. This reticence is a result of negative myths surrounding Black actors.

IT'S A BLACK FILM

Hmmm! Well, have you ever heard anyone say *'It's a white film?'* No! Of course you haven't. Because a white film is not defined by its race, it is regarded as the norm, as the industry standard. See how that socialisation process works yet? A white film doesn't get or require a racial status. If it is a white film – apparently – it's going to appeal to everyone... across the whole world. It's an interesting if not arrogant take. Unfortunately, that is where we are at. A white film is normal. So much so, that it can be marketed in Asia, Africa and the Middle East despite those continents consisting of predominantly people of colour. The language used about white films is problematic. They are regarded as mainstream, or regular, or the norm, or the standard. In that context, anything not regarded as white is deemed as other, not the norm, not the standard and, let's be honest, when you're saying those things you mean less!

The problem with calling something a Black film is the separation it creates. Apparently a Black film is only meant to be watched by Black people. Think about that for a moment: a white film can be watched by Blacks, whites, Middle Eastern people, South Asians, East Asians and everyone else. It can be watched by people of all races across the globe. But a Black film can only be watched by Black people!

WHY?

Yes, you've guessed it, you know what I'm going to say. It is because that is a result of the socialisation process known as white supremacy, that it is so intricately and intrinsically woven into our society and consciousness that it very often goes unnoticed and the white racial frame that Joe R. Feagin discusses in his book ensures white dominance and inequality at the expense of all other races. You probably never gave it a second thought if you are white. You may well have simply accepted the white film as the norm, as the mainstream. At this stage I'd like you to interrogate your thoughts and the status quo.

....

EXERCISE 13

1. It's a Black film! Is it?
2. Before this chapter what did this mean to you?
   - It will only appeal to Black people?
   - It won't appeal to the mass audience?
   - It won't sell as well as a (white) mainstream film?
3. Having read this book, what does it mean to you now?
4. What do you understand the white racial frame to be and how would you regard its impact?

....

If it is exceptionally well written and highly entertaining, if it is a superbly acted and a well-made piece of work, why don't you believe it will sell? Is it because you have added a racial connotation to it? Because a racial connotation, i.e. Black, has been added, in many minds it immediately gets demoted. Once that demotion appears, myths are created to enforce them. So before you label something a Black film, ask yourself what you mean by that? What are the implications of your label? Are those labels objective and fair?

A BLACK ACTOR CAN'T SELL A FILM OR TELEVISION SERIES INTERNATIONALLY

This is one of the biggest and most problematic myths of all. It is born of racism and the perception of racism, even pandering to racism. The latter has often been an issue for film and television executives. It is clearly not the case that the film or television series will not sell across the globe simply because it has a Black lead, and that has been the case for decades. I'll be looking at some films and television dramas that have starred Black actors. But first I will start with Will Smith.

FILM

Will Smith

One of Hollywood's most bankable stars, Will Smith was in large part responsible for busting the myth that a Black lead cannot sell a film internationally. In an article by Eithne Quinn for Taylor & Francis[102], Quinn points out that Hollywood is one of the most minority-free industries in America, with barely any people of colour in any high-level positions at any major studio, talent agency or management firm. According to the article Will Smith had commercial ambition and was determined to become the biggest movie star in the world. He engaged in cross media releases, for example releasing a song at the same time as the film, increasing and improving its branding. Smith had come up against the myth that *'Black doesn't travel'* and *'African Americans don't sell around the world'*. Smith attended overseas locations to market and promote his work and it paid off. Below is a list of Will Smith's commercial successes:

- *Bad Boys*
- *Independence Day*
- *Men in Black*
- *Suicide Squad*
- *Aladdin*
- *The Pursuit of Happyness*
- *King Richard*

Blade (1998) – Wesley Snipes

Blade cost $45 million to make and made $131,237,688 at the box office worldwide. It was regarded as a commercial success.

Passenger 57 (1992) – Wesley Snipes

Passenger 57 cost $15 million to make and grossed $66.5 million.

Black Panther (2018) – Chadwick Boseman

Dispelling the myth for all time that a film with a Black lead could not sell was *Black Panther* starring Chadwick Boseman, which made

$1.347 billion at the box office. It made money in every country according to IMDb including:

- China $105,062,459
- South Korea $42,859,368
- Taiwan $12,778,780
- Thailand $8,996,694

Also worthy of note is that it made $19,265,532 in Russia and $6,971,750 in the United Arab Emirates.

Aladdin (2019) – Will Smith

According to IMDbPro, *Aladdin* cost $183 million to make and it made $1,050,693,953 at the box office. Its box office sales in China were $53,481,575. In India it made $9,076,831 and in Russia it made $18,844,721.

Fast & Furious 9 (aka *F9: The Fast Saga*) (2021)

The *Fast & Furious* franchise has become a global phenomenon. *F9* made $726,229,501 at the box office worldwide dispelling the myth yet again that Black actors cannot sell a film internationally. Worthy of note in respect of the countries are:

- China $216,935,282
- Japan $33,257,802
- Mexico $26,260,884
- South Korea $19,269,286
- Brazil $13,956,552
- UAE $6,030,386
- Middle East $3,200,776

F9 sold in all continents across the globe. Nine films later the *Fast & Furious* franchise is still a commercial success. I'd wager that the diverse cast and portrayal are factors in its success, not to mention family being at the heart of the films. If people can see themselves or someone like them on the screen, they are more likely to watch.

The Bodyguard (1992) – Kevin Costner and Whitney Houston

It is well known that this film had the best-selling soundtrack of all time. Behind the scenes executives were reluctant to cast Whitney Houston as the co-star because she was Black. However, according to Wikipedia *The Bodyguard* grossed $411 million and was the second highest grossing film of 1992.

Sister Act (1992) – Whoopi Goldberg

According to IMDbPro this film cost $31 million to make and grossed $231,605,150 at the box office. Wikipedia lists it as one of the most financially successful comedies of the early 1990s.

Hidden Figures (2016) – Taraji P Henson and Octavia Butler

This was a film telling the story of a group of African American women who were genius mathematicians and instrumental in developing the space programme at NASA. According to IMDbPro the film cost $25 million to make and grossed $235,956,898. That is a return of nearly ten times. Worthy of note are some of the international sales which I set out below:

- USA & Canada $169,607,287
- South Korea $3,152,987
- Taiwan $1,1881,419
- Mexico $1,664,308
- Brazil $2,107,819

It is clear from the evidence of the selected films that it is a myth that a Black actor, male or female, cannot sell a film internationally. The hysterically funny *American Fiction* is also a global success and has won a 2024 BAFTA and a 2024 Critics Choice Award for best actor and has a flurry of Oscar nominations. The aforementioned films have been commercial successes in Europe, Africa, Asia, the Middle East and Russia.

One issue may be the lack of marketing in certain circumstances. Will Smith dispelled the myth when he marketed himself across the globe. If the attitude starts with 'it won't sell', then lacklustre or no effort is put into marketing strategies and that plays into Howard Becker's self-fulfilling prophecy – that is – if you believe something about yourself or situation then it becomes true.

TELEVISION

Television series with Black lead actors have also had success in the United Kingdom, the United States, and have also sold well internationally and received critical acclaim.

The genius and formidable Michaela Coel has had notable success in television, and her shows have gone on to receive critical acclaim and awards.

Chewing Gum (2 seasons) (2015–2017)
Created, written and produced by Michaela Coel. According to IMDb this comedy went on to win two BAFTAs in 2016, one for Best Female Performance in a Comedy Programme, and one for Best Breakthrough Talent. It also won Best Breakthrough at the 2016 Royal Television Society Awards and Favourite Comedy Production at the 2016 Screen Nation Awards. The show was also nominated in the British Screenwriters' Awards and the Broadcasting Press Guild Awards. Chewing Gum was available on Netflix but has since been moved to HBO.

I May Destroy You (2020)
A drama comedy about sexual assault, written and created by Michaela Coel, this won five BAFTAs, a BANFF World Media Festival Award, three Black Reel and three Broadcasting Press Guild Awards, two Dorian TV Awards, two Film Independent Spirit Awards, a GLAAD Media Award and two Emmys, to name but a few. The New York Times called it 'Touching and quietly hilarious'.

Luther (2010–2019)
Idris Elba played DCI John Luther for five seasons. Luther went on to win sixty-nine awards with fifty-eight nominations. Wikipedia states

that the show had a 91% approval rating and Rotten Tomatoes gave it a Metacritic score of 82 out of 100.

Scandal (2012–2018)
As previously mentioned, Shonda Rhimes has been instrumental in changing the face of television in many ways with race blind casting being used in *Grey's Anatomy* and *Scandal*. The latter ran for seven successful seasons and won Outstanding Drama in the Image Awards; it was also awarded TV Programme of the Year by the American Film Institute... and many, many more.

Greenleaf (2016–2020)
A predominantly Black cast star in this soap opera about church and family life. It has been well received by critics and audiences alike and aired in the United States and internationally via Netflix. Starring Keith David and Lynn Whitfield, it was executive produced by Oprah Winfrey through her production company OWN in conjunction with Lionsgate.

Empire (2015–2020)
Starring Taraji P Henson and Terrence Howard, this was a six season television drama focusing on the lives of a Black family who are moguls and musicians in the industry. According to Wikipedia, it was one of the most watched television shows on Fox. It also surpassed *The Big Bang Theory* as the highest-rated scripted programme in the 2014 to 2015 television series. It too has won a number of awards including a Golden Globe, Television Critics Association Award, a Teen Choice Award and four BET Awards.

BLACK ACTORS CAN'T LEAD

I'm not going to list another set of shows to prove my point. The aforementioned shows clearly demonstrate that such assertions are simply myths. Myths that are not supported by the evidence. There is also nothing to suggest that there is an issue with Black actors being unprofessional or problematic on set. As one actor stated in interview, Black actors making it in America are welcomed because the American industry sees British training as excellent... and they welcome excellence. If there was an issue with Black actors not being able to work professionally, capably and diligently on set then they would not be having such repeated successes in America.

BLACK ACTORS OR BLACK SHOWS ARE A RISK

Everything is a risk. Every show that is produced and greenlit has at one stage been a risk. This is a perception not based on objective or empirical evidence; it is one based on racial prejudice. If that isn't the case then why are certain white producers and actors allowed to fail repeatedly, yet there is no connotation attached to their race. We should all be striving for excellence. If a producer, director, writer or actor produces something excellent, then it is less of a risk. It appears that anything not regarded as white seems to have the added burden of an unfair label by virtue of the race of the actor or producer. This is not objective or helpful and certainly not profitable.

Each one of the aforementioned statements is a myth. A myth created by racial prejudice, pandering in some ways to racial prejudice. Ask yourself: has every single white film been a success? Have there been no white failures? In respect of the former question, of course not; with regard to the latter, of course there have. This demonstrates the racial advantage that white filmmakers, writers and actors have. Their position is not racialised, they are given opportunities and even if they fail, they are still given further opportunities.

So, if a project is brought to you, or you want to cast a lead role as white and definitely not Black or another race, if you are starting your thought processes with *'Black people can't'*, then you are racialising matters and doing so in a negative way. If you have one or more of the thoughts above I would ask you to do the following:

1. Stop and think, why do you believe that?
2. Is your belief based on any objective or empirical evidence?

3. Conduct some in-depth and empirical research on your assertion. What were the results?
4. Consider the aforementioned television programmes and films that were led by Black actors. Is your assertion or thought sustainable?

I will leave the chapter on this note. Consider the first ten chapters in this book. Consider what racism is and how it manifests. Remember the white racial frame and how it perpetuates racial inequality. An aspect of racism and discrimination is that it dehumanises and reduces a person to a stereotype. In the preceding chapters I hope you have realised that Black people have been enslaved, subjected to genocides, suffered apartheid and segregation. They have been brutalised, mutilated, experimented upon and murdered with impunity. Black people have overcome much of what was done to them by white people. Today Black people still have to deal with racism in all its forms. Today though, as we have always been, we are human beings. We are a part of society. Despite the past, today we are doctors, lawyers, scientists, inventors, engineers, teachers and carers. We are family members, we are friends, we are parents, we are sons and we are daughters. We are many things in many ways. So when you reduce us to a stereotype you are taking away our humanity, our complexity, our character and our experiences. When you say Black people are... and then follow it through with a generalisation you are engaging in negative stereotyping and, to be blunt, it is racism. When those assumptions and decisions based on those assumptions are made you are maintaining the status quo of the white supremacist socialisation process. In reality, if you truly want to take race out of the picture and you want to make a great television series or film then you really only need to ask the following questions and answer them objectively.

1. How does the script read?
2. What is the person's track record?
3. If the lead/producer/director was white, would I greenlight this project?

4. If the lead/producer/director was white, would I be reacting in the same way?
5. Is my objection/refusal to consider this project objective and if so, on what basis?

'The beauty of anti-racism is that you don't have to pretend to be free of racism to be an anti-racist. Anti-racism is the commitment to fight racism wherever you find it, including in yourself. And it's the only way forward.'

Ijeoma Oluo

CHAPTER 14

MOVING FORWARD:
SOLUTIONS NOT PROBLEMS

At times this was a difficult process and at times I'm sure that this has been a difficult read for you – particularly if you are white. But like I said, if you're white you can put this book down, go on with your life and not have to think about race because, let's be frank, you're not going to have to endure racism. If you're still here, that's great, because I want to end on a constructive note; but make no mistake, that doesn't mean it's necessarily an easy task. So, now you are aware of what racism is, the extent of it, and how it manifests, the question is: what can be done about it?

ANTI-RACISM

It has been said many times that it is not enough to be non-racist; to combat and eliminate racism, we need to be anti-racist. So what does that look like?

1. CHALLENGE IT

If you hear racist remarks or see racist behaviour call it out. You can simply say to the offending person *'that is not appropriate,'* or 'that is racially offensive – stop.' What did it cost you to say that? Particularly if you are in a position of power such as a senior writer, producer, director or executive. If a person replies 'I didn't mean anything by that,' then challenge that assertion with 'then why say it?' Or 'You clearly did because it pertains to a person's race.' The key here is to not let racism slide. To not condone racism by being silent. In her book So You Want to Talk About Race, Ijeoma Oluo asks you this question: 'If these behaviours are being replicated across the organisation, what impact do you think it is having on Black people or people of colour within that organisation?' So next time you hear a racist remark or see racist bullying I would ask you to challenge it politely and firmly and ask yourself that question. Ask the offending person that question then consider how a Black person or person of colour feels about working in an organisation where they are subjected to racism with impunity.

2. STATE YOUR INTENTIONS

Whenever a new project begins, if you are a leader of the organisation or the project then you can explicitly state in the presence of everyone that you want the project or organisation to be a safe and good working environment for all people of all races and all genders and all abilities. As such bullying, harassment and discrimination will not be tolerated. In order to state that though you will have to have proper policies in place because such inappropriate behaviour should come with warnings and sanctions that can be dispensed fairly and justly.

3. WARN PEOPLE

If you are in a position of power and you see or hear racism, warn the person who is engaging in it that they will not be welcome on the set and if it continues that you will not consider hiring them for future opportunities.

4. SANCTION APPROPRIATELY

As in #3, if the racist behaviour is particularly egregious or is confirmed to have happened then there should be an appropriate sanction in place. One possible sanction would be terminating the contract or the work.

5. LISTEN AND ACT ACCORDINGLY

When there are complaints about racism and discrimination, listen to what is being said by the complainant. Do not dismiss or gaslight the person who has come to you. If an allegation is made, consider how to deal with the situation. It is worth having a policy on discrimination and harassment. If you don't have one and can't draft one, then consider adopting the standard policies designed by ACAS which can be found here: www.acas.org.uk/templates-for-employers.

Another resource for creating policy documents and helping you to think about which policies you want to put in place can be found at: www.resourcecentre.org.uk/information/equality-and-diversity-policies-for-small-groups/.

6. MYTH BUST

If there are thought processes that are engaging in mythical thinking, or stereotyping in a negative way then remember to myth bust. It can be done in the following ways:

    i.   identify the thinking as mythical
    ii. provide empirical evidence
    iii. provide evidence of success
    iv. challenge the perception.

It is worthy of note that in order to challenge such behaviours and perceptions and engage in anti-racism you are not required to create conflict. You can challenge things politely and firmly and you can stand your ground, particularly so if you are in a position of power.

7. CHALLENGE STEREOTYPING

If a character is identified by race and is then tasked with engaging in a negative act associated with that race, then that is textbook stereotyping and should be challenged. Examples of stereotyping are:

- Black male, 20s – thug/gangster/drug dealer/drug user/ inmate
- Black woman – prostitute/drug addict/inmate
- Asian/Middle Eastern – terrorist.

The above are not characters they are racial stereotypes. Now you may argue that it is not stereotyping and it is simply casting and it's part of the story. Well ask yourself why so many Black male actors receive the role of mugger, gangster, robber, drug dealer, inmate; and why so many Black women get roles as angry Black woman, drug addict, prostitute, inmate. These roles have no characterisation or humanising aspect – why is that? Let me ask you the question in reverse. Have you ever heard twenty white actors complaining about receiving stereotypical roles based on their race? I think not, so as I've said before and will say again, please do not write a stereotype – it is racist and dehumanising. It is also unoriginal and lacks intellect or imagination. If you are a producer or director, I would ask you to challenge the stereotypical role and ask for more from the writer.

In his lecture on racism Joe R. Feagin is asked how to combat racism and how to engage in anti-racism. Some of his suggestions were:

- Teach real history, or rather the truth of history.
- If a person makes a racially offensive comment, ask them what they meant by it.
- Ask the person if they really think that's fair.

Sasha Salmon who wrote Think-Piece on Anti-Racism in the UK Film & TV Industry on behalf of the Film and TV Charity made a number of recommendations to facilitate anti-racism.

I am most grateful to Sasha Salmon and the Film and TV Charity, who with their kind permission enabled me to set out her recommendations below. They are as follows:

Recommendations for the Film and TV Charity and the UK film and TV industry

1. Make a clear commitment to anti-racism underpinned by meaningful and measurable actions – and assess staff and organisational performance in correlation with this. Ringfencing 30% of spend and output is meaningful and representative.

2. Ensure that the anti-racism agenda is not limited to HR departments, but that all teams including creative teams, governors and executive teams have ownership of this issue and clear action plans with proportionate ringfenced funding.

3. Be publicly accountable on all work on anti-racism and redressing wider inequality.

4. Be transparent and collaborative when working with researchers to evaluate any anti-racism work.

5. Work together with other industry partners to move the needle on racism and creative diversity in the industry.

6. Work together to establish a body to support people of colour to report any discrimination, as outlined in Marcus Ryder's review for Bectu in 2021.

7. Meaningfully listen to, and invest in, anti-racism projects and interventions designed and led by people of colour.

8. Centralise the lived experience of people of colour and other marginalised groups in our work – from decision-making to Writers' Rooms.

In respect of Sasha's final comments, she made a closing statement and listed a number of questions for people within the industry to consider. What she said is reproduced below:

I wanted to close with a page of questions to help readers consider their own role in anti-racism in the industry. I hope this is shared widely and helps open up conversations for readers to explore their own complicity in racism in the industry and to think about new behaviours and structures going forward.

Racism is a fact of the UK's film and TV industry, and everyone in the industry needs to be actively anti-racist. If you read this report and want to check your own anti-racism practice, then consider the questions below. Where do you feel you're making progress? Where do you know you could do better? How will you continue to grow? If you work with people who don't see racism as an issue in our industry then perhaps you can find a way to share one of these questions with them, too.

1. Do you understand what racism is and what it looks like in your life and work?

2. Do you understand what it means to be actively anti-racist?

3. Have you ever been in a situation where you have seen someone treated differently because of their race? If so, what did they do about it? What did you do about it? Did you know who or where to report this to?

4. Do you have people of colour in your inner circle? How many? If you do not, how do you expand your networks and build trust? Would you feel comfortable giving someone a paid opportunity or to lead a project without anyone in your circle personally knowing that person well?

5. Have you ever been in a team or room of decision-makers and had no people of colour in that room? How many times?

6. In your current or most recent places of work, how many people were Black, Asian or belonged to another minority ethnic group? Did any have decision-making powers?

7. Do you have a protégé, or spend extra time investing in the career of someone more junior? Have you given them references? Helped them get more opportunities? Have you advocated on their behalf? Do you have regular contact? Are they the same race and social background as you? Have you ever supported a person of colour in this way?

8. Who is responsible for improving representation and diversity in the work you do and in the industry more broadly? Do you feel you have a role to play? Is there more you could be doing within the power you have?

9. Has any person of colour told you what they think is needed to improve representation, diversity, and ability to tackle racism where you work? If so, did you or others listen? Were these changes made?

10. If you are positioned to allocate funding or commission work, how much of your funding and commissions go to representing and supporting Black, Asian and minority ethnic communities and people? Is it representative of where you live and are based? (At least 42% for London, 42% in Birmingham, 15% in Leeds, 14% Nationally. NB this is from the 2011 census and numbers will now be higher.)

11. Do you think the UK public want to hear stories that are new to them and go beyond the stories they've already heard? Do you think white people want to hear stories of other communities and races?

12. If someone has lived experience and you do not, do you defer to them on what that experience would look and feel like and make changes to your project in response to their experience?

13. Have you ever been in a situation where a person from the marginalised community raised concerns about how their community was being portrayed in a certain project? If so, did you listen and make changes?

14. How many times have you seen racist characters in film and TV and was this discussed overtly within the piece?

15. Do you understand the concept of intersectionality? When you tell stories of white characters, do you explore their personality, sexuality, likes and dislikes, interaction with their family and community, their abilities, their physicality, their politics, their faith, their desires? Do you do the same when you are presenting Black characters, Asian characters, and characters from other minority ethnic communities?

16. Do you feel there needs to be 'different voices in a room?' How are these voices heard?

17. Have you ever watched a film or TV show that helped you to understand racism and changed your perceptions? Have you ever watched a show where you learnt something about a new community or race?

'If you have knowledge, let others light their candle in it.'

Margaret Fuller

CHAPTER 15

RESEARCH

The more knowledgeable you are on the subject the more you will be able to write about it. The importance of research cannot be overstated. This has clearly been about race, racism and the entertainment industry and so it required research in a number of areas. If you are going to write a hospital drama I suggest you would need to research the workings of a hospital, its structure, its operations and management. You would also want to research the medical side, or at least have a medical advisor. If you are going to write a Black character into that show and you are white, you would probably want to look at the report and reviews in respect of race and hospitals. The same can be said of law and order, the media and any other institution. It is imperative therefore to have a basic understanding of research and how to conduct it.

QUALITATIVE DATA

This is usually in-depth data acquired through close and careful study of a person or a situation. It can arise from observations, interviews, questionnaires and books. The benefit of qualitative data is that it gives you more depth, more knowledge and therefore greater insight and understanding of what you are going to write about. From a writer's perspective this is golden.

BOOKS

Depending on the time you have it is always informative to read a couple of books on the topic you are researching. A book will give you the information that you need. Sometimes it will give you avenues of further research and information.

ARTICLES

Academic articles are a great way to understand the crux of the issues and what the pressing concerns are in the current climate. They are also an excellent source for analysis and counterarguments – I assume there's going to be some conflict between your characters! Journalistic articles can of course be a great way to learn about an event or a pressing issue. However, a caveat is needed. Some journalistic articles have been discredited. There are also issues surrounding bias and credibility in respect to certain media outlets.

INTERVIEWS

This is a great way to glean information and insights not just about a person but also about the industry in which they work. If you don't know the person you are meeting then it would be advisable to take some safety precautions:

- Meet in a public place.
- Make your own way to and from the venue.
- Do not give out your home address.
- Tell people where you are going and who you are meeting and what time you expect the meeting to finish.
- Give an estimated time for when you are expected to return.

I tend to meet people for lunch or coffee in public venues although I am amenable to meeting people in their offices. Interviewing a person gives you great insight into their work, their views on work and how they work. I believe that it gives your writing a sense of credibility. I find that a combination of questions is also helpful. Closed and open questions usually make up my interview.

In respect of race and racism I would advise speaking to Black and white people or other people of colour. The key here is to listen. The answers may surprise you and they may make you uncomfortable. If you are white and you speak to other white people you can do so informally, just to gauge their opinion, or you could do it formally and ask to interview them.

You might want to ask the following questions:

1. How do you feel about immigration?
2. How would you feel if your son or daughter was in a relationship with a Black person?
3. Would you ever date or marry a Black person?
4. How would your parents feel if you married or dated a Black person?
5. Are there any racial groups that you don't like?
6. If so, why not?
7. Would you hire a Black person?
8. If not, why not?

The answers may surprise you. Particularly if it is someone you know or thought you knew. It may also be worth asking yourself the same questions. You could, too, interview Black people and people of colour; however, I would start with friends if you have any. If not then try colleagues. If you are going to interview colleagues or other people I would stress to them that you will keep things confidential and that you will not repeat what they say. I can't stress enough that the key is to listen and not to defend or judge.

STUDIES

It is worth looking at the studies that have taken place in respect of race and racism. There were a number of studies referred to in *Biased*, but more can be found with further research. Studies give you an insight into how people behave in certain situations, towards other people, or on receipt of information.

DATABASES AND WEBSITES

Wikipedia is a fantastic resource to start getting information on people and events and it also contains a number of links to its references. But I will say that in respect of some of the Wikipedia articles I have read, it has been silent in respect of race and racism and it sometimes just gives you the bare facts, so it would be wise to engage in further research. Databases can also give you basic and/or in-depth information on a person or subject you are researching.

DOCUMENTARIES AND LECTURES

This is a great way to gather well-researched information on an event, issue or person. Lecturers in academic circles are usually very knowledgeable in their chosen field and can provide a wealth of information. Television documentaries will usually have a team of researchers so again will be able to provide you with a great deal of information. Two great documentaries to start with are *13th* and *Stamped From The Beginning*, both available on Netflix.

INQUIRIES, REVIEWS, REPORTS AND FINDINGS

It is always worth looking at the inquiries, reviews, reports and findings that have been published in respect of an institution or organisation. Sometimes, the organisation will publish a report, at other times their governing body or oversight committee. These reports often start by setting out the purpose and scope, the facts, any evidence that they have received or which has been given. The findings and recommendations are usually set out last. Once again, such reports can give you a fantastic insight into the issues and problems that arise within an organisation or institution. Where evidence has been taken, it can also give you an idea of how people give evidence, the testimonies they give and, to a degree, how the people assessing their evidence regard them. Again, it's great research but is also great for character building.

QUANTITATIVE DATA

Statistics tell their own story. They can also identify the scale and scope of the story. Often government departments will have statistics on various issues and so will organisations. In the United Kingdom the main source of statistical data is the Office of National Statistics www.ons.gov.uk.

QUESTIONNAIRES

There are numerous sociological findings using quantitative and qualitative questionnaires. A quantitative questionnaire will simply obtain its data by asking simple closed questions that will elicit a yes/no answer or a grading. You can obtain your own data by creating your own questionnaire for research. If you want qualitative data as well, you can ask open-ended questions such as 'describe a time when…'.

INSTITUTIONS

It is also worth visiting institutions to get your information or research; you can go to places like the British Library or the National Archives – they are a great way of researching your topic.

SHADOWING

Shadowing a person on the job can also provide you with great information and insight about the institution or organisation. You could explain your interest in the work and request the opportunity to shadow an employee or department. They may want you to get a DBS check or they may want to conduct some security clearance. I would advise getting a DBS check and work and character references in advance and explain that they are available on request. An organisation may refuse to give you the opportunity to shadow them because they may have individuals and data to protect but it is always worth a try. If they don't allow you to shadow them, then you could perhaps ask someone to be interviewed or you could give them the option of answering a list of questions.

CONCLUSION

Research is a gargantuan topic in its own right. The collection of data informs governments and organisations in various ways. Above is just a basic idea and provision of certain research tools that may assist you with a view to building your world and creating your characters.

'Where do we go from here?'

CHAPTER 16

FINAL THOUGHTS

Whenever I lament the state of society, politics or injustice, at some point in time the same thought springs to mind: *'It doesn't have to be this way.'* That thought obviously applies to racism. It really doesn't have to be this way and we can all take steps to eliminate racism.

It was difficult to write this book at times, not to mention depressing and painful. I researched the chapters on law, entertainment and healthcare to demonstrate and articulate the level of racism in this country, the West and its institutions. Those institutions are made up of people, so let's be honest – individuals act in racist ways and as a collective they protect each other and the institutions they work for, either through complicity or by supporting wrongdoing; and in this case the wrongdoing is racism. Racism is individual, collective, institutional and systemic. One race benefits from that racism at the expense of Black people and other people of colour. The beneficiaries of racism are white people.

Now that I have come to the end of this book I'm gathering my thoughts and pondering what note to end on. Should I end on a positive note? Why? The evidence doesn't suggest an end to racism and discrimination. Should I end on a hopeful one? Again, why? Activists have been striving for decades for racial equality and to highlight the prevalence of racism – only to be met with denials or stony silence from governments, the media and the numerous institutions where racism has been revealed. As I was writing this book there were more news stories and reports about police brutality and neglect and obscenity on the basis of race. There were adverse findings in respect of racism within healthcare, and the media reporting on Ukraine has also had a racist element to it. So, I simply leave this book with a number of thoughts and observations.

1. IF YOU CAN MISTREAT SOMEONE, YOU CAN MISTREAT ANYONE

I always say this, because history has shown that when a group of people are subjected to violence, abuse, extermination and overall mistreatment on the basis of a trait, more often than not the perpetrators are only starting with that group. Scholarly writing has suggested that slavery and colonisation was a precursor to the Jewish Holocaust. The precursor to slavery was the kidnapping and shipping abroad of British white people to America to become indentured servants. Each act of mistreatment builds on another. So, if a racial group are being mistreated it won't be long before another identifiable group are subjected to the same fate.

2. MALEVOLENCE KNOWS NO BOUNDS

I believe that this ties in to the one above. Malevolence does not stop in its tracks. I believe it spreads and unless it is stopped, it will behave like cancer. Consider the genocides committed by the powerful against racialised groups. How did they treat women in their societies? How were the disabled treated? How were gay people treated? Remember the systematic abuse of children in care perpetrated by powerful elites and the Catholic and Protestant churches in the United Kingdom. The abuse of children by the Catholic Church has been systematic and global. Malevolence knows no bounds, so as individuals we should take every care to stand up to it and stop it in its tracks. To be clear, racism is a force of malevolence.

3. RACISM MAINTAINS AND FURTHERS EVIL

It's been a long and winding road getting to fifty. I've had my own mental health battles to deal with. Some time ago I embarked on a spiritual path. The reason was twofold. I'd been struggling with insomnia, a condition that on many occasions made me contemplate suicide. A condition that modern medicine couldn't and didn't help with. As a result of the insomnia I was prone to episodes of depression and suicidal ideations. I was also aware at the time that there was a lot of fear, anger and darkness in society and the world. And I remember thinking that I didn't want to add to that and so it meant going within and addressing my own flaws, wounds, traumas and issues. It's been a long journey and, if I'm honest, I'm still on it but it's helped me to see things from a spiritual perspective. Now you don't have to accept anything I say in this regard because spirituality is a deeply personal issue and what I say may either resonate with you or not, but I will set out what I believe and how it relates to the above heading.

I believe human beings consist of mind, body and soul. That makes us sacred. That makes us unique and divine. Now if we realised how sacred and wonderful we are as human beings we would perhaps live different lives. And if we realised how sacred other people were, we would treat them differently. There would be no room for hatred, racism, sexism or homophobia. We wouldn't support colonialism, slavery or imperialism. We wouldn't support environmental destruction and we wouldn't support the systematic incarceration of people on the basis of their race or their lack of means. Our society, our world would be completely different. But that is not how our society has been CONSTRUCTED. It has been constructed to make people believe there is a hierarchy of humanity in factors such as race, gender, sexual orientation, class and wealth and that that determines who fits where.

The construction of racism fills a human heart with hatred and the human mind with ignorance. It allows humanity to keep one race down to be murdered, to be abused and mistreated. So yes, racism is a method of maintaining and furthering evil, because it fills human hearts with darkness and evil and makes many do terrible things. So we should all be doing our best to deconstruct and eradicate it for the peace of our own hearts and minds and for the benefit of our society.

4. A HIERARCHICAL SOCIETY WILL BE OUR END

Have you seen the state of the world lately? I'm sure you have. It's a hot mess. We appear to be heading for cataclysmic disaster in more than one area of global society. One of the first things that came to mind when collecting my thoughts for this final chapter was the book *Lilith's Brood* by Octavia E Butler. I read this last year and it was so profound and beautiful it stayed with me for some time. Lilith wakes up in a containment cell. The earth has been destroyed and an alien race has rescued her. She is one of the few survivors. In discussions with the aliens they talk about humanity's destruction and how it came to be. The aliens conclude the reason for our downfall... is hierarchy. This sat with me for some time and I still think about that today, particularly in light of humanity's predicament. Our inevitable destruction is assured if we do not change our ways.

Hierarchy is what makes a person feel entitled. Entitled to do and take what you want, regardless of the cost and impact on others and the environment. If you are at the top of the hierarchy, you can steal land, perpetrate genocide on innocent people and destroy the very planet you live on. If you are at the top of the hierarchy you can abuse other people with impunity. Hierarchy divides us and the finite resources that the planet has are stolen and distributed unfairly and unevenly. Hierarchy can dehumanise us, so we can look down on others and treat them less well. Hierarchy can make a person believe they are better than others even if they don't have any great talent or admirable character traits.

Of course in organisations and institutions there needs to be a hierarchy of management but perhaps we have made a grave error by creating a hierarchy of humanity because it is turning out to be a very destructive force against people and the planet.

5. YOU CAN EFFECT CHANGE

We all live together in society and, together or individually, we could do great things. Bear in mind that you are part of society and you can effect change in many ways big or small. You can make someone's life at work a joy, or you can make it a misery. You are not helpless. You are an adult with agency. You can tear people down or you can lift them up. As an individual you can reject racism in all its forms. You can choose to educate yourself as to what racism is and how it manifests and you can take an anti-racist stance at home and at work and in life. You can ascertain if racism exists within you – take the steps to face it head on and remove it.

6. RACISM CAN BE ELIMINATED

Now that you have learned something about racism and how it operates in the entertainment industry, I hope that as individuals and organisations, you will take positive steps to combat racism and eradicate it. It will take time, but great strides can be made now and hopefully one day it will be gone completely – and then you can make a film about it!

7. LIFE IMITATES ART

Well then, let's make some beautiful art. Art that tells the story of all of humanity in all its forms. Art can be so many things. It can show the best and worst of humanity. But it can also give hope and inspiration to people. So I leave this book in the hope that we in the entertainment industry strive to do just that.

RIGHT TO REPLY

Where any person or organisation is freshly criticised or named in an adverse manner, journalistic integrity requires that they have the right of reply.

I had contacted the FBI, in respect of their report, however no response was received.

END NOTES

CHAPTER 3

1   Joe R. Feagin, Hernan Vera and Pinar Batur, *White Racism: The Basics*, Routledge, 2000

2   Nick Hazlewood, *The Queen's Slave Trader: Jack Hawkyns, Elizabeth I, and the Trafficking in Human Souls*, HarperCollins, 2004

3   Ibid – page 62

4   Eric Williams, *Capitalism and Slavery*, Penguin, 2022

5   Ibid – page 46

6   Ibid – page 49

7   Hugh Thomas, *The Slave Trade: The History of the Atlantic Slave Trade 1440-1870*, Macmillan, 1998

8   Ibid – page 136

9   Ibid – page 140

10   Martin Bernal, *Black Athena: The Afroasiatic Roots of Classical Civilization Volume One: The Fabrication of Ancient Greece 1785-1985*, Vintage, 1991

11   https://www.dw.com/en/africas-forgotten-world-war-ii-veterans/a-53358115#:~:text=More%20than%20a%20million%20Africans,rest%20serving%20France%20and%20Belgium

12   https://foreignpolicy.com/2019/02/23/britains-abandoned-Black-soldiers/

13   https://www.nationalww2museum.org/war/articles/african-americans-fought-freedom-home-and-abroad-during-world-war-ii#:~:text=More%20than%20one%20million%20African,and%20in%20the%20US%20military

14   https://encyclopedia.1914-1918-online.net/article/war_losses_africa#:~:text=In%20all%2C%20about%202%2C350%2C000%20Africans,civilians%20perished%20in%20this%20effort

15   Caroline Elkins, *Imperial Reckoning: The Untold Story of Britain's Gulag in Kenya*, Holt McDougal, 2005

16 *The Unremembered: Britain's Forgotten War Heroes*, Channel 4, 2019

17 Jennifer Eberhardt – *Biased* – page 38

18 The Scarman Report into the 1981 Brixton riots, 1981

19 The Macpherson Report into the murder in 1993 of Stephen Lawrence, 1999

20 Commission on Race and Ethnic Disparities: The Report - https://assets. publishing.service.gov.uk/government/uploads/system/uploads/ attachment_data/file/974507/20210331_-_CRED_Report_-_FINAL_-_ Web_Accessible.pdf

21 Report of the Working Group of Experts on People of African Descent, dated 2 August 2019 document number A/74/274 (https://undocs.org/ en/A/74/274)

22 Robin DiAngelo, *White Fragility: Why It's So Hard for White People to Talk About Racism*, Penguin, 2018

23 https://www.prb.org/resources/Black-women-over-three-times-more-likely-to-die-in-pregnancy-postpartum-than-white-women-new-research-finds/

24 https://www.npeu.ox.ac.uk/assets/downloads/mbrrace-uk/reports/ maternal-report-2021/MBRRACE-UK_Maternal_Report_2021_-_Lay_ Summary_v10.pdf

25 Brad Greenwood et al, 'Physician–patient racial concordance and disparities in birthing mortality for newborns' (August 2020), https:// www.pnas.org/doi/epdf/10.1073/pnas.1913405117

26 https://www.theguardian.com/education/2021/mar/24/exclusion-rates-Black-caribbean-pupils-england

27 https://www.gov.uk/government/publications/the-report-of-the-commission-on-race-and-ethnic-disparities-supporting-research/ethnic-socio-economic-and-sex-inequalities-in-educational-achievement-at-age-16-by-professor-steve-strand

28 https://www.kcl.ac.uk/news/racism-embedded-in-nhs-organisational-culture-and-norms-prevents-progress-on-healthcare-staff-inequities

29 *Biased, Uncovering The Hidden Prejudices That Shape Our Lives*, Eberhardt – page 263

CHAPTER 4

30 Portrayal of Minorities in the Film, Media and Entertainment Industries, Horton, Price and Brown, Poverty and Prejudice: Media and Race, Stanford University 1 June 1999

31 https://en.wikipedia.org/wiki/The_Birth_of_a_Nation

32 https://www.washingtonpost.com/posteverything/wp/2015/03/03/ the-birth-of-a-nation/

33 Portrayal of Minorities in the Film, Media and Entertainment Industries, – Horton, Price and Brown, Poverty and Prejudice: Media and Race, Stanford University, 1 June 1999

CHAPTER 5

34 https://en.wikipedia.org/wiki/Gene_Roddenberry
35 https://en.wikipedia.org/wiki/Star_Trek:_Discovery

CHAPTER 6

36 https://www2.bfi.org.uk/sites/bfi.org.uk/files/downloads/bfi-press-release-new-bfi-research-reveals-representation-of-Black-actors-in-film-2016-10-06.pdf
37 https://filmtvcharity.org.uk/wp-content/uploads/2021/09/Racial-Diversity-Initiatives-in-UK-Film-and-TV-FilmandTVCharity.pdf
38 The report can be downloaded from here: https://www.bcu.ac.uk/media/news/blog/survey-shows-racism-widespread-in-uk-entertainment
39 Ibid page 23
40 https://filmtvcharity.org.uk/wp-content/uploads/2021/09/Think-Piece-Anti-Racism-FilmandTVCharity.pdf
41 Link to the report can be found here: https://bectu.org.uk/r2bh-campaign/

CHAPTER 7

42 Eric Williams, *Capitalism and Slavery*, Penguin, 2022
43 The Brixton Disorders by the Rt Hon Lord Scarman OBE – Nov 1981, Command Paper 8427
44 The Stephen Lawrence Inquiry: Report of an Inquiry by Sir William Macpherson – February 1999 Cm4262-I https://assets.publishing.service.gov.uk/media/5a7c2af540f0b645ba3c7202/4262.pdf
45 https://www.met.police.uk/SysSiteAssets/media/downloads/met/about-us/baroness-casey-review/update-march-2023/baroness-casey-review-march-2023a.pdf
46 https://www.inquest.org.uk/bame-deaths-in-police-custody
47 https://www.ohchr.org/en/press-releases/2018/04/un-human-rights-experts-says-deaths-custody-reinforce-concerns-about
48 Report of the Independent Review of Deaths and Serious Incidents in Police Custody – https://assets.publishing.service.gov.uk/government/uploads/system/uploads/attachment_data/file/655401/Report_of_Angiolini_Review_ISBN_Accessible.pdf

49   https://www.ethnicity-facts-figures.service.gov.uk/crime-justice-and-the-law/policing/stop-and-search/latest

50   https://www.equalityhumanrights.com/sites/default/files/ehrc_stop_and_search_report.pdf

51   http://news.bbc.co.uk/1/hi/uk/2246331.stm

52   https://www.theguardian.com/uk/2010/oct/17/stop-and-search-race-figures

53   https://www.policeconduct.gov.uk/sites/default/files/documents/Operation%20Hotton%20Learning%20report%20-%20January%202022.pdf

54   www.bbc.co.uk/news/uk-england-london-59185137

55   https://chscp.org.uk/wp-content/uploads/2022/03/Child-Q-PUBLISHED-14-March-22.pdf

56   Big, Black, Mad and Dangerous – Sharon Walker

57   https://lordslibrary.parliament.uk/accusations-of-racism-in-the-metropolitan-police-service/

58   https://www.independent.co.uk/voices/met-police-cressida-dick-no-longer-institutionally-racist-racism-Black-officer-a9001176.html

59   https://www.bbc.co.uk/news/stories-53224394

60   https://www.theguardian.com/commentisfree/2020/jun/15/Black-police-officer-met-institutionally-racist-bame-officers

61   *Racist America: Roots, Current Realities and Future Reparations* - Joe R. Feagin 2nd Edition 2003, Routledge

62   https://hollywood.colorofchange.org/wp-content/uploads/2020/02/Normalizing-Injustice_Complete-Report-2.pdf

CHAPTER 8

63   Brewer, H – Creating a Common Law of Slavery for England and its New World Empire – *Law and History Review* November 2021, Vol 39 No 4

64   *The Sugar Barons: Family, Corruption, Empire and War* by Matthew Parker Windmill Books 2012

65   Ibid page 147 - 148

66   *Racist America* by Joe R. Feagin – kindle edition location 392 - 397

67   https://calmatters.org/justice/2021/04/california-long-waits-jail-bills/

68   https:///.prisonpolicy.org/racialjustice.html

69   Prison Policy Initiative – The Racial Geography of Mass Incarceration - https://www.prisonpolicy.org/racialgeography/report.html

70   Patrick Williams and Becky Clark, 'Dangerous Associations: Joint enterprise, gangs and racism' (2016), https://www.crimeandjustice.org.uk/sites/crimeandjustice.org.uk/files/KEY%20FINDINGS%20

Dangerous%20Associations%20Joint%20Enterprise%2C%20 gangs%20and%20racism.pdf

71 Race at the Bar: A Snapshot Report – November 2021 - https://www.barcouncil.org.uk/uploads/assets/d821c952-ec38-41b2-a41ebeea362b28e5/Race-at-the-Bar-Report-2021.pdf

72 The Specialist Commercial Bar and Black Inclusion: First Steps - https://tecbar.org/wp-content/uploads/2022/05/Black-Inclusion-Group-First-Report-27-April-2022.pdf

CHAPTER 9

73 The mystery of why people go missing and are never seen again – Liverpool Echo 24 October 2016 https://www.liverpoolecho.co.uk/news/liverpool-news/mystery-people-go-missing-never-12055470

74 https://www.ethnicity-facts-figures.service.gov.uk/uk-population-by-ethnicity/national-and-regional-populations/regional-ethnic-diversity/latest/

75 Insider, Missing White Women Syndrome, https://www.insider.com/experts-missing-women-of-color-are-not-centered-news-coverage-2021-9

76 *Journal of Criminal Law and Criminology*, Spring 2016

77 Racism, the Press and Black Deaths in Police Custody in the United Kingdom (2018), Institute for Race Relations, London UK

78 https://pressgazette.co.uk/news/two-third-journalists-uk-media-bigoted-or-racist/

CHAPTER 10

79 https://en.wikipedia.org/wiki/Josiah_C._Nott

80 *Atlanta Journal-Record of Medicine 5* (1903) p46

81 https://ibw21.org/reparations/how-false-beliefs-in-physical-racial-difference-still-live-in-medicine-today/

82 Honor Smith, 'Medicine in Africa as I have seen it', *African Affairs*, Volume 54, Issue 214 pages 28–36

83 https://aninjusticemag.com/white-shooters-are-most-often-responsible-for-mass-school-shootings-6e7b647b5cce

84 https://scholars.csus.edu/esploro/outputs/graduate/School-shootings-race-and-the-media/99257927763801671

85 *Medical Apartheid: The Dark History of Medical Experimentation on Black Americans from Colonial Times to the Present*, page 295

86 Extreme Violence and the British Way: Colonial Warfare in Perak, Sierra Leone and the Sudan https://pure.royalholloway.ac.uk/ws/portalfiles/

portal/28666886/British_Colonial_Violence_in_Perak_Sierra_Leone_and_the_Sudan.pdf

87   Brad Greenwood, Rachel Hardeman, Laura Huang and Aaron Sojourner, 'Physician–patient racial concordance and disparities in birthing mortality for newborns', August 2020, https://www.pnas.org/doi/10.1073/pnas.1913405117

88   Richard Majors, *The International Handbook of Black Community Mental Health*, 'Black Mental Health and the New Millennium: Historical and Current Perspective on Cultural Trauma and 'Everyday' Racism in White Mental Health Spaces – The Impact on Psychological Well-being of Black Mental Health Professionals', Emerald Publishing, 2020

89   https://royalsociety.org/blog/2020/10/west-africans-and-the-history-of-smallpox-inoculation/

90   https://www.maryseacoletrust.org.uk/learn-about-mary/

CHAPTER 12

91   http://www.thenewBlackmagazine.com/view.aspx?index=3216

92   https://www.belfasttelegraph.co.uk/entertainment/film-tv/news/Black-actors-like-david-harewood-are-leaving-britains-lazy-stereotypes-for-hollywood-says-chuka-umunna-29717060.html

93   https://www.vibe.com/news/entertainment/john-boyega-typecasting-576765/

94   https://www.independent.co.uk/arts-entertainment/films/news/daniel-kaluuya-interview-queen-and-slim-racism-uk-hollywood-baftas-a9280206.html

95   https://www.radiotimes.com/movies/selma-star-david-oyelowo-i-had-to-leave-britain-to-have-an-acting-career/

96   https://www.vulture.com/article/thandie-newton-in-conversation.html

97   https://www.theguardian.com/film/2014/jul/04/sophie-okonedo-interview

98   https://www.glamourmagazine.co.uk/article/naomie-harris-glamour-cover-interview-2020

99   https://www.tatler.com/article/gugu-mbatha-raw-interview

100 https://www.mckinsey.com/featured-insights/diversity-and-inclusion/Black-representation-in-film-and-tv-the-challenges-and-impact-of-increasing-diversity

101 https://www.theguardian.com/culture/2021/nov/05/david-harewood-were-still-dealing-with-perceptions-of-what-Black-can-be

CHAPTER 13

102 https://www.tandfonline.com/doi/full/10.1080/15405702.2013.810
070?af=R

●LDCASTLE BOOKS

POSSIBLY THE UK'S SMALLEST INDEPENDENT PUBLISHING GROUP

Oldcastle Books is an independent publishing company formed in 1985 dedicated to providing an eclectic range of titles with a nod to the popular culture of the day.

Imprints include our lists about the film industry, KAMERA BOOKS & CREATIVE ESSENTIALS. We have dabbled in the classics, with PULP! THE CLASSICS, taken a punt on gambling books with HIGH STAKES, provided in-depth overviews with POCKET ESSENTIALS and covered a wide range in the eponymous OLDCASTLE BOOKS list. Most recently we have welcomed two new sister imprints with THE CRIME & MYSTERY CLUB and VERVE, home to great, original, page-turning fiction.

oldcastlebooks.com

OLDCASTLE BOOKS		CREATIVE ESSENTIALS		THE CRIME & MYSTERY CLUB
POCKET ESSENTIALS		PULP! THE CLASSICS		VERVE BOOKS
KAMERA BOOKS		HIGHSTAKES PUBLISHING		